CUBA

SAGE FOCUS EDITIONS

Cuba
Internal and International Affairs

edited by
Jorge I. Domínguez

Written under the auspices of the center for
International Affairs, Harvard University

SAGE PUBLICATIONS
Beverly Hills / London / New Delhi

For information address:

SAGE Publications, Inc.
275 South Beverly Drive
Beverly Hills, California 90212

SAGE Publications India Pvt. Ltd.
C-236 Defence Colony
New Delhi 110 024, India

SAGE Publications Ltd
28 Banner Street
London EC1Y 8QE, England

Printed in the United States of America

Library of Congress Cataloging in Publication Data

Main entry under title:

Cuba

(Sage focus editions ; 50)

Includes index.
Contents: Revolutionary politics / by Jorge I.
Domínguez—The mass media / by John Spicer Nichols—
The economy / by Carmelo Mesa-Lago—[etc.]
1. Cuba—Addresses, essays, lectures. I. Domínguez,
Jorge I., 1945-   . II. Harvard University. Center
for International Affairs.
F1758.C98   972.91'064   82-5700
ISBN 0-8039-1843-7   AACR2
ISBN 0-8039-1844-5 (pbk.)

FIRST PRINTING

2199958

Contents

Preface

This book results from the joint interests of the authors in Cuba's internal and international affairs. We have written a book that, we hope, will be useful to economists, political scientists, journalists, sociologists, and to students and practitioners of international relations—in Cuba, the United States, and in other countries.

We have benefited from each other's suggestions and criticisms and from comments made by others, especially at two small conferences open to a diverse public, hosted by the U.S. Department of State and held during the preparation of the draft chapters.

The research and writing of the chapters by Domínguez, Gonzalez, LeoGrande, and Mesa-Lago were funded in part by the Office of Long Range Assessments and Research of the U.S. Department of State. We are very grateful for the support we have received. The authors alone, of course, bear responsibility for the findings, conclusions, and all other statements in this book. We were especially pleased because the scholarly independence and integrity of the work was a common objective of both the authors and the donor. Unfettered and impartial research serves the interests of all. In particular, we wish to thank Kenneth Roberts for his support and assistance in facilitating our work. These authors, in addition, are grateful to the respective institutions with which they are affiliated for general research support received.

The chapter by Nichols was funded in part by a Research Initiation Grant from the Pennsylvania State University (R. G. Cunningham, Vice President for Research and Graduate Studies) and sponsored by the U.S. International Communication Agency (Charles S. Spencer, Jr. and Norman Painter,

Office of Research). The author is grateful to these institutions and individuals for funding and also for supporting that same open inquiry. The author alone bears responsibility for the conclusions and judgments in his chapter.

We are all jointly grateful to the Center for International Affairs at Harvard University that sponsored the research and under whose auspices this book is published.

—Jorge I. Domínguez

Introduction

Seven U.S. Presidents ago, Fidel Castro led his revolutionary forces to power in Cuba in January 1959. The survival of revolutionary rule in Cuba, in frank opposition to successive U.S. governments, has been perhaps the most striking achievement of the Cuban leadership during the past quarter century. No other revolutionary movement had survived in power in Cuba since its independence in 1902 in opposition to the United States, nor had any such movement done so in Central America or in the Caribbean. Thus, from its very beginning, revolutionary rule in Cuba has signified not only a dramatic shift in Cuban twentieth-century history, but also an international event of worldwide significance. This book seeks to explore these twin dimensions of the Cuban experience as the 1980s have opened.

The central features of revolutionary rule in Cuba can be summarized through paradoxes that illustrate the achievements and the failures of the regime at home and abroad, and that suggest the reasons why Cuba has been feared, admired, defended, and attacked internationally in the recent past as few other governments have been with such intensity.

Today, Cuba has an authoritarian political system, though its leadership employs the rhetoric of democracy and has implemented policies that could lay the groundwork toward a democratic political system. Political decision making in Cuba is highly centralized; the structure of political power is deeply stratified and hierarchical; the mass of the population lacks, in

9

practice, the means to remove the top and middle leadership of the party, the government, and the constitutional organs of the state; it also lacks the power to shape the norms at the work-place in ways consistent with a serious commitment to pro-letarian rule. There is only one legal political party—the Communist Party of Cuba. All mass media are in the hands of state organs, but the Cuban press does show some criticism, though not challenging the continuity of incumbents.

The impressive social transformations achieved by the Cuban revolutionary government in the area of education, broadly construed, may have laid the groundwork for a possibly more democratic society if other institutional and structural changes were made to allow this potential to flourish. With median schooling levels in the junior high school range, Cuba has one of the more educated populations of any less developed country, with virtually complete literacy and rising enrollments of people of all ages in senior high schools. "Education" in Cuba has also entailed active partici-pation in a great many discussions about the affairs of the country, domestic and international, so that Cubans are very informed and aware of politics. Such politicization is, of course, highly biased in the government's favor. Political par-ticipation in neighborhoods and municipalities is also quite substantial. Citizens can affect the local decisions that concern their lives (though, of course, not as much as they might wish). They can also remove some local officials from municipal office in elections that are somewhat competitive (there are at least two candidates per post, although there are other limits on competition). Thus, although there are some democratic tendencies in Cuba, they remain constrained within a predom-inantly authoritarian framework.

The sheer volume of information in Cuba is extraordinarily high, almost certainly at the peak of its history. Through books, magazines, radio, television, the arts, theatre, and music, Cubans are provided with information about the country and the rest of the world. Textbooks and technical publications abound. Translation services for many languages are impressive. Rare among less developed countries, Cuba has developed its own computer hardware and software.

And yet Cuba is also largely cut off from much of the existing global flow of information. While the origins of this information isolation can be traced in part to U.S. policies that sought to strangle the Cuban revolution in the early 1960s, the persistence of the isolation is the responsibility of the Cuban government. The government does not accept the free circulation of ideas. While its libraries accept books and other publications from abroad, only some of these, judged consistent with predominant views and policies, are made available to the public; others are available only by obtaining special permission. Cuban government agencies are slow to respond to invitations from abroad that promise, at times free of charge, an increase in the flow of information. There is, then, much of a "self-blockade" in information that has not been previously screened, even as there is also an avid search for materials that would transfer technical "how-to" information to enlighten and instruct the population.

The Cuban revolutionary government has been massively involved in the country's economic development, with a single-minded commitment unprecedented in the country's past. And yet, with the exception of the first half of the 1970s, Cuban economic growth performance has been very poor by any standards—compared to its own prerevolutionary past, compared to other Communist countries, or compared to other Latin American countries. High rates of investment are wasted at times through persistently inefficient practices. Projects are begun and developed, often with little appreciation for the costs of delayed completion or of substandard operation.

The Cuban revolutionary government brought about, within the half-decade of coming to power, an extraordinary shift in the distribution of income and wealth, not only to the benefit of the state through expropriation, but also among families and individuals, to the benefit of the poor. The rationing mechanisms that stand as a symbol of the failure of the economy to grow in real terms per capita are also a symbol of the commitment to equality. Nevertheless, policies inaugurated in the 1970s and the 1980s to improve the country's economic growth performance rely heavily on incentives—cash as well as nonmonetary material benefits—that heighten inequalities among individuals to the benefit of professional elites.

The revolution in power sought to make changes for the long term, asking today's citizens to sacrifice for the sake of future generations. While many of Cuba's young people are certainly strongly committed to the revolution, stand willing to die to defend it, and have benefited from government policies, it is also true that "youth problems" feature prominently in the leadership's recent concerns about the country's present and future. The overwhelming majority of emigrants in 1980—the desperate boat exodus across the Straits of Florida—were people from their late teens to mid-30s in proportions far in excess of their share of the Cuban population.

The revolutionary government sought independence from the United States in every sphere of Cuban affairs. Some of the confrontations that have involved the United States and Cuba mark key events in the recent history of international relations: the failed Bay of Pigs (or Playa Girón) invasion, the dramatic October 1962 missile crisis, the fear of a "second Cuba" in the Dominican Republic that led to the landing of U.S. forces in that country in 1965, U.S. fears about the possible establishment of a Soviet naval base in Cuba in 1970, U.S. anger over Cuban intervention in the wars of Angola and in the Horn of Africa in 1975 and 1978, and worry about Soviet forces in, and arms weapons deliveries to, Cuba in the late 1970s, and, as the 1980s have opened, bitter disputes over the nature of Cuba's engagement in support of the Sandinista government of Nicaragua and over the U.S. and Cuban roles in El Salvador's civil war.

In order to be able to stand up to the United States, Cuba aligned itself increasingly with the Soviet Union. Cuba is today among the Soviet Union's closest allies, and the only one that has committed large numbers of combat troops to advance allied goals in Africa. Within this tight alliance, both the USSR and Cuba can exert leverage over each other, although the former, of course, is by far the stronger power. The distinct, independent character that Cuban foreign policy had as recently as the mid-1960s has waned as the alliance with the Soviet Union became more intense. Thus, the search for independence from the United States, and for international influence more generally, that led to the Soviet alliance served also to constrain Cuban foreign policy and to limit its independence of action.

Cuba has aspired, however, to be more than just a Soviet ally. It joined the Non-aligned Movement of countries shortly after the revolution came to power, and Fidel Castro rose to become its president at the 1979 summit of member countries. Cuba's foreign policy vision portrays the country's role as a bridge between the Soviet Union and Eastern Europe, on the one hand, and the less developed countries, and especially the peoples of Latin America, on the other hand. President Fidel Castro has argued that there is an understandable and natural affinity among all of these countries that facilitates Cuba's foreign policy role. The Soviet intervention in Afghanistan—within months of Castro's rise to the presidency of the Non-aligned Movement—undercut that basic premise and undermined Cuba's potential for leadership in the movement. The war between Iraq (Cuba's designated successor in the movement's presidency) and Iran further weakened the movement and limited the scope of Cuba's initiatives during its term.

Cuba had been spectacularly successful throughout most of the 1970s in improving state-to-state relations with many of the countries of the Western Hemisphere. For many reasons, however, Cuban relations with most of these same countries deteriorated very sharply in 1980 and 1981. A still underdeveloped country with serious problems on its development path, Cuba has nevertheless been able to project its influence throughout much of the less developed world in ways unmatched by any other country but the major powers and the major former colonial powers. Cuban armies, victorious in Angola in 1975 and in the Horn of Africa in 1978, have been tied down, however, in wars without end in those same settings since "victory" had seemed to be at hand years ago. The burden of war abroad has begun to be felt on the homefront, although the genuine extent of the cost is difficult to assess.

Cuba supplies as well large quantities of nonmilitary foreign assistance in a wide number of sectors, including construction, health care, sports training, education, and many others. There is much selflessness in these efforts that demonstrate the internationalism of the leadership and the people, and yet Cuba has also begun to charge fees to some of the wealthier, typically oil producing, recipients of Cuban programs. Cuban construction contracts overseas have now become major earners of foreign exchange in convertible currency. Thus some Cuban state enterprises have become transnational firms as well. From internationalism to foreign profits, the country in the Americas that most dramatically expropriated the property of transnational firms has now begun to learn from them.

Cuba is a curiously ideological country. There is much discussion of ideology. There are particular ways of forming questions, of seeing and understanding the world, that stem from deep ideological convictions that are often well thought out. Still, there have been dramatic changes in the substantive content of ideological pronouncements over time that are difficult to reconcile and explain to the public. Examples are the relative weights of moral and material incentives, the relative degrees of commitment to egalitarianism, or the role of the People's Republic of China in the international Communist movement and the events that have transpired in that country. Moreover, Cuba's official ideology, Marxism-Leninism, was expounded through texts inculcated in party members and others only rather late in the experience of revolutionary rule. Even today, the speeches of Fidel Castro are a more important guide to ideological thinking and trends than the sayings of grand classical texts.

Cubans themselves have become an internationalized people. The two major cities where Cubans live are metropolitan Havana and metropolitan Miami. Cubans serve many governments and many state and private enterprises throughout the world, bearing many citizenships and intermarrying with many other peoples. From the military command rooms in Ethiopia and Angola to the company board rooms of the United States, Cubans are among the few peoples of the world who have become truly international. And yet the various branches of the Cuban nation, to say the least, do not get along well. Cubans were profoundly split by the revolutionary experience—as only great revolutions can do—and have been impoverished as well as liberated by that experience. They have been impoverished because much oppression and suffering has occurred on both sides of this great divide which, for good or ill, must be traced to the revolutionary cleavage. They have been liberated because many have been able to do what they wished, individually or collectively, in Cuba, in the United States, or elsewhere, in ways that would probably have been impossible in the absence of the revolution. The revolution unleashed the energies of the Cuban people to fight among themselves, within their families and neighborhoods, but also to build constructively varied and different futures.

This book addresses some of the main concerns of Cuba's internal and international experience as the 1980s have opened. Three of the chapters that follow deal principally with internal affairs and two with international affairs. We have thus sought to underline the varied dimensions of the long-run consequences of the Cuban revolution in power.

Jorge Domínguez (Chapter 1) argues that the Cuban political system has evolved toward a "consultative oligarchy" where centralized power at the top was strengthened as the 1980s opened. There is considerable political continuity in major organs. Organizational representativeness has become an increasingly important criterion for membership in top organizations at the same time that lines of rank and authority are being delineated more clearly. Performance has become more important. Political stratification has become the defining feature of the political system, observable among elites, intermediate cadres, and in the mass of the population. Political stratification widens the participation opportunities for middle elites but constrains those below that level. It stimulates the use of organizational techniques for problem solving, and it strengthens the role of the master of the country's bureaucratic politics—the armed forces. While Fidel Castro's personal role remains, of course, paramount, his behavior responds, too, to this new organizational context; he acts more as the arbiter among competing organizational claims.

John Nichols (Chapter 2) notes that the Cuban mass media are not just an instrument of political control, but that they also reflect economic and technological constraints, and social conditions, that transcend political ideology. All media systems serve to provide feedback to correct or to regulate problems in the country at large. The task of providing feedback is affected by the extent of social differentiation and social conflict: the media can serve as a channel to regulate debates arising from diversity and they can manage, increase, or decrease levels of conflict. Nichols found that Cuban print media have different agendas and that they vary especially in geographic coverage; these agendas tend to be related to levels of social differentiation and of social conflict. He shows that the Cuban press is not monolithic in content and function, pointing to substantial changes that have occurred, particularly during the 1970s. Cuban publications, not unlike publications in other countries, serve different functions for different readers at different times.

Carmelo Mesa-Lago (Chapter 3) analyzes the performance of the Cuban economy in the second half of the 1970s and assesses the prospects for the next half-decade. He found that the Cuban economy performed much worse in the late 1970s than it did in the early 1970s. A great many output targets of the first five-year plan (1976-1980) were unfulfilled. Outcomes in the social sphere were mixed. There were many reasons for these serious failures. These range from mistakes in planning, to the problematic introduction of new management and incentives policies, to the decline of the value of sugar, and even to natural disasters and plagues. Man-made disasters, such as labor indiscipline and low productivity, and the costs of African wars weakened the economy as well. Foreign trade was reoriented dramatically to emphasize bilateral relations with the Soviet Union. The prospects for the second five-year plan (1981-1985) are not good, and targets may be missed again on a large number of items. The concentration of trade with the Soviet Union is projected to increase, while uncertainties remain concerning international debt as well as energy and sugar prices and supplies. Economic policy, Mesa-Lago argues, combines many strands of earlier years, from the pragmatic to the romantic.

William LeoGrande (Chapter 4) discusses Cuban policies toward Third World countries. The strategy of the 1960s that emphasized support for "national liberation" struggles was supplemented in the 1970s by a more conciliatory policy toward other Third World states, seeking to establish normal state-to-state relations in Latin America and elsewhere. Through most of the 1970s, Cuban influence among Third World states increased considerably as Cuba became a broker between socialist and Third World countries. By the late 1970s, however, some Third World countries had begun to criticize aspects of Cuba's support for the Soviet Union, especially in the Horn of Africa (1978) and later in Afghanistan (1980). Because Cuba has invariably sided with the Soviet Union when there are conflicts between Soviet policies and Third World preferences, Cuban leadership among Third World states suffered in the late 1970s and early 1980s. Simultaneously, the resurgence of the Cold War in the Western Hemisphere and the active competition between Cuba and the United States in Central America have also contributed to a deterioration of Cuban relations with many former friends. LeoGrande concludes that Cuban foreign policy is reaching the limits imposed by ideology and by its relations with the Soviet Union. He suggests there may be no more easy gains to be made by Cuban diplomacy.

Edward Gonzalez (Chapter 5) turns his attention specifically to U.S.-Cuban relations, surveying their recent history and thinking about prospects for the years ahead. Gonzalez assesses the costs and benefits of the conciliatory versus the punitive strategies that have been, and can be, tried by the United

States to deal with Cuba. He argues that the first is unlikely to
alter Cuban behavior sufficiently to meet basic U.S. policy
goals, and that the second is likely to be either unfeasible,
counterproductive, or too costly. Instead, he proposes a
"leverage strategy" that would combine elements of the
punitive and the conciliatory policies to elicit behavior changes
from Cuba that would meet U.S. goals. Leverage, Gonzalez
notes, entails the ability of the United States to influence
Cuba's behavior to the former's advantage through Cuba's
own recognition that it can minimize its vulnerabilities and
maximize its interests only by satisfying U.S. demands. To
accomplish this, pressures as well as inducements are likely to
be part of the array of policy instruments. A leverage strategy,
of course, is open to any state that wishes to use it, although the
specific content will necessarily differ. While Gonzalez illus-
trates his case with reference to U.S. policy toward Cuba, in
principle the same type of analysis can be developed for Cuban
policy toward the United States, or for policies among other
states.

In sum, the authors' findings point to three principal conclusions to assess the Cuban experience as the 1980s opened.
In domestic politics and the mass media, the strengths of the
revolutionary regime are still impressive, despite evident
problems, making it highly likely that it will remain in power
with considerable capabilities. In economics, there is also
continuity—unfortunately so for both the Cuban elite and the
Cuban people. Performance has been poor, and the prospects
for the short to medium term are not encouraging. The major
changes may have occurred in international affairs, due to the
increasing problems faced by Cuban foreign policy in its
relations with most countries of the world outside of the Soviet
Union and its close allies. Cuba's margin of discretion in the
world has narrowed and, by choice or default, its ties to the
Soviet Union have been strengthened and become even more
important. The balance sheet as the 1980s opened had little
cheerful news for the revolutionary leadership. These leaders
seem certain to hang on to power, but they find it increasingly
difficult to invest that power effectively at home or abroad to
serve ends that they value.

1

Revolutionary Politics

The New Demands for Orderliness

JORGE I. DOMINGUEZ

"Demand for orderliness," President Fidel Castro told the Second Congress of the Cuban Communist party in December 1980, "should never be neglected in a revolution."[1] Thus he summarized his response, and that of the government and party that he led, to the tumultuous events in Cuba in 1980. He also pointed to a principal political outcome in Cuba in the late 1970s that would shape the political structure of the early 1980s, that of "political stratification."

Only some of this political stratification was the result of deliberate policies consciously pursued by the leadership, such as those that increased the scope of power of the Cuban armed forces in the society. Some was the result of the unintended consequences of such policies, such as the excessive successes of judicial restraint or the appearance of managerial lobbying in the late 1970s. The links between social and political stratification occurred despite the best efforts of the leadership, suggesting structural obstacles that even a highly powerful and committed leadership finds difficult to overcome.

AUTHOR'S NOTE: Parts of an early draft of this chapter appeared as "Cuba in the 1980s" in *Problems of Communism* 30, 2 (March-April 1981): 48-59.

The consolidation of political stratification in contemporary Cuba affects the understanding of its internal politics and the development of the politics of a consultative oligarchy. Fidel Castro's personal power in Cuba remains, of course, supreme, but it works increasingly (although not exclusively) in organizational settings, e.g., acting as a judge to settle competing policy arguments or organizational positions. Second, the boundaries that separate sets of people in Cuban politics have jelled. It became clearer in the late 1970s, for example, who was "within the revolution" and who was not. Third, hierarchical relations were clarified. The control of the top leadership (not just Fidel Castro's) became more evident as changes were made to the political structures adopted earlier in the 1970s.

Fourth, participation opportunities were stratified as well. The opening of political participation opportunities at the local level, developed in the mid-1970s, was consolidated but not extended. The favored modes of mass participation remained either political mobilization or citizen contacting. Effective control of the top ranks of Cuban politics remained at the top, not the bottom, of the political system. Participatory stratification, however, also meant that the participation opportunities for middle-level personnel increased. Participatory chances in Cuba, therefore, are becoming institutionalized as they relate to rank.

Fifth, the stakes of politics are increasingly organizational. Fundamental decisions now must be made about relations among organizations and about membership in them. Sixth, while there is still an occasional reliance on the traditional political methods of the Cuban leadership, especially in crises, the techniques for problem solving as well as longer-range programs are also increasingly organizational. Finally, the leadership's own explanations of success and failure point increasingly to organizational consciousness and criteria. Even when individuals are blamed for mistakes, it is less for the failings of revolutionary virtue, as was the case at times in the late 1960s, and more for sheer incompetence. Organizational responsibility rather than revolutionary good intentions are becoming the essential criteria for judging personal performance.

THE EVENTS OF THE LATE 1970s: BACKGROUND[2]

When the First Party Congress of the Cuban Communist party met in December 1975, guarded optimism about the future appeared justified. The Cuban economy had benefited from a half-decade of economic recovery, making up for the severe economic crisis of the 1968-1971 period. Cuban relations with the Soviet Union had become very close; Soviet assistance to Cuba had increased markedly. The Cuban Armed Forces had been professionalized and were winning in the Angolan war. The international situation looked very favorable: the United States was highly restrained in the wake of the Vietnam war; the Portuguese empire collapsed; Latin American governments showed greater independence from the United States; and fresh possibilities appeared for Cuban leadership in the Non-aligned Movement.

The Cuban Communist party had grown and become better articulated internally; the party had become a recognizable organization rather than merely a conglomerate of individuals singled out for praise. The party began, in effect, to exercise its so-called "leading role." An experiment in local participation in Matanzas province had gone well enough that the Congress ratified its extension nationwide; other state organs, including a National Assembly and a Council of State, were added to the existing national organizational network. A new Constitution and new procedures for law enforcement, the courts, and government and party behavior were about to be approved. The mass organizations had reached new heights in membership and activity. Performance in education and health continued to improve. All this had created new bases of legitimacy and popular support for the regime.

Five years later, much had been accomplished, but many unanticipated and genuinely surprising problems appeared.

The other chapters in this book discuss the trends in the areas of economics, mass media, and international relations. Suffice it to say here that the economic problems that Cuba faced, especially in 1979 and in early 1980, were among the most severe since the revolution came to power in 1959 and served as the background to the major political events of those years. The rising conflict with the United States in the late 1970s brought to the fore within Cuba new concerns about national security, providing a rationale for the expansion of the Cuban military. This chapter will turn specifically to the political questions. The most dramatic events of the 1979-1981 period were the departure of over 125,000 Cubans to the United States and other countries, the replacement of many top party and government office-holders, and the new concern with internal and international security.

THE ELITE: ORGANIZATIONAL HIERARCHY AND STAKES[3]

Changes of the Cuban party and government elite strengthened those at the very top. These delineated lines of hierarchical authority more clearly and expanded the representation of organizations in the Central Committee. Performance became the operative criterion for promotion or demotion for elites just below the very top.

Notwithstanding the events of the second half of the 1970s, not one of the members of the Political Bureau of the Communist party, as constituted in 1975, was dropped five years later. Blame and responsibility for errors committed during that five-year period were born exclusively by subordinates. The 1980 Political Bureau was increased by three members, all of whom had belonged to the Central Committee and the higher ranks of party and government since the revolution came to power. This confirmed the political strength at the top of the stratification hierarchy.

Only one of the members of the 1975 Secretariat appears to have been demoted (Raúl García Peláez, the Ambassador to Afghanistan), even though he remains a member of the Central Committee in an important post. The two most elderly members of the Secretariat (Roca and Rodríguez) left that office but remained as members of the Political Bureau; Isidoro Malmierca also left the Secretariat, but only to shift to the roughly comparable rank of Foreign Minister. Four new members were added to the Secretariat, thus keeping its size intact. The rank of alternate member of the Political Bureau (with eleven members) was created. This enlarged the top leadership by drawing from heretofore weakly represented organizations. Three Division Generals lead the list of alternate Politbureau members. No military officers (other than the Armed Forces and Interior Ministers) had served on either the Political Bureau or the Secretariat. The Presidents of the four principal mass organizations have also become alternate Politbureau members. The other alternates are two members of the Secretariat, a provincial party first secretary, and the President of the Central Planning Board, who speaks for high-ranking technical and managerial personnel.

Political Bureau members are generalists who serve in many roles. Eleven of the sixteen are also members of the Council of Ministers, with direct line responsibility; fourteen of them belonged to the Council of State. In contrast, all of the alternate Political Bureau members (including the two party Secretariat members) are organizational specialists; none belonged to the Council of Ministers, although five of the eleven belonged to the Council of State. The creation of this new rank at the top, therefore, has added to the inner high councils of the regime people who are most likely to be representatives of the organizations in which they work. The Cuban top elite had lacked this component of organizational representativeness. Even so, the combined ranks of Political Bureau, alternate Political Bureau, and Secretariat membership include only 29 people, because several belong to two of these ranks.

There were also changes at the Central Committee. The number of full members, which had only increased from 100 to

TABLE 1.1   Primary Area of Activity of Communist Party Central
Committee Members (Percent)

Area of Activity	1965 full members (N = 100)	1975 full members (N = 112)	1980 full members (N = 148)	1975 all members (N = 124)	1980 all members (N = 225)
Politics	10.0	28.6	20.3	26.6	21.3
Bureaucracy	17.0	17.9	16.9	17.7	17.3
Military	58.0	32.1	24.3	32.3	27.1
Foreign relations	3.0	8.9	7.4	8.1	6.2
Mass organizations	7.0	6.3	18.9	8.1	15.6
Education, science, and culture	4.0	5.4	6.8	5.6	5.8
Other	1.0	0.8	5.4	1.6	6.7

NOTE: All those on active military duty are classified as military. All nonmilitary personnel who held principal posts in the Communist party or the Communist Youth Union are classified under politics (only 4 of 225 members were in the Youth Union in 1980). All those whose principal job appears to be in government or state organizations are classified as bureaucrats, except the ministers of armed forces and interior, all those working in education, science or culture, or in foreign relations. In 1980, there are 1 and 4 unknowns, respectively, in the full- and all-member columns.

SOURCE: See Notes 2 and 3.

112 from 1965 to 1975, was 148 in 1980. There had been no alternate members from 1965 to 1975, when 12 such positions were created; there were 77 in 1980. The composition of the Central Committee also changed. There has been a marked increase in mass organization leaders acting as full members of the Central Committee, matched by a comparable decline in the share of the military. The latter decline, as can be seen from Table 1.1, is the continuation of a long-term trend.

The decision to expand the Central Committee probably responded to the difficulty in deciding who might be dropped. Indeed, 78.7 percent of the 108 full members still alive in 1980 were reelected. Six of the twelve alternates were promoted to full members, and only two of these twelve were dropped. The number of military members of the Central Committee remained unchanged (at 36). Because a number of people on active military duty in 1975 had taken up civilian responsibilities by 1980, this opened up posts as full Central Committee members for other military officers. The share of Central Committee membership employed in the bureaucracy, foreign relations, and in education, science, and culture remained remarkably consistent from 1975 to 1980. The number of those in the party and the Communist Youth Union fell slightly but was compensated by the increase in mass organization representation—people whose work is akin to that of the party and Youth Union. Considering all the members of the Central Committee (full and alternate), the changes are a bit more modest. The decline in the military share is much less because officers account for one-third of all alternates; thus, the actual number of officers who belong to the Central Committee in either category has increased considerably, as one might expect from the great services that they have performed in the Angolan and Ethiopian wars. Fewer than one-tenth of the alternates were mass organization leaders, a proportion far closer to the historical pattern.

In sum, the composition of the entire membership of the Central Committee exhibits considerable stability, despite the relative shift between military and mass organization shares. The expansion of membership accommodated more easily the organizational stakes of politics, sharing growth rather than having to choose among worthy claimants for power. The need for organizational representativeness accounts best for the changes in structure and composition. The strength of the organizational hierarchy has been preserved. The role and representativeness of the Political Bureau were enhanced, thanks to the alternates. The interlocking patterns of power at the top of party, government, and state organizations were maintained.

Organizations and Performance Criteria

Central Committee membership patterns also illustrate other features of the organizational stakes of politics. One is the importance of performance on the job. Among the most public jobs are those of the fourteen first secretaries of the Communist party in each province (including the first secretary of the special independent municipality of the Isle of Youth, formerly the Isle of Pines). Five of the fourteen were dismissed from their jobs between 1975 and 1980, indicating the high stakes in assuming such a post. They were held responsible for poor political and economic performance. Three of these five were also dropped from the Central Committee. A fourth, Faure Chomón, remained in the Central Committee but continued his long decline within the leadership (he had once been a member of the National Secretariat). Only one of the five, Raúl Curbelo, was transferred to a job of comparable rank as head of the civilian assistance efforts in Ethiopia. Of the five new provincial first secretaries, only one had previously belonged to the Central Committee and was so continued. The other four were reminded of their probationary status by being added only as Central Committee alternates.

Three provincial first secretaries were singled out for promotion. Julio Camacho, the first secretary for the city of Havana (an independent province), became a Political Bureau member and Miguel Cano, from Holguín province, became a Political Bureau alternate. Julián Rizo, the Matanzas province's first secretary, who helped to launch the first experiment in local government in 1974, joined the Secretariat. While Camacho's promotion may depend on the importance of his job and on his long-lasting closeness to the top elite, Rizo's and Cano's promotions appear to be related to performance.

Cano's promotion is especially interesting because his rise has been recent even though he has been a party official since the early 1960s. The performance of Holguín province from 1976 to 1980 on some key indicators was far superior to that of the other eastern provinces: Holguín's gross production increased 67 percent and productivity jumped 46 percent. In contrast, Granma province did not even fulfill its plan, and its provincial first secretary was fired. Guantánamo and Santiago provinces' first secretaries held to their posts in 1980, but their respective rates were 38.9 percent and 21.1 percent for the first, and approximately 30 percent and 35 percent for the second. Neither number matched Holguín province's, so that only Cano was promoted from these eastern provinces.[4]

The result has been that the fourteen provincial first secretaries came to reflect hierarchical orderings far more than had been the case in 1975. Three of them joined the top elite, five were virtually on probation, and the balance remained as ordinary Central Committee members. Their experience thus shows the new and clearer links between policy performance and organizational position and power.

Other highly visible office holders are the members of the Council of Ministers. Beginning in late 1979, many ministers were held responsible for poor performance in broad areas of the economy, society, and internal security. Three were replaced in December 1979. A month later, eleven ministers, presidents of state committees (also of ministerial rank), or presidents of other central state organs responding directly to the Council of Ministers, were dismissed. Nine others were dropped from the Council of Ministers, or from direct access to it, because their agencies were dismantled or subordinated to others, thereby losing their independence. Never had such a massive political shakeup occurred in the upper reaches of the government since 1959. Nine of these 23 had been Central Committee members or alternates as well; six of these nine were dropped from the Central Committee.

These changes have clarified the role of the Council of Ministers subordinate to top party organs. The Executive Committee of the Council of Ministers is one of the key organizations that interlocks with top party organs. Of its fourteen members, eight are in the Political Bureau, one is a Politbureau alternate, and the others belong to the Central Committee. For the 22 ordinary ministers, the pattern is rather different. None belong to the Political Bureau. Only ten belong to the Central Committee (two others are Central Committee alternates). Ten ministers do not belong to the Central Committee at all (in contrast, all Division Generals in the Armed Forces do).

Many of the ministers who belong to the Central Committee are former military heroes of the revolution in the 1950s who have since assumed civilian jobs. A clearer picture of the limited political weight of ministers who lack such "historic" merit emerges by looking at the recent career patterns of those who were ministers in 1980 but who were not elected to the

Central Committee when the first party Congress met in 1975. There were nine ministers in 1980 who were also ministers in 1975 and who were left out of the Central Committee at that time. Only two of these were added to the 1980 Central Committee as full members, and one other as an alternate. There were also six ministers in 1980 who had become so only between 1975 and 1980 and who had not been members of the 1975 Central Committee. Only two of these six were in the 1980 Central Committee.

The stratification of the Council of Ministers, therefore, is far sharper and precedes the stratification of the provincial first secretaries. At the top there is the Executive Committee of the Council of Ministers with close ties to high party organs. At the bottom there are the more technically oriented ministers who are not even Central Committee members. In between there are the ministers who do belong to the Central Committee. Unlike the provincial first secretaries (all of whom are at least Central Committee alternates), a large minority of the Council of Ministers is excluded altogether from the Central Committee. Among those who belonged to the Central Committee, there is the entire range from Central Committee alternate to full Political Bureau member. This organizational hierarchy is related not only to historic merit but also, increasingly, to performance. Good performers are promoted; bad performers are dismissed; new ministers tend to be virtually on probation.

Two other aspects of the changes in the Council of Ministers clarified hierarchical relations. The first was the recentralization of power in the hands of the Vice Presidents who constitute the Executive Committee of the Council of Ministers. Instead of appointing new ministers to replace those dismissed, the Vice Presidents assigned new responsibilities to themselves. While only two of thirteen Vice Presidents had direct ministerial responsibilities prior to December 1979, all but three had acquired them by the end of January 1980. Instead of a "circulation of elites" at the very top, there was a reconcentration of power that reversed some of the modest trends from the mid-1970s toward decentralization.

A second factor was the manner in which the changes were made. According to the 1976 Constitution, the National Assembly—Cuba's national legislature—is supposed to approve the appointments of ministers. The leadership could have waited to announce the changes made in early December until the National Assembly met later in the month, and it could have made the changes announced in mid-January a bit sooner. Instead, all the changes were authorized formally by the much smaller Council of State, to which all the Political Bureau members at the time belonged. While, as we will see, the National Assembly is not a trivial organization, top personnel decisions remain effectively beyond its real authority.

Factional Politics

One long-standing concern in studies of the Cuban elite has been the relative weight of "factional politics," specifically the rivalry evident in the 1960s between former members of the prerevolutionary Communist party (the *Partido Socialista Popular* or PSP) and former members of the Twenty-sixth of July Movement and of the less important Revolutionary Directorate.

There is no evidence that that historical factional split has much relevance to Cuban politics in the 1980s. Nevertheless, the "balance of origins" that has characterized top party organs remains. Former PSP members accounted for 23 percent of the 1965 Central Committee and for 20.5 percent of the full members of the 1975 Central Committee.[5] While the data on prerevolutionary background for the 1980 Central Committee remain incomplete, the PSP share would be expected to decline. The reason is, of course, chronological age. Former PSP members are much older than the rest of the elite; two of the four Central Committee members who died between 1975 and 1980 were PSP members. Moreover, many of the new Central Committee members born in the 1930s and early 1940s were too young to have participated much in prerevolutionary Cuban politics. What, then, does the fragmentary evidence show?

The old PSP share of the Political Bureau was diluted slightly by enlargement, but it is still 19 percent. Among the alternate Political Bureau members, old PSP members accounted for 18 percent. Cuba's daily newspaper, *Granma,* published the biographies of new 1980 Central Committee members. Of 48 new full members for whom biographies have been published, the PSP accounts for 15 percent. The PSP's contribution to the 23 demotions of full members in 1980 from the 1975 Central Committee (excluding the four dead) was 17 percent. And of 33 new alternate members for whom biographies have been published, the PSP accounts for 24 percent. Thus, the PSP accounts for about 19 percent of all the new members for whom evidence has become available.

These numbers are far too consistent to be random. How, then, might this apparent fixation with historical political origins be explained? Perhaps efforts to alter the historical share, except through natural death, might be taken to mean a change of policy that is otherwise unintended. Thus, paradoxically, historical factional shares may have to be maintained to prevent their renewed politicization. Another explanation might be the continuing need to amend for purges undertaken against former PSP members in the 1960s. To develop current elite harmony, good performers who had been punished for their factional affiliations in the past should be rewarded now, with the effect of maintaining the historical PSP share. There is some evidence to support this hypothesis.

Of the fifteen new, former-PSP (full or alternate) members of the Central Committee identified so far, eight had only belonged to the youth wing of the old party; none of these appeared to have had their careers interrupted in the 1960s. Of the seven who had been full PSP members, one had been a simple worker, now promoted to the Central Committee primarily for symbolic reasons (see below), and two others made their careers as military officers in the Interior Ministry (one of whom became a war hero in African wars). Two remained bureaucratic technicians. The two remaining, Evaristo Baranda and René Peñalver, had nontechnical, political careers that did suffer interruptions.

Baranda joined the party, then called the Integrated Revolutionary Organizations (ORI) when it was led by Aníbal Escalante (later fired from the job of Organization Secretary by Fidel Castro) in 1962. Baranda appears to have been expelled from the party at about that time, along with many other former PSP members, because he is said to have joined the Communist party only in 1965. No information is given of his whereabouts during the intervening three years.[6]

Peñalver joined the party in 1962 and rose quickly through the ranks. He served as first party secretary of several important regions in western Cuba. Then the second major factional dispute surfaced in late 1967, with many former PSP members once again clustered around Aníbal Escalante. Peñalver lost his high party rank. He ran a repair shop from late 1967 until 1970. Peñalver reemerged as second party secretary in a region of western Cuba in 1972, later to become national secretary general of the agricultural workers union.[7]

In short, then, factional politics do not seem to matter much for active political disputes or for policy formulation, but the historical shares have been maintained partly not to give offense and partly to make amends to those who had suffered, perhaps unjustly, from factional disputes in the 1960s.

Symbolic Politics

As organizational stakes and procedures become important, the principles that legitimate political rule are affected. Political legitimacy since 1959 has depended on several factors, only one of which has been Fidel Castro's personal appeal. During the 1970s, the organizational bases for legitimacy became more important, complementing the earlier sources. Organizational representativeness in top party organs may be becoming a basis to legitimate rule for middle and upper ranking elites. Decisions are right not only because they may make sense but also because there are varied organizational inputs. This is not a generalized, but a bounded participation, within the hierarchical channels. It is consistent with some lines of argumentation about politics in the Soviet Union, too.[8]

As organizational representativeness rises in importance, however, a political leadership, part of whose legitimacy derives from its links with humble people, is likely to feel the need to include some non-elites in the Central Committee's membership, thus giving rise to symbolic representation. This symbolic representation did not occur in the 1965 Central Committee, when the organizational framework of Cuban politics was in its infancy, and it is at most barely noticeable in the 1975 Central Committee. In the 1980 Central Committee, however, at least seven of the full members lack a high political, economic, or military rank. They are only "exemplary" workers—"vanguards" in their work place or "National Heroes of Labor." This is "affirmative action" on the grounds of social class. The most spectacular is Antonio León del Monte Pérez, a technician in a textile factory, born in 1924 and an old PSP member, who has been cited numerous times within his industry for his good work, and who was honored as "National Hero of Labor" for five consecutive years, from 1974 to 1978.[9] In addition, seventeen leaders of the Cuban Confederation of Labor became full members of the 1980 Central Committee—an unprecedented number.

Another feature of symbolic politics that has surfaced in Cuba, as in other countries, is "affirmative action" for women. Women accounted for only 5.4 percent of the full members of the 1975 Central Committee, but for almost half of the dozen alternates. Only the high share (though small number) of the women alternates served as a glimmer of affirmative action politics in the 1975 Central Committee. There was also some evidence of affirmative action in the election of women to the Organs of People's Power (local and provincial government) in the 1970s. By 1980, women accounted for 12.2 percent of the full members of the Central Committee and for 14.3 percent of its alternates. This more-than-doubling of the share of full members would not have occurred unless specific steps had been taken to accomplish it. For example, four of the seven full members and three of the four alternate members of the 1980 Central Committee who appeared to be there only for their "exemplary work" merits were women; these women did not even have national responsibilities in the women's federation. Eight leaders of the Women's Federation also became full members of the 1980 Central Committee. If these affirmative action cases were to be excluded, the women's share of the Central Committee would approximate its historical level.

The use of Central Committee membership for symbolic representation is an innovation to convey political messages and policy orientations through organizational means. The limits of symbolic politics are also clear, however. There have never been women members in the Political Bureau or the Secretariat of the party, nor in the Executive Committee of the Council of Ministers. There is only one woman minister (there had been three others until early 1980, when two were dismissed from their posts and one died).

The one area where symbolic politics might apply (but has not) is race. The proportion of full members of the party's Central Committee who are blacks or mulattoes has changed little; it is about 11.5 percent; among the alternates, the proportion is about 14.3 percent.[10] No fewer than one-quarter of all Cubans are nonwhite. While the proportion of nonwhites in the 1980 Central Committee is slightly higher than in the 1975 Central Committee, there is no evidence of the kind of affirmative action in the area of race that has become plain with regard to social class and gender. Racial politics remain behind a political veil in Cuba, as has always been the case.

STRATIFIED ELITE PARTICIPATION: THE NATIONAL ASSEMBLY

The study of policy formation in Cuba is among the more inaccessible topics for research by outsiders. However, the debates in the National Assembly have become somewhat open. The Cuban National Assembly was established in the 1976 Constitution as the State's highest legislative organ. Over 90 percent of the members of the National Assembly are also members of the Communist party, so that National

Assembly debates can also be taken as a reflection of intra-
party discussions. National Assembly members are elected
indirectly. In effect, membership is an appointment that
reflects decisions by the national leadership. The structure and
origin of the National Assembly virtually ensures that major
leadership policies will not be challenged. The National
Assembly has little discernible impact on foreign policy,
military policy, or economic planning and budgeting. It would
be an error, however, to consider the National Assembly to be
only an adornment. Some genuine debates have occurred in
committee and in plenary meetings. Because information
about the latter is more available, the two 1980 sessions are
examined as a proxy for some of the new context of Cuban
politics.[11]

Case 1: As usual, little debate occurred over most issues
that surfaced at the typically brief session of the National
Assembly in December 1980, but considerable debate ensued
over a bill on environmental protection and on the rational use
of natural resources. This debate was rather open, apparently
not manipulated. While the National Assembly committee
that guided the legislation prevailed on most issues, an exception was the decision on where the new organizational power
would be. The committee, and the bill, recommended that the
Academy of Sciences would have "direction and control" over
new policies. Vice President José Ramón Fernández, of the
Executive Committee of the Council of Ministers, objected
that the bill would reduce ministerial authority unnecessarily;
instead, he proposed that the Academy's powers be limited to
"coordination." The matter was solved only upon President
Fidel Castro's personal intervention. He proposed to assign
the overall responsibility to the Council of Ministers which
could decide, entirely at its discretion, what the proper role of
the Academy and the Ministries should be in enforcing this
legislation. His proposal was approved unanimously.[12]

Case 2: During the discussion of this law, six other amendments were proposed by Faustino Pérez, a member of the
Central Committee. Although Pérez did not at the time have

organizational responsibility relevant to this bill, he had professional expertise because he once directed the Institute of Hydraulic Resources. Four of his amendments were rejected or withdrawn. One that was approved simply inserted in the preamble a section on the advantages of a socialist system to implement this kind of legislation. The only one of his substantive amendments that was approved went on to prohibit the dumping of garbage in rivers and waterways. It passed, at least in part, because Fidel Castro spoke in its favor.[13]

Case 3: At the equally brief earlier session in July 1980, there was a major debate over a bill to rehabilitate soils and to preserve inland wetlands. The bill had been proposed personally by Armed Forces Minister Raúl Castro and had been debated extensively. It was formulated at the level of the Executive Committee of the Council of Ministers, not at a lower level, perhaps because it was proposed by Vice President Castro. However, the Executive Committee had to amend it and distribute it for comment by appropriate agencies three times before it was ready to be submitted to the National Assembly. A major change from the original design was the insertion of the previously neglected subject of inland wetlands.

In the plenary session, Vice Minister of Culture Antonio Núñez Jiménez argued that the bill should be expanded even more to include soil preservation. Núñez had no organizational responsibility over this subject, but he is recognized as an expert on geography and associated sciences. He was supported by Félix Duque, the chief officer of the Agriculture Ministry in Matanzas province, who claimed that the bill should be discussed further with his own Ministry and with the Academy of Sciences. A number of leading figures, including Vice Presidents Rodríguez and Cienfuegos, and city of Havana first party secretary Camacho, defended the existing bill. Vice President Raúl Castro, however, proposed that the bill be withdrawn for further study. Some of the bill's original critics then switched positions, suggesting that his bill be passed and another one drafted, but President Fidel Castro put an end to the discussion by supporting Raúl Castro's motion for withdrawal.[14]

Case 4: A new Traffic Code was also approved at the July 1980 Assembly session. The Committee on Internal Order steered the bill, and all of its proposals but one were approved easily. The exception was the committee's proposal that cargo trucks be used to transport people for recreational purposes on weekends or on vacation. It was opposed, for a variety of reasons, by Havana city first secretary Camacho and others. Interior Minister Ramiro Valdés urged the Assembly to approve the bill as drafted, leaving to the Interior Ministry the issuance of regulations that would address this problem. Secretariat member Jesús Montané reminded the country's chief law enforcement officer that the Interior Ministry could issue no regulations unless authorized to do so by law. President Fidel Castro resolved the debate by retaining the committee's language but adding a phrase to give the Interior Ministry the necessary discretion to issue further regulations.[15]

Case 5: A related debate ensued concerning the severity of sanctions in the Traffic Code against those driving under the influence of alcohol. Some, including Secretariat member Montané, wanted a tougher bill. Others opposed a total ban on drinking before driving on the grounds that it was impractical. As Vice President Rodríguez put it: "We must bear in mind our country's specific conditions, not to establish a penalty that does not elicit compliance from our society." The debate was solved when President Castro moved to establish a committee that would redraft this section.[16]

These cases illustrate several aspects of policy debates in Cuba. The first, of course, is Fidel Castro's personal role as a judge among contending opinions. He rarely spoke early; he allowed the debate to unfold, and then took decisive action to settle the controversy. He was never challenged. Equally important is the kind of solution he favored. He sought to create political discretion for top government authorities to act with less constraint than originally envisaged. This was so in the first and fourth cases, and to some degree in the fifth.

The cases also indicate some vigorous debate. It is extremely unlikely that these were staged or prearranged. Even a bill introduced by Raúl Castro had to be withdrawn temporarily.

Indeed, the discussions are the best public manifestation of substantial freedom of expression at the elite level. The latter is, of course, the fundamental qualification: this is only an intraelite debate. Serious and sustained challenges are mounted only by those National Assembly members of a high and secure rank.

While lower ranking National Assembly members do participate, their interventions tend to be formalities; only by exception have they attempted to challenge the leadership so far. One such exception occurred at the December 1979 National Assembly when a deputy from the city of Manzanillo complained about inadequate drainage systems in her home city. President Fidel Castro chided the delegate for representing only the interests of the local community, since all delegates should represent the interests of the whole country. President Castro then went on at great length, and apparently with considerable passion, to detail the benefits the revolutionary government had conferred on Manzanillo. No comparable challenge to the leadership has been reported since that time.[17]

In short, political stratification has occurred within the National Assembly. Certain topics, such as the budget or foreign and military policy, are in effect the exclusive prerogative of elites in the Council of State, the party's Political Bureau, and the Executive Committee of the Council of Ministers. Other issues may be debated at National Assembly plenaries, provided one has either appropriate organizational rank or recognized expertise. Those who have neither ordinarily play minor roles.

The National Assembly cases also show the organizational context of much of the debate. In the first, third, and fourth cases, the organizational powers of the Ministries generally, or of specific agencies such as the Academy of Sciences and the Agriculture and Interior Ministries, were at the heart of the debate. There is also evidence of much prior discussion among organizations. The fourth and fifth cases also show the renewed importance of routinized procedures. In the fourth case, the view that discretion was implicit in the general powers of the revolutionary government, as the Interior Minister suggested, was criticized and did not prevail. Discretion was retained, but the value of established legal procedures was preserved, too. In the fifth case, although the matter was not settled, the debate was about the appropriateness and the efficacy of law. This is plainly different from earlier times, when the view that Interior Minister Valdés manifested had been the ordinary practice.

Those who had no direct organizational responsibility and who took part in debates were either very high-ranking government and party leaders, such as Camacho or Montané, or had recognized expertise, such as Faustino Pérez or Antonio Núñez Jiménez. The top leaders are necessarily involved, even if they do not have direct line responsibility. "Expert" interventions are to be expected more as the importance of the historical merits of prerevolutionary times, and of mere "revolutionary virtues," declines.

There is no evidence of permanent factions. Perhaps because the issues do not lend themselves to factional debates, the historical origin of leaders seems to be unimportant. However, the personal predilections and temperaments of leaders are shown. For example, the positions taken by Ramiro Valdés and Carlos Rafael Rodríguez in the fourth and fifth cases are almost caricatures of their reputations.

Finally, although concern for following legal procedures prevailed, there is no civil libertarian consensus as a result. For example, Montané's position in the fourth and fifth cases is not opposed to government discretion or to severe sanctions; it only seeks to uphold the importance of procedures. The opponents of severe sanctions in the fifth case did so on the grounds of practicality, not principle.

STRATIFIED PARTICIPATION IN MASS POLITICS

Participation opportunities outside of these elite settings are more limited. They also exhibit further ranges of political stratification. Budget legislation mandates that the Provincial

Assemblies discuss the budget bill before it is submitted for the consideration of the National Assembly. This has not happened in practice. The budget bill has been discussed only by the Executive Committees of the Provincial Assemblies and not by the Assemblies themselves. Evidence of this violation of the law has been given by the national coordinator of People's Power (which includes both provincial and municipal government levels), as well as by the Executive Committee Presidents in some of the provinces. While the Provincial Assemblies might begin to discuss budget laws in the early 1980s, the precedent of budget law discussion at the National Assembly level is not encouraging; there is no real discussion of the budget. Thus, the provincial executive is likely to retain real discretion.[18]

This problem was noted with greatest eloquence by Vice President Rodríguez, who observed that blaming practical difficulties to justify the lack of genuine discussion and participation has the effect of "transforming democracy into technocracy and allowing a group of people to decide everything." He warned of the danger of "turning the dictatorship of the proletariat into a dictatorship of the Secretariat."[19]

The presidents of the provincial executive committees, in turn, have lower rank than the party first secretaries in the provinces. For example, all of the first secretaries are Central Committee members or alternates. Only one provincial president (a former General) belongs to the Central Committee, and two others are alternates.

Discussions of the planning and budget laws are also supposed to be a means for enterprises and, especially, for workers to have an input into regional, provincial, and national decision making. The experience so far is discouraging. In 1978, 34 percent of all enterprises failed to discuss at all the 1979 plan with the workers. An additional 58 percent of the enterprises brought the 1979 plan before a workers' assembly, but then paid no attention to suggestions made. Thus, only 8 percent of the enterprises had some resemblance of effective participation—and only they were in compliance with the law. Even in this minority of enterprises, the pattern of participation tends to be very heavily weighted toward those in positions of responsibility, such as party officers or labor leaders.[20] Partly in response to these deficiencies, some improvement occurred in the discussion of the 1980 plan. The proportion of enterprises that held meetings and that made changes in response to suggestions rose sharply to 58.8 percent (although stratification within the enterprise continued). Still, 5.7 percent of the state firms were in complete violation of the law by holding no meetings, and the balance held meetings but subsequently ignored suggestions.[21]

The text of the 1980 plan bill said that it had been discussed previously with the workers. Party Secretariat member Jorge Risquet noted that while there had been difficulties for several years in discussing the plans with the workers, the situation had gotten worse in the case of the 1980 plan. The Assembly approved Risquet's proposal that the bill's reference to prior participation by workers be deleted. Form came to correspond to fact.[22]

The pattern of stratification, therefore, ranges from complete (and illegal) exclusion, to merely formal meetings, to those where some substantive discussions occur; in the latter, the local plant political, managerial, and labor leaders, in turn, account for the bulk of the participation. As will be seen in the later discussion of managerial participation, however, the degree of participation by anyone at any rank at the enterprise level remains very modest—another feature of stratification and of persisting centralization of decision making.

It is more difficult to assess the extent of participation at the local level outside of the workplace, that is, in the relationship between ordinary citizens and the delegates to the municipal assemblies of People's Power. The innovations of the mid-1970s had two principal features. Elections for delegates to municipal assemblies were introduced; these, in turn, elected delegates to the Provincial Assemblies and deputies to the National Assembly. The municipal elections—the only direct ones—were competitive in the sense that there were at least two candidates per post, but the electoral system restricted the meaning of competition. There was no freedom of association; candidates opposed to the government could not coalesce to advance their views. There was no freedom to campaign as an individual on behalf of a program. Only the party and the government could campaign. Party-controlled nomination procedures above the municipal level guaranteed elite control. These features have not changed. They provide for limited elements of electoral participation, greater than in the USSR, but under sharp constraints.

The second innovation legalized, legitimated, and to some degree promoted citizen-contacting of public officials to bring to their attention community problems and inefficiencies. This innovation was an impressive manifestation of concrete democratic commitments that also sought to improve the efficiency of the delivery of government services.[23]

The citizen-contacting mode of participation remains.[24] However, the responsiveness of government officials to citizen complaints is weak at times. Vice President Humberto Pérez has said that the meetings at which municipal delegates are to render an account of their work before the assembled local citizenry have become a "liturgy," the fulfillment of a duty without content or purpose. Discussions in the National Assembly of these problems confirm Pérez's observation. President Fidel Castro's Main Report to the Second Party Congress noted that many of these meetings had become nothing but "mere formalisms."[25]

Part of the explanation for the behavior of the local delegates is that they have such limited resources to meet the numerous citizen demands. All municipal and provincial governments have authority over only about 20 percent of the country's budget. While central state revenues (in current prices) were to increase by 18.2 percent from the 1980 to the 1981 budget, all subnational government revenues were to rise by only 14.7 percent. And although subnational governments have formal authority over a large number of enterprises within their jurisdiction, these enterprises accounted for only 9 percent of the country's state sector gross production in 1978.

Subnational government resources, therefore, remain inadequate to meet the needs posed by the volume of citizen demands.[26]

Political stratification thus operates at the local government level as well. The levels of government above the municipal remain subordinate to the party and rather insulated from direct electoral contact, even under electoral procedures that are weighted to ensure that the regime will not be threatened fundamentally. Municipal elections are competitive only in a limited way. The most open channels of participation are those of citizen-contacting, with the apparently growing limitation of formalistic responsiveness from government officials and the continuing inadequacy of subnational government resources to meet citizen demands. The most open channel is precisely that which does not determine who shall rule.

Another means for organized mass participation has been membership in local voluntary organizations that render specific community services. These include community councils, neighbors' committees (independent of the formally organized mass organizations discussed below, such as the Committees for the Defense of the Revolution), local sports councils, and the like. Because these organizations are somewhat depoliticized, in contrast to the formal mass organizations, they may indicate how many citizens actually choose to participate on their own rather than responding to the inducements of political mobilization. A study conducted in December 1976 in 282 rural communities showed a complex associational life, with 2714 different community organizations, or an average of almost ten per community. However, only about 25 percent of the adult population (ages 15 and over) participated in these community organizations. This might be taken as the level of participation that would occur in the absence of much political mobilization. It is a substantial level, but it does leave three-quarters of the population outside of the voluntary participatory strata.[27]

The oldest means of political participation in Cuba is membership through mass organizations. In the late 1970s, political stratification has also surfaced most clearly with regard to the

Committees for the Defense of the Revolution and the Women's Federation. Up to the mid-1970s, with only minor interruptions, both of these mass organizations increased steadily the share of the adult population included within their ranks. Approximately 80 percent of the adult population was included in the Committees by 1973, and a comparable proportion of adult women was included in the Federation by 1975.[28]

At the end of 1980, the proportion of adult women who belonged to the Federation stood at 80.3 percent, and at the end of 1981 it was 81 percent. At the annual mass meeting of the Committees for the Defense of the Revolution (CDR) in September 1980, their share of the adult population stood still at 80 percent. One year later, that proportion remained unchanged. There has been no other five- or six-year period since 1959 during which the share of the population participating failed to increase. In the Committees' case, Fidel Castro explained: "The only reason for the membership not being larger is that, in the past few years, the organization has been especially careful in choosing new members." Most of the CDR membership growth in recent years has simply kept up with the population growth. The CDR Statutes forbid a local neighborhood Committee to accept new members over age 18 unless the admission is ratified by a higher-ranking "Zone" or other CDR officer. This procedure seeks to maintain political coherence, though at the cost of limiting mass participation and local democracy.[29]

The decision to establish a clearer political boundary between those within and outside the revolutionary mass organizations has defined sharply who is on the margins of political life. This, too, consolidates political stratification—it identifies the polar opposite of the national elite. Including an estimate for children, this "politically marginal" population may amount to about two million people.

In conclusion, political stratification has come to delineate the Cuban population. The elites have considerable opportunities for participation structured around organizational stakes. Participation opportunities below the elite are much more limited, but middle-ranking elites in the provinces or in the workplace still have some input. The most open channel for participation for ordinary citizens is the one that has no impact on incumbent identity or replacement. Finally, the trends in political stratification have rigidified the boundary, setting apart the "politically marginal" with greater precision than ever.

THE "POLITICALLY MARGINAL"

The "politically marginal" includes those who do not belong to the mass organizations for which some political "merit" is required and also those who do belong but who are still disaffected with the regime. The 125,000 people who migrated to the United States in 1980 (and a few thousand more to other countries) included many who had belonged to such organizations. Those who were excluded from membership entirely—by their own choice or not—are of course at the bottom of the political stratification pyramid.[30]

At the most extreme level, violent and illegal political participation resurfaced in Cuba in 1980 in ways unparalleled during the preceding decade. These acts of violence were not aimed at overthrowing the government but at securing political asylum in embassies (Peru, the Vatican, and Ecuador) accredited in Havana. The assaults on these embassies reveal the existence of an organized and occasionally armed underground society beyond the reach of the government.[31]

Less extreme is the case of those who left the country in 1980 without recourse to armed violence. Many left voluntarily; others did so because the government induced them to depart. In some instances, the choice was between remaining in prison and exile, and they naturally chose the latter. This is the third wave of emigration from Cuba since the revolution came to power. It is also the most demographically representative. The occupational and racial composition of the emigration appears to match that of urban Cuba; the most recent exodus is unrepresentative only in that it is still overwhelmingly urban. Comparing the three waves of emigration, there is a gradual universalization of the exile pool, suggesting that support and opposition to the government are much less related now to social and economic cleavages than they were in the early 1960s. Except for the rural-urban cleavage, support or opposition appears to depend more on political beliefs than on one's position in the social structure. This is, however, a self-liquidating participation. The exiles are no longer a problem at home for the Cuban government. The opposition has been exported once again, contributing to the regime's consolidation in a difficult time.[32]

Many of those who left have complained of consumer shortages in goods and services. The "consumerist" critique of the Cuban government's performance is, at times, devastating. For example, the national newsmagazine *Bohemia* conducted a small survey among 135 respondents in the cities of Havana and Matanzas concerning the supply and quality of clothing. Clothing, a basic need, has been included in the rationing system since 1962, but it has also become available legally in recent years at higher prices in the so-called "parallel market" in government stores. The respondents to the *Bohemia* survey were citizens whose political views on other subjects remain unknown; there is no reason to think that they are other than a random sample of the population of these two cities. What, then, do they think?

A substantial majority (59 percent) believe that the supply of clothing is good or sufficient, consistent with its availability through both the rationing and the parallel market systems. But 78 percent of the respondents believe that clothing does not respond to fashions; 84 percent find little variety in the clothing supply; 62 percent believe that the clothing available is neither functional nor practical; 76 percent complained about the quality of materials; 47 percent specifically mentioned that the materials were inappropriate for Cuba's climate; and 76 percent had difficulty finding clothing for their size. In addition, 65 percent believe that the enterprises responsible for the clothing supply do not take into account the opinions of consumers and, most surprisingly, reflecting the increasing importance of the parallel market, 91 percent believe that prices are too high.[33]

The consumer's dissatisfaction with economic performance is thus not limited to those who have chosen exile. It is a fact of Cuban public opinion. While the government has attempted to meet this criticism by improving the supply and quality of production, its principal approach to its critics in 1979-1981 was to increase internal security controls.

The leadership has thus turned much of its attention to the alleged weaknesses in the work of the Interior Ministry and the courts. The most extensive official criticism was made by Fidel Castro in his report to the Second Party Congress. He chided the Interior Ministry for its "tendency toward bureaucratism and a weakening sense of discipline and rigor." He said that its efficiency had declined not so much against the clearly counterrevolutionary enemy but against other manifestations of "highly dangerous elements with serious crime records." These crime records, of course, include activities only some of which are strictly "common crime." Efforts to leave the country without an exit permit, or violations of the rationing system, are considered crimes in Cuba, but in fact they result from aspects of the Cuban political and economic system that generate crime. Nonetheless, Fidel Castro criticized the Revolutionary National Police because it did not respond well to these tasks of "crime control"; he also complained of "some legal mechanisms that did not promote a more active and efficient struggle against crime."[34]

The only government sector whose top leadership was changed entirely in December 1979-January 1980 was that of internal order, law and courts. The Ministers of Interior and Justice, the Attorney General, and the President of the Supreme Court were all replaced (the latter through retirement). Why did this happen?

In addition to the rise in political and economic discontent, the revolutionary government may have encountered the "excessive success" of the Constitution and the new legal codes approved in the mid-1970s. These helped to set a climate for laws being observed and arbitrariness reduced.[35] Such measures worked too well. Beginning in 1979, the courts were criticized for their enforcement of procedural safeguards whose consequence was to set free people accused of crimes. For example, 22,138 cases (37.1 percent of those on file) were dismissed in 1978. About one-third of these were dismissed for lack of sufficient evidence, and the balance because the guilty party could not be determined. In addition, there were also 3,830 acquittals, of which almost half occurred because the prosecution withdrew the charges. A storm of protest broke out over the leniency of the police and the courts. President Fidel Castro summed up the mood by saying that the effect had been to create "guarantees for the criminal"; instead, the rights of society had to prevail.[36]

That criticism set the stage for the personnel changes and for the toughening of the laws and of law enforcement. Political Bureau member Armando Hart summarized the policy as it had evolved a year later: "the general policy, with regard to the penal regulations, . . . is that legislation be made more severe."[37] There were also extralegal moves, particularly the promotion of "asambleas de repudio," where members of local Committees for the Defense of the Revolution were to express their disgust at those who had chosen to leave the country in 1980. These often served as settings for uncontrolled violence. A street brawl at the U.S. Interests Section was also a part of this increased legal and extralegal repressive climate as a means to deal with opponents. Repressive measures were also applied within the intellectual community. For example, a number of professors and students at the University of Havana were dismissed or placed on probation on the grounds of insufficient ideological zeal. More generally, the Committees for the Defense of the Revolution made 180,000 reports to the police for various reasons from 1977 to 1981.[38]

The repressive apparatus was strengthened in 1980 compared to immediately preceding levels as one response to the crisis of those months. Combined with measures already discussed, the boundary between those within and outside the revolution has been sharpened. Patterns of political stratification are clearer. Participation for the "politically marginal" is severely constrained. The procedures to deal with this minority of the population are confrontational and repressive. And, as the extralegal measures have again subsided from their temporary reappearance in 1980, the mechanisms for the state to relate to its opponents have also come to rely on formal, albeit tougher, procedures.

INTERMEDIATE ELITES

The evolving pattern of political stratification does not simply separate elite from mass. It has also led, albeit cautiously, to the development of organizational politics at the intermediate level. Intermediate-level organizations struggle over degrees of centralization or autonomy, regulation and deregulation that have been critical issues in Cuban revolutionary politics. At stake is a challenge to central power. Two examples will be used to illustrate opportunities and problems: managers and the Peasants' Association (ANAP).

Managers

One political consequence of the changes in Cuban economic policies, alluded to by Carmelo Mesa-Lago in his chapter in this book, has been the emergence of a managerial interest. There is, to be sure, no national association of managers. Managers belong to labor unions as do other workers, and they subordinate to ministerial bureaucracies. But managers have begun to articulate their interests at meetings called to discuss management issues; their views also appear to be represented in part by the officials in charge of implementing the new planning and management system.

At the second meeting on the implementation of this management system, held in 1980, some managers argued publicly about the need to enhance managerial autonomy from the central state organs in order to improve general economic efficiency. They complained of bureaucratic restrictions imposed from above.[39]

The officials of the Central Planning Board in charge of the management system are also blunt. Their main report in 1980 notes that a serious problem is how to establish, maintain, and enhance enterprise autonomy: "At present, there is excessive tutelage or paternalism by the majority of central state organizations over the firms that are subordinate to them." The report notes that this is a violation of the law as well as undermining economic efficiency.[40] Moreover, while enterprise participation in the formulation of the national plan has increased, progress made "is still insufficient and occasionally formalistic."[41] The report details examples of gross centralization of economic decision making which, in effect, nullify the policy toward greater managerial independence.

In turn, managers are being criticized both by central state organization technocrats and by labor union leaders. Technocrats criticize managers for talking about enterprise autonomy but doing little to defend it in practice. For example, managers have been slow to use available legal marketing mechanisms that require entrepreneurship to sell their marginal or lower quality products or byproducts ("seconds" as they might be called in the United States). Managers complain that the quantitative targets embodied in the plans are sometimes illusory; they do not reflect adequately the reality of the work center and, just as importantly, they reduce the funds to be distributed at the year's end to management and labor. Technocrats counter that they are opposed to designing plans that can be fulfilled effortlessy just to generate such funds; technocrats also argue that it is management's responsibility to make certain that all numbers in the plan are based on objective facts.[42]

Because labor unions have little impact on wages and benefits at the enterprise level (these are set centrally), much of their effort turns toward problems of occupational health and safety and to disciplinary relations between labor and management. Early in 1981, the Cuban Workers' Confederation (CTC) inspected health and safety job conditions and found about 3.5 million violations of the law in 2,386,874 labor files surveyed. Only 400,000 cases could be resolved quickly.[43] The unions have also complained of managerial "excesses" in the application of labor discipline regulations. They have also complained that regulations covering managerial transgressions and abuses are being applied too leniently and, in some egregious cases (such as in the rather vast educational establishment for Cuban and foreign students in the Isle of Youth), not at all.[44]

The future of organized managerial politics in Cuba remains uncertain because the observed behavior is so new. The limited increase in managerial autonomy has generated a debate about the kinds and extent of autonomy. Many managers are clearly unaccustomed to behaving as innovative and risk-taking entrepreneurs because their experience has been with rigid centralization. The increase in managerial autonomy has also given rise to an increase of labor union activity in the limited areas where managers can be held personally responsible: the work environment and discipline. Discussions over managerial abuses in turn indicate the reappearance in public of concerns about stratification and inequality in the workplace.

So far, managers' fates seem closely linked with those of officials in the Central Planning Board, under the general supervision of Vice President Humberto Pérez. The emergence of managerial politics is yet another indication of the rising organizational stakes in Cuban politics: The disputes are focused at the core of the political system: centralization versus autonomy and authority in the workplace.

ANAP

The National Association of Small Peasants (ANAP) has the most interesting history of all Cuban mass organizations. Early in the 1960s, it behaved somewhat as an interest group, seeking advantages for its members even at the expense of others.[45] The ANAP became a more typical mass organization later in the 1960s, eschewing such autonomous goals and practices. It entered the 1980s with two major projects in political balance. For the sake of the party and government, ANAP pursues the promotion of cooperatives; for its own peasant members, ANAP has promoted and defended the new free peasant market. Early in 1980, in response to the economic crisis, the Cuban government legalized the free peasant market. Peasants, cooperative members, and all those who raise crops may sell in the free peasant market at any price that the market will bear, in the absence of all government price controls, all surpluses that remain after commitments to state agencies recorded in the national plan targets have been met. Until 1975, the government had opposed any private sales by peasants. The First Party Congress reversed that policy, but it set strict limits on the quantities that could be sold freely, and no marketplaces were set up to facilitate such sales. In 1980, controls were relaxed entirely for surplus production, and marketplaces were established to facilitate private sales. Supply and demand have operated since then. Peasants have set prices many times higher than those set under price control because the demand is so great. This undoubtedly serves the need of upper income consumers, and it is likely to stimulate peasant crop production, but it is also a financial breakthrough for the peasantry. No other sector of Cuban society has been deregulated (albeit only partially) as much. But ANAP cannot claim all the credit. One reason for the policy change was probably the belief of the Central Planning Board staff that this was a more efficient agricultural policy. Nonetheless, the ANAP's constituents are the principal gainers. Conscious of the political problems already posed by high prices in the free peasant market, ANAP remains committed to preventing excessive speculation. ANAP's President, alternate Political Bureau member José Ramírez, continues to uphold the view of a "worker-peasant alliance" despite high prices.[46]

ANAP's principal ideological concession to the government has been to promote peasant cooperatives to lead the peasants to pool resources to obtain credit and share services (already widespread practices) and also to share land and labor collectively. Notwithstanding many efforts during the first

decade and a half of revolution, cooperatives of this latter type
were few. Their number actually declined from 328 in 1963 to
126 in 1967 to 43 in 1975. The fifth peasant congress, under
party prodding, approved new efforts to promote these cooperatives. As the Second Party Congress met at the end of 1980,
the number of these cooperatives reached 1,017, accounting
for 11.4 percent of all the land in the hands of ANAP members,
and including 26,454 members (approximately 13.7 percent
of the total ANAP membership).[47]

It remained difficult to convince peasants to join these
cooperatives. ANAP President Ramírez explained the slow
growth of this ideologically visible program: Because peasants
had to choose voluntarily to join, it was necessary to "woo and
convince" them. The drafters of the 1981-1985 five-year plan
were more impatient with ANAP foot-dragging. While most
political statements in the published plan outline are very
discreet, this reference to the slow growth of cooperatives is
uncharacteristically blunt: "The cooperative process in the
countryside has been delayed and there must be an effective
economic, ideological and political work to bring this task to
the level that is required." ANAP responded by raising the
number of cooperative members to 38,000 by the end of
1981.[48]

ANAP has thus entered the 1980s with substantial success
in obtaining favorable partial deregulation to benefit its
members. To retain political support, it may have to work
harder to promote among the peasants a still unpopular
cooperative movement. ANAP's political skills depend greatly
on its small but durable top leadership. Only two ANAP
leaders belong to the party Central Committee. In ANAP's
case, what has made the difference has been the quality of that
leadership's organizational bargaining skills rather than the
quantity of their representation in top organs. ANAP's reappearance as an effective lobby is also consistent with the view
that more autonomous intermediate-level organizations may
become more important in a politically stratified system. As in
the case of managers, they are challenging past practices of
political centralization.

THE ARMED FORCES: RENEWED IMPORTANCE

The Armed Forces have been essential for the survival of revolutionary rule. They were among the first entities to be professionalized and institutionalized; the rest of the party and government subsequently learned from them. The Armed Forces have also been very capable over the years of protecting their organizational stakes and expanding their influence.[49] In the second half of the 1970s, Cuba fought two wars abroad (in Angola and in Ethiopia) and came to maintain a large permanent overseas military presence. In the fall of 1980, that amounted to approximately 35,000 troops.[50] To support them, the Armed Forces undertook new programs that increased their social weight and claimed additional resources. Partly as a result of those commitments, and partly because of deteriorating relations with the United States since 1978, the Cuban Armed Forces induced these policy changes. This section will discuss only the political and organizational aspects of the recent growth of the Cuban Armed Forces.

The Cuban military still accounts for a very high proportion of the party Central Committee. Although their share of the membership has declined, the absolute number of military full and alternate Central Committee members has increased. Military overrepresentation in the Central Committee, compared to the military share of party membership, apparently also increased from 1975 to 1980. It should be assumed that the membership composition of the party Congress reflects the composition of the party membership rather more closely than does the Central Committee. The latter necessarily overrepresents the top elites. Therefore, the ratio of Central Committee membership shares to Congress membership shares (as a proxy for party membership shares) is a measure of the relative strength of representation of a given category of people.

The military accounted for about 19 percent of the First Party Congress but for only 13.7 percent of the Second Party Congress. The party was formed most quickly within the armed forces in the late 1960s and early 1970s; the military share of the entire party probably declined in the late 1970s because the party's civilian sector grew more rapidly. This would also explain the relative decline of the military shares from one party Congress to the next. The military share of Central Committee membership, however, declined more slowly than the military share of the Congress (see Table 1.1). Relative military overrepresentation thus increased from 1975 to 1980. The ratio of the military's share of the full membership of the Central Committee to its share of the membership of the party Congress was 1.69 in 1975; in 1980, that statistic grew to 1.77. For all members (full and alternate), that statistic grew from 1.70 in 1975 to 1.98 in 1980. The Armed Forces and the Interior Ministries thus entered the 1980s claiming a rising relative share of party power.[51]

The Armed Forces have obtained the approval of "veteran's preference" for returning troops in jobs and housing, especially for those left vacant by those who became exiles in 1980. The Society for Patriotic-Military Education (SEPMI) was established in January 1980. It helps to prepare low-skill specialists who might work eventually in the Armed Forces, and it promotes sports that help to train people in militarily useful activities (target shooting, parachuting, and the like). The SEPMI is also a propaganda organ for the Armed Forces, building support for the military and its programs. Within a year of its founding, SEPMI had 80,721 affiliates in 671 local associations; its 371 sports clubs had over 13,000 members. By January 1982, SEPMI had 117,363 members in 987 local associations. Given that most of the equipment for these sports is expensive and must be imported, the commitment to this program is all the more remarkable.[52]

Also in 1980, the government established a new Territorial Militia. These units are to be financed largely by the people's donations beyond the formal military budget; the militia's training, which occurs during weekends and vacations, amounts to forty class hours a year. Thus the military have successfully claimed more resources from the rest of the society. The Territorial Militia's creation has been justified publicly as a response to threats from the Reagan administration in the United States. In fact, as Armed Forces Minister Raúl Castro has explained, the Armed Forces had pushed earlier for the establishment of these units out of their strategic and organizational perspectives: "The organization of these units is necessary in order to round out our defense system." "We have accelerated the process," added General Castro, "to meet the threats hurled by the new U.S. administration."[53] The basic rationale, then, comes from the Armed Forces' need for organizational growth, now only made politically easier within Cuba by the changing international situation.

The Territorial Militia revives in part the old notion of the militia that had disappeared as the professional military reserves and the civil defense were developed. The Territorial Militia seeks to include students who are not yet in the military or the reserves, women, able-bodied people above military reserve age limits, and workers who cannot leave the factories to serve in the Armed Forces on a regular basis. The Territorial Militia is to be included in military planning and exercises. It will be used primarily in military construction, rear guard operations, and the protection of factories and farms. The units most closely linked to the regular Armed Forces are commanded by regular officers.

To implement this organizational innovation, a military officer has been assigned to every municipal and provincial government to coordinate national defense at the grass roots. Never before had the Armed Forces penetrated subnational government so effectively. The ideological rationale also hearkens to a pattern of role expansion familiar in the Cuban military in earlier years. As General of the Army Raúl Castro put it, "the organization of the militia is also related to a broader concept of national defense, which should be seen as the unity of all factors of defense and production."[54]

The Armed Forces have also obtained full recognition of their five top schools as equivalents of a university. When the reform of higher education in 1976 established the Ministry of Higher Education, only the Military Technical Institute was designated as a center of higher education. By academic year

1977-78, all five of the top military schools qualified as higher education centers. Finally, in December 1980, the Executive Committee of the Council of Ministers established full equivalency between the engineering degrees granted by these five military schools and the universities. The Armed Forces Ministry retained full control over these schools; they were not turned over to the Ministry of Higher Education, even though the latter is headed by a former general. More importantly, this reflects the continuing upgrading of the professional quality of the Cuban military officer corps. Beginning with the class of 1982, the Cuban Armed Forces will receive only officers who are university graduates. That had not been the norm previously.[55]

The Armed Forces have also obtained resources to raise the standard of living of officers and troops. Facilities have been improved; housing has been built; social and recreational clubs for officers and troops have been established. Wages, pensions, and other social security benefits have been increased. These benefits maintain differences by rank, so that in each instance the rewards to officers are greater.[56]

The Armed Forces succeeded as well in changing the draft recruitment policy. Beginning in 1979, they began to draft the male graduates of technological and senior academic secondary schools before they went on to the university, thereby markedly improving the quality of draftees. The terms of service were also changed. Draftees who distinguished themselves militarily and politically could get a reduction of up to one year in the ordinary three-year term of service so that they could continue their university education. While the Armed Forces were thus allowed for the first time to systematically tap better trained young people, the intention has also been announced of generalizing this practice so that the completion of secondary education (academic or vocational) will become a prerequisite for military service, raising the draft age from 16 to 18. Given the extraordinary expansion of the Cuban educational system, this further policy change should be feasible soon.[57]

The changes in draft policy clarify the motivations for the other policy changes. The Territorial Militia and the SEPMI will reach students not in active military service either before or after they serve in the Armed Forces. The quality of military personnel will be improved without interrupting the links between the Armed Forces and the country's youth from age sixteen on. A probable corollary policy (not, however, yet mentioned) is that young people with poor academic records and discipline problems might be excluded from the regular Armed Forces and channelled to the Army of the Working Youth, devoting their time to burdensome economic tasks (sugar cane harvest, construction, and so forth) under military discipline for three years.[58]

The Armed Forces began training regular university students as reserve officers in the 1976-77 school year. As of 1981, over 5,000 new reserve officers were made available by these university programs; the inflow should remain at least at that number through 1985. Indeed, as the program is extended to all universities (and comes to include women) in the early 1980s, General Raúl Castro expects to be receiving 10,000 new reserve officers per year. As a part of the policy of strengthening the Armed Forces, these regular university students are called up for one month's intensive military training at the end of each school year and for six months' training upon graduation.[59]

Reserve call-ups for training also became more frequent and all-encompassing in the early 1980s. Reservists who had not been called up for military training in a number of years, including many over age 40, were called back for further military training in 1980 and in 1981.[60]

The formal military budget has changed little in the late 1970s (after doubling in real terms from its level in the early 1970s). Military expenditures in the 1981 budget are 842 million pesos, the highest sum ever, but account for only 7.5 percent of the total expenditure budget, the lowest share in recent years.[61] However, the military's economic burden is much higher upon adding the new extrabudgetary costs, such as the financing of the Territorial Militia. But the most important way to assess the military burden is its impact on personnel. More than 100,000 military have been sent to Angola and Ethiopia (original troops, plus replacements) in 1975-1980. Thus, the combined effect of past practices (including a large and active military reserve), recent changes, and foreseeable innovations in the military's relations with society have greatly increased the scope and weight of the Armed Forces' authority and influence in a systematic, organized fashion.[62]

The Armed Forces have, of course, maintained the most hierarchically strict command relations within their own organization. Systematic politicization by the Communist party has not challenged the military rank structure. The proportion of officers who belonged to either the party or the Communist Youth Union rose from 86 percent in 1976 to over 90 percent in 1981. The persistence of the military hierarchy within the party can be shown in part by an analysis of the ranks of delegates to the Second Party Congress in the leading military units. Combining the three territorial armies (West, Center, and East), the Air Force, and the Rear Guard Forces, the delegates elected through normal processes in these units were: 17 division and brigade generals, 35 colonels and lieutenant colonels, 8 other officers, and no one below the rank of First Lieutenant (4 civilian workers of the Armed Forces were also elected).

Partly in compensation, the Central Committee developed a procedure (applied generally, not just in the military) to reach into any organization to pick delegates with outstanding work records to the party Congress. The "direct" delegates, thus selected, included no generals, 2 colonels and lieutenant colonels, 7 other officers, and still no one below the rank of first lieutenant (7 civilian workers were also selected). Even after these efforts, the military delegation to the Second Congress remained top-heavy. The Navy, too, adhered to this pattern. No one below the rank of ship captain was a Congress delegate (2 civilian workers were also sent). In addition, no one below the rank of colonel became a full member of the Central Committee. All division generals but for the head of

TABLE 1.2   Social Stratification in the Cuban Communist Party:
             National Level, 1980

	N	% mass	% elites	Members as % of mass in labor force[a]	Members as % of elites in labor force[a]
Labor Force[a]	2,397,500	84.8	15.2	—	—
Communist party civilian membership[b]	434,143	62.3	37.7	13.3	27.5
II Party Congress civilian membership[d]	1,520	52.4	47.6	39[c]	198[c]
II Party Congress full membership	1,780	44.7	55.3[e]	39[c]	—

a. Refers to state civilian labor force in 1977. Excludes military and small private (mostly peasant) sectors.
b. Assumes that military and "other" shares of the Second Party Congress are exactly proportional to their share of the party membership. Military and "other" party members are thereby excluded from this row. Includes peasant sector.
c. Per 100,000.
d. Excludes 13.7 percent of the Congress who are military and 0.9 percent classified as "others." Includes peasant sector.
e. Includes military and "other."

SOURCE: *Granma,* December 20, 1980, pp. 1, 5; *Granma Weekly Review,* December 28, 1980, p. 12; Comité Estatal de Estadísticas, *Anuario estadístico de Cuba, 1978* (Havana), p. 58.

the Air Force made it as full Central Committee members (the Air Force Chief remained a Central Committee alternate).[63]

The Armed Forces have shown once again that they are Cuba's most politically skillful bureaucracy. Their achievements in organizational politics far exceed what ANAP has accomplished; managers, in contrast to the military, have hopes, but few successes, to their credit. The mixture of a plausible international threat, a considerable weight within the party elite, and extraordinary organizational skills have prepared the Armed Forces well to continue to succeed in a politically stratified Cuba.

SOCIAL AND POLITICAL STRATIFICATION

There is also a relationship between political and social stratification. Tables 1.2 and 1.3 present some information relating party membership and rank to occupational categories.

TABLE 1.3   Social Stratification in the Cuban Communist Party, 1980: Local Examples

| | Labor force | | PCC (N = 244) | | | |
	% mass	% elite	% mass	% elite	Members as % of mass in labor force	Members as % of elite in labor force
"René Arcay" cement factory, Mariel, (N = 938)	79	21	57	43	19	53
"La Conchita" fruit and vegetable preserves factory (N = 849)	93	7	62	38	6	48

SOURCE: Computed from *Granma*, July 9, 1980, p. 1; January 7, 1981, p. 2.

In each table, the term "mass" refers to those directly linked with production, services, and education (a category that also includes professionals and technicians). This is the key statistic reported by the Cuban Communist party at all levels. Despite its fuzziness, it sets apart this large conglomerate of people from those referred to as "elites" in the tables. The latter are political and administrative leaders and staff. In the fourth row of Table 1.2, the term "elite" also includes all Second Party Congress members who are not "mass" (most of the additions are military officers who should, indeed, be considered elites).

The elite faction is far better represented in the party than is the mass (Table 1.2). Whereas the civilian elites account for only 15.2 percent of the State civilian labor force, they account for 37.7 percent of the civilian party membership, and for 47.6 percent of the civilian membership of the Second Party Congress. Because most military party members are officers, and because more military members of the Second Congress were officers, it is plausible to add the military to the elite category. The elite share of the Second Party Congress then rises to a high of 55.3 percent. The elites' share of the Second Congress is over three times their share of the labor force. At the Second Party Congress, there were 39 civilian mass delegates for every 100,000 mass members of the state civilian labor force, but there were 198 civilian elite delegates for every 100,000 elite members of the state civilian labor force. (This is in fact a very conservative estimate of elite over-representation. Because most military members of the Second Congress are elites, too, the combined elite overrepresentation score is likely to be much larger). Thus, at a minimum, the elites were five times more likely to be represented at the Second Congress than was the mass.

At the level of the party, the computation in Table 1.2 is extremely conservative. It assumes that the military's share of the party is exactly proportional to its share of the membership at the Second Party Congress. In fact, a better guess is that the military share increases from the party at the base all the way to the Central Committee. It has already been shown that the military share of the Central Committee is twice the military share of the Second Congress. (Recall also that most military party members are officers.) Nevertheless, the computation in Table 1.2, conservative as it is, shows that the civilian elite has at least twice the representation in the party as the civilian mass. While over one-quarter of the state civilian labor force elites belong to the party, somewhat less than one-seventh of the state civilian labor force mass belongs to the party.

Another problem with Table 1.2 is that there are no pertinent data on the entire labor force; peasants are excluded from the available statistics. While it is difficult to assess what difference this makes for the analysis, it is likely that peasants contribute fewer members to the party than does the rest of the society. If so, the party would be even more unrepresentative of the labor force than is suggested in Table 1.2. It is also difficult to say whether the mass-elite ratio in the peasant sector is different than in the state civilian labor force. My guess is that more peasants are likely to be in the "mass" category. If so, the underrepresentation of the mass of the population in the party would be even more severe than is reflected in Table 1.2.

Table 1.3 confirms at the local level the patterns identified at the national level. Bear in mind that these plants are described in the Cuban press because they are considered to be good examples. It is likely that other work centers perform much less well. Both factories have a mass majority within the local Communist party consistent with the national party figures in Table 1.2. However, only 19 percent of the mass at the cement plant and only 6 percent of the mass at the preserves plant belong to the party, whereas 53 percent and 43 percent of the elites do so, respectively. (These latter figures give further credence to the argument that the 27.5 percent statistic in the right-hand column in Table 1.2 is a serious underestimate).

There is, therefore, a close and striking relationship between social class and party membership, and between social class and party rank. This can be seen at both the national and the local levels.

Nevertheless, it is equally correct that the Cuban Communist party has made great efforts to increase the mass share of the membership. Figures on social stratification's link to party membership were much more lopsided at the First Party Congress. President Fidel Castro rightly pointed out that the number of mass party members increased very substantially from one Congress to the next. The rate of increase of mass members was greater than the rate of increase of elite members, and that is why the mass share of the party civilian membership rose to 62.3 percent.[64]

The arithmetic of social stratification, however, has some often unsuspected effects. Let us return to the example of the "René Arcay" cement plant. If we assume that the plant's labor force in 1976 was the same as in 1980, then 24 percent of the elites at the plant belonged to the party in 1976 as versus only 7 percent of the mass.[65] By 1980, the mass statistic had risen by a factor of 2.7 and the elite statistic by a factor of 2.2— the "right" trend for a party at the vanguard of the proletariat. However, the percentage gap between elite and mass in 1976 was only 17 percent; by 1980 it had widened to 34 percent. Inequalities had thus doubled during a five-year period notwithstanding the best, most sincere efforts of the Communist party.

Educational data also show a widening of inequalities. In 1975, the modal party member only had a sixth grade education; only 16 percent had completed senior high school at the time of the First Congress. The educational gap between party and people was narrow. While 59 percent of the people had at least a sixth grade education by the mid-1970s, 80 percent of the party had reached such a level. At the time of the First Congress, the situation could be described as a junior high school elite leading a grammar school people. By the Second Congress, the average educational level in the Cuban population was sixth grade, so that one could speak of a junior high school population. But the rate of educational increase has been much faster for party members. In 1980, 75.5 percent of all party members had at least a high school education, almost five times the rate five years earlier.[66] What had been a gap of only about three years of education between party and people had more than doubled too.

A somewhat similar stratification was evident in elective posts. For example, only 22.6 percent of all municipal officials elected in October 1981 were workers. The proportion of agricultural and industrial workers elected to the National Assembly in November 1981 was 17.6 percent; the proportion that included all workers "directly linked with production, education and services" was 37 percent—less than half their share of the work force.[67]

Evidence of stratification has begun to appear in interpersonal relations. At the "Manuel Martínez Prado" sugar mill, reporters for the news magazine Bohemia found that university-trained technicians who had recently joined the mill's workforce complained that the experienced workers did not trust them and did not communicate what they knew about the mill's operations. The experienced workers, in turn, complained that some of the university-trained technicians were arrogant and impractical. These feelings, of course, are not unique to Cuba or to its mills; but the spread of these feelings of inequality reflects the increasing social and political stratification in Cuba in recent years.[68]

Social and political stratification acquire a dynamic of their own. Cuba is simply finding out how difficult it is to overcome the difficulties of strong stratifying patterns.[69]

CONCLUSION

Cuba enters the 1980s having witnessed impressive changes during the previous two decades. Cuba has become a major factor in the international system. Its revolutionary government has transformed many aspects of its own society, economy, and politics. To its credit, it continues to build on its already impressive accomplishments in certain areas such as education and public health. This chapter has had a much more modest goal: What are the demands for orderliness in the Cuban revolution?

They are those of a regime that could be described as a "consultative oligarchy." The Cuban political system is neither the one-man terroristic dictatorship that its enemies claim nor the participatory egalitarian paradise painted by some of its supporters. Hierarchy, bureaucracy, performance, bargaining over organizational stakes—these are the hallmarks of Cuban politics. Cuba is not unique in this regard, of course, but the two alternative descriptions just cited seem to be more prevalent.

The political authority of the top leadership remains, in effect, unchallenged. Centralized power at the top was strengthened as the 1980s opened. There is also impressive stability, albeit with some changes, at the Central Committee of the Communist party. Organizational representativeness became an increasingly important criterion for membership at the same time that lines of rank and authority were delineated more clearly. Performance also became more clearly related to organizational rank, promotions, and demotions. While the importance of historically grounded factionalism has declined, the symbolic politics of "affirmative action" on the grounds of class and sex (but not race) have appeared.

The demands for orderliness in the revolution have also led

to stratified political participation. There is a good deal of many kinds of political participation in Cuba. Most of it, however, is only consultative, with very little discernible impact on decision making. Again, this does not make Cuba unique, but it does characterize it. The political participatory channel that is most open to independent actions by the mass of the population—citizen-contacting of public officials—is precisely the one that has little bearing on incumbent identity. This consultative participation is itself stratified.

For the top and the intermediate elites, participation is more meaningful. Party members, the overwhelming majority of the National Assembly (many of them are Central Committee members, too), argue and bargain with each other, at times openly, with important effects. Disputes at this lofty level do matter for policy. The stakes have become organizational as well; arguments rage over jurisdiction and rank, over responsibility and institutional power. This widened organizational context has revived the lobbying skills of an organization such as that grouping the small peasants, and it has provided a possible opening—as yet more potential than realized—for managers. It has been a boon to that long-standing master of Cuban bureaucratic politics, the Armed Forces, whose influence over Cuban social life has climbed markedly since 1978. At the bottom of the stratification pyramid are the "politically marginal." The party and government deal with them primarily through the exercise of naked state power. The lines separating them from the majority of the population have hardened as well.

Techniques of problem solving have become organizational, too, from the armed forces to the running of the economy. Even Fidel Castro's political style has begun to take into account his new role as the arbiter among competing organizational claims.

For the world beyond Cuba, there are some significant implications from this analysis. First, the combination of the conflict-ridden international situation around Cuba's world role in the late 1970s and early 1980s with the stronger organizational position of the Cuban Armed Forces in a more stratified context has strengthened the hand of the military over society, economy, and politics. There have been a series of military policy successes.

Second, foreign policy is one of the last vestiges of extremely centralized political decision making, less subject to the organizational competition that has become more important in other policy arenas. Foreign policy remains a matter for the Political Bureau, the Executive Committee of the Council of Ministers, and the Council of State—with considerable overlaps in their memberships. Above all, it remains Fidel Castro's domain.

Third, despite the above, the tendency in the Cuban political system away from rule by a few "heroic" individuals toward rule by organizations that are represented in the top councils of decision making by their leaders, suggests that foreign policy, too, might become an arena for competitive organizational bargaining. Virtually all agencies of the Cuban government now have international links and programs. One-third of the delegates to the Second Party Congress have served abroad in military or civilian tasks (compared to one-twelfth at the First Party Congress).[70] The stakes of much of Cuban foreign policy may also need to respond in the next few years to the demands for orderliness in the revolution.

Fourth, for those who seek to affect internal affairs within Cuba from the outside, beyond foreign policy concerns, the new organizational context and the sharpening political stratification are all the more important.

For Cubans themselves, there might be even more important questions. Do the demands for orderliness in the revolution compete with, overcome, or exclude altogether the demands for a revolution within the revolution? Are the dreams of the late 1950s, which turned the revolution into a national epic for many Cubans, to be realized through rising political and social stratification? Will Cuba respond more to order or to revolution? Can these be combined, as Fidel Castro's formulation hopes for? These questions are only opened, not settled, by this analysis, but they are indeed at the heart of Cuba's future.

NOTES

1. Granma Weekly Review, December 28, 1980, p. 13.
2. For background material, see Jorge I. Domínguez, *Cuba: Order and Revolution* (Cambridge: Harvard University Press, 1978). I will refer to this book for historical background to simplify the references.
3. My biographical files are the principal source. The Cuban daily newspaper, Granma, published short biographies of new Central Committee members in the first months of 1981. A very helpful reference work is the National Foreign Assessment Center, Central Intelligence Agency, *Directory of Officials of the Republic of Cuba* (February 1981).
4. Granma, December 1, 1980, p. 2; ibid., December 5, 1980, p. 2; ibid., December 15, 1980, p. 2; ibid., December 16, 1980, p. 2.
5. For a list, see Domínguez, Cuba, pp. 533-534.
6. Granma, February 17, 1981, p. 2.
7. Granma, February 7, 1981, p. 2.
8. See, for example, Jerry Hough, "The Soviet system: petrification or pluralism?" in Leonard J. Cohen and Jane P. Shapiro, *Communist Systems in Comparative Perspective* (New York: Anchor Press, 1974).
9. Granma, February 10, 1981, p. 2.
10. For a complete set of photographs, see Granma, December 27, 1980, Supplement.
11. See Domínguez, *Cuba,* pp. 243-249 for background. As should become clear, I believe that I underestimated the utility and importance of the National Assembly in those pages. In the paragraphs that follow, I describe not only the limitations that I expected and that have occurred in the Assembly's work but also a surprising (at least to me) level of discussion with somewhat greater policy consequences than I had thought likely.
12. Granma, December 27, 1980, p. 1.
13. Ibid.
14. Granma, July 4, 1980, p. 3.
15. Granma, July 3, 1980, pp. 1-2.
16. Ibid.
17. Departamento de Versiones Taquifráficas, "Discurso pronunciado por el Comandante en Jefe Fidel Castro Ruz, Primer Secretario del CC del Partido Comunista de Cuba y Presidente de los Consejos de Estado y de Ministros en la clausura del II período de sesiones de 1979 de la Asamblea Nacional del Poder Popular," December 27, 1979. This speech has circulated in mimeographed form only. Pagination varies. Section quoted is around the beginning of the third part of the speech.
18. Granma, July 4, 1980, p. 3.
19. Ibid.
20. "¿Cómo marcha la implantación del sistema de dirección y planificación de la economía?" *Bohemia* 71, 27 (July 6, 1979), p. 36; Domínguez, *Cuba,* pp. 300-301.
21. Comisión Nacional de Implantación, Sistema de Dirección y Planificación de la Economía, *Informe Central: Reunión Nacional* (Havana: July 1980), p. 48. These sharp limitations on participation in the workplace—especially violations of the law—also surprised me, especially because they are so unnecessary to the maintenance

of elite control. In my book, I had thought that the norm was what had turned out not to have occurred at all in 41.2 percent of the firms, even in 1980.

22. Granma, December 27, 1979, p. 4.
23. Domínguez, Cuba, pp. 281-291.
24. Susana Tesoro, "Primero vivir, luego filosofar," Bohemia 71, 38 (September 21, 1979), pp. 40-42.
25. Granma, July 4, 1980, p. 4; Granma Weekly Review, December 28, 1980, p. 9.
26. Computations from Bohemia 73, 1 (January 2, 1981), p. 58; Granma Weekly Review, January 6, 1980, p. 3; and Comité Estatal de Estadísticas, Anuario estadístico de Cuba 1978 (Havana), p. 54. For a quantitative breakdown of citizen demands, see Granma, April 6, 1981, p. 4.
27. Mario Escalona Reguera and Nisia Agüero Benítez, "La participación popular en la gestión estatal en Cuba," Revista cubana de administración de salud 5, 3 (July-September 1979), pp. 218-219.
28. Domínguez, Cuba, pp. 265, 267.
29. Granma, January 31, 1981, p. 1; ibid., October 23, 1981, p. 4; ibid., January 23, 1982, p. 2; Gramna Weekly Review, October 5, 1980, p. 2; Bohemia 73, 44 (October 30, 1981), pp. 48, 52.
30. For a review of events and a statement of U.S. policy, see U.S. Department of State, Bureau of Public Affairs, Current Policy 193 (June 20,1980). For a discussion closer to the Cuban government's views, see Lourdes Casal, "Cuba, abril-mayo 1980: la historia y la histeria," Areito 6, 23 (1980), pp. 15-25.
31. On the Vatican and Ecuador embassy seizures, the official Cuban view is available in Granma Weekly Review, December 21, 1980, p. 1, and ibid., March 1, 1981, p. 12. For information on those who seized the Ecuador embassy, see Granma, February 14, 1981, p. 1.
32. See survey conducted by the U.S. Federal Emergency Management Agency, cited in Boston Globe, June 4, 1980, p. 73. For historical comparisons, see Domínguez, Cuba, pp. 139-141.
33. Computed from Tania Quintero and Magda Martínez, "Desde el diseño hasta la talla: encuesta de Bohemia sobre las confecciones textiles," Bohemia 73, 3 (January 16, 1981), pp. 32-37.
34. Granma Weekly Review, December 28, 1980, p. 10.
35. For a good discussion, see three articles by Max Azicri in the Review of Socialist Law (Leyden) 6, 2 (1980): "An introduction to Cuban socialist law," pp. 153-163; "Change and institutionalization in the revolutionary process: the Cuban legal system in the 1970s," pp. 164-182; and "The Cuban family code: some observations on its innovations and continuities," pp. 183-191.
36. Verde olivo 20, 28 (July 15, 1979), pp. 11, 14; Granma Weekly Review, July 15, 1979, p. 2.
37. Granma, July 3, 1980, p. 2.
38. See Casal, "Cuba, abril-mayo 1980"; some of this information was also culled from observations and conversations during my visit to Havana in August 1980. See also Granma, Oct. 23, 1981, p. 4.
39. Raúl Lazo, "Notas sobre la autonomía empresarial," Bohemia 72, 48 (November 28, 1980), p. 19; Granma, January 5, 1981, p. 2.
40. Comisión Nacional de Implantación, Informe, p. 249.
41. Ibid., p. 12.

42. Raúl Lazo, "El tritón y otros mitos," *Bohemia* 73, 13 (March 27, 1981), pp. 32-33.

43. Granma, March 14, 1981, p. 4.

44. Granma, March 16, 1981, p. 2.

45. For a discussion of the ANAP from its foundation until 1977, see Domínguez, *Cuba,* pp. 445-463.

46. For a national listing of free peasant markets, see *Magacin,* August 1, 1980, p. 7. This is a monthly paper with information on retail facilities. For a discussion and defense of the market by peasant leaders and central planners, see, respectively, Granma, January 30, 1981, p. 2; and Granma Weekly Review, November 9, 1980, Supplement, p. 5.

47. Elsa Blaquier and Luis López, "¿Qué nos trajo este quinquenio?" *Verde olivo* 21, 51 (December 21, 1980), pp. 34-43; Granma Weekly Review, December 28, 1981, p. 11.

48. Granma, January 30, 1981, p. 2; Granma, December 12, 1981, p. 2; and Departamento de Orientación Revolucionaria, Comité Central del Partido Comunista de Cuba, *Proyecto de los lineamientos económicos y sociales para el quinquenio 1981-1985* (Havana: 1980), p. 5, section 003.

49. For background, see Domínguez, *Cuba,* Chapter 9.

50. Computed from Granma Weekly Review, August 3, 1980, p. 3; and ibid., November 30, 1980, Supplement, p. 3.

51. Granma, December 20, 1980, p. 5; Domínguez, *Cuba,* p. 332.

52. Granma Weekly Review, June 22, 1980, p. 3; Granma, January 5, 1981, p. 1; Granma, January 28, 1982, p. 3; *Bohemia* 71, 33 (August 17, 1979), p. 54; Lesmes La Rosa, "Primer aniversario de la SEPMI," *Verde olivo* 22, 5 (February 1, 1981), pp. 14-15.

53. Granma Weekly Review, February 8, 1981, p. 12; Granma, January 27, 1982, p. 2.

54. Ibid. See also ibid., February 1, 1981, p. 2.

55. Lesmes La Rosa and Jorge Luis Blanco, "Las FAR en el primer quinquenio," *Verde olivo* 21, 51 (December 21, 1980), p. 8; Mario Rodríguez, "Convertirse en oficial-ingeniero," ibid., 21, 46 (November 16, 1980), p. 34; and Concepción Duchesne, "Incremento y desarrollo de la educación superior," *Bohemia* 72, 48 (November 28, 1980), p. 36.

56. For examples, see Jorge L. Blanco, "Casa de Oficiales," *Verde olivo* 20, 16 (April 22, 1979), pp. 35-36; ibid., 20, 30 (July 29, 1979), p. 52; La Rosa and Blanco, "Las FAR en el primer quinquenio," pp. 4, 7-8; and José Cazañas Reyes, "Nace una comunidad," ibid., 21, 49 (December 7, 1980), pp. 11-13.

57. *Verde olivo* 20, 32 (August 12, 1979); "Ejército Occidental: primera década," ibid., 21, 51 (December 21, 1980), pp. 53-55; La Rosa and Blanco, "Las FAR en el primer quinquenio," p. 6; Granma Weekly Review, December 28, 1980, p. 10.

58. For an update on the Army of the Working Youth, see Luis López, "Un trienio de intensa labor," *Verde olivo* 21, 44 (October 12, 1980), pp. 48-49.

59. Granma Weekly Review, April 19, 1981, p. 2.

60. Jorge Luis Blanco, "Reservistas," *Verde olivo* 22, 5 (February 1, 1981), pp. 38-40.

61. See Granma Weekly Review, January 11, 1981, p. 4, for the 1981 budget. For earlier ones, see Domínguez, "Political and military limitations and consequences of Cuban policies in Africa," *Cuban Studies* 10, 2 (July 1980), pp. 23-24.

62. Granma Weekly Review, December 28, 1980, p. 10, carries the military section of Fidel Castro's main report to the Second Party Congress.

63. Domínguez, *Cuba,* p. 366; Granma Weekly Review, November 29, 1981, Special Supplement, p. 5; José Cazañas Reyes, "IV conferencia del partido en el ejército occidental," *Verde olivo* 21, 41 (October 12, 1980), pp. 50-51; Rubén Fonseca, "VII conferencia del partido en la MGR," ibid., pp. 52-53; Jesús Casal Guerra, "VII conferencia del PCC en la DAAFAR," ibid., 21, 40 (October 5, 1980), pp. 50-51; "Sexta conferencia del Partido-Jefatura de Retaguardia," ibid., pp. 52-53; Lesmes La Rosa, "VI conferencia del partido en el ejército oriental," ibid., pp. 53-55; Pablo Noa, "VIII conferencia del PCC en el ejército central," ibid., pp. 55-56.

64. Granma Weekly Review, December 28, 1980, p. 12.

65. Granma, July 9, 1980, p. 2.

66. Granma Weekly Review, December 28, 1980, p. 13; ibid., July 5, 1981, p. 3; Domínguez, *Cuba,* pp. 170, 317.

67. Granma Weekly Review, October 25, 1981, p. 3; ibid., December 6, 1981, p. 3.

68. "Dentro del 'Martínez Prado,' " *Bohemia* 73, 1 (January 2, 1981), p. 18.

69. For comparable examples from other socialist countries, see Sidney Verba and Goldie Shabad, "Workers' councils and political stratification: the Yugoslav experience," *The American Political Science Review* 72, 1 (March 1978), pp. 80-95; David Lane, *Politics and Society in the USSR* (New York: New York University Press, 1978), pp. 394-414.

70. Granma, December 20, 1980, p. 5; Domínguez, *Cuba,* p. 331.

2

The Mass Media

Their Functions in Social Conflict

JOHN SPICER NICHOLS

The Cuban mass media are an essential channel for mass mobilization and control, management of domestic conflict, and the maintenance of the Cuban revolutionary process. Rather than an inert link between the Cuban leadership and masses, the media are integral threads woven into the fabric of Cuban society that reciprocally affect and are affected by the course of the Cuban revolution. In fact, mass media have been so important in the political process that the late Herbert Matthews of the New York *Times* once described the Cuban revolution as "government by television."[1]

The Cuban leadership, understanding full well the significance of mass communication in the revolution, has placed heavy emphasis on the development and control of the country's print and broadcast media. By allocating a considerable portion of its scarce economic resources and plentiful human resources to the communication sector, Cuba has built one of the most developed media systems among countries of a similar level of

AUTHOR'S NOTE:The author wishes to thank Professor Larry M. Newman, Drexel University; Professors R. Thomas Berner and Robert E. O'Connor, Pennsylvania State University; Orville L. Freeman, President of Business International Corporation; Professor Jorge Reina Schement, University of Southern California; and Elizabeth Mahan, University of Texas at Austin.

economic development. Radio and print media reach virtually all Cubans, and most now receive television.[2] The personnel who staff the media are deeply entrenched in the national power structure. Cuban journalists are members of the Cuban Communist Party (PCC) in greater proportion than most other employment sectors and the population at large,[3] and in addition, most editors, directors, and top-level media policy-makers also hold positions in the PCC, government, or mass organizations.[4] Most important, however, President Fidel Castro and the Central Committee of the PCC have given prominent attention to the role of the media in ideological formation in reports to both the First and Second Congress of the PCC and through other policy statements.[5]

The emphasis placed on the mass media by the Cuban leadership has not been matched by foreign scholars studying the country. While the academic literature is filled with significant research and interesting analyses about the party, military, government, and a wide variety of social sectors and mass organizations, the quantity and quality of research on the media are sadly lacking. The little that does appear in the Cuban studies literature is usually written by academics from disciplines other than mass communication who often lack an understanding of mass communication processes and effects or by mass communication researchers and working journalists who frequently lack an understanding of Cuba as unique social system. The latter group particularly tends to compare the "communist aspects" of the Cuban media to a nonexistent U.S. media utopia and, consequently, arrives at the simplistic conclusion that the U.S. media are "free" and the Cuban media are "not free." This chapter attempts to go beyond simple ideological classification and to explain the functions of the Cuban mass media.

SYSTEMS PERSPECTIVE

This research is rooted in the systems perspective of mass communication developed by Tichenor et al., a research group that views the mass media as a subsystem interdependent with all other parts of the total social system.[6] In the process of encoding essential messages and delivering them to various audiences, the mass media become intertwined in the complex societal network. Moreover, as an organic part of the larger social system, the mass media have the power to control, and in turn are controlled by, other subsystems with which they are linked. Under these conditions, no single social subsystem (much less one individual) could maintain exclusive control over any other subsystem, including the mass media. In sum, mass communication cannot be understood apart from the society within which it operates, and vice versa.

All social systems, especially those that are experiencing rapid social change, are subject to a considerable amount of tension or social conflict. This conflict can be either functional or dysfunctional, depending on a nexus of conditions within and surrounding the system. Conflict could be a sign of vitality and arouse power-holders and power-contenders to seek creative solutions to existing problems, or it could be a sign of turmoil leading to the disintegration of the system. In either case, the mass media are an important, probably essential mechanism through which the social system attempts to control conflict. Under some circumstances, the mass media could initiate or accelerate social conflict and thereby help to revitalize a stagnating system. Under other conditions, they could reduce conflict that is fostering disorder and threatening society.

In both cases, the mass media generally operate in the interest of system maintenance. Tichenor et al. say that "maintenance" does not necessarily mean perpetuating the status quo, although that may be the outcome. Rather, the research team defines "maintenance" as sustaining the system and its dynamic processes. The Cuban revolution is, of course, an example of a dynamic process.

The mass media perform two different but overlapping functions in maintaining the social system—feedback control and distribution control. In the feedback control function, the mass media apply corrective pressure on subsystems that may be out of functional balance with the total system or on the system itself. For example, Watergate-style investigative reporting contributed to the realignment of power-contenders in the U.S. government in the 1970s. Similarly, the Cuban mass media could perform a regulatory function by reporting debates in Committees for the Defense of the Revolution and citizen complaints about public services or by setting new or perhaps competing agendas for public discussion. This is not to say that the media take direct action to solve the problems or that the media act autonomously. Tichenor et al. use the analogy of a thermostat which senses a change in temperature, thereby triggering a heating or air conditioning unit. However, the thermostat is not an independent mechanism. It can be set on high or low by powerful actors in the environment that it helps to regulate.[7]

In the distribution control function, the mass media withhold, selectively distribute, or restructure tension-laden information in order to maintain the system. In the United States, the mass media may avoid potentially dysfunctional messages ranging from national security issues to small town gossip. All advertising and public relations activities by both public and private organizations are examples of the distribution control function. In Cuba, announcements of favorable production figures, government decrees, speeches by the leadership, schedules of cultural activities, and other information intended for routine consumption (rather than to stimulate social reaction) serve a distribution control function.

"Newspapers, or mass media generally, function as a necessary component of a system's institutional technology for dealing with conflict, a major process associated with social change and adaptation," say Tichenor et al. "Media constitute a part which is necessary, but not sufficient in and of itself or causal in the conflict process."[8] Therefore, all mass media, whether local or national, capitalist or communist, developed or developing, appear to perform the feedback control and distribution control functions for the maintenance of their respective social systems. The extent to which the media perform these functions depends on a variety of political, economic, and social conditions in the system. Herein lies the major research question in this chapter: Under what conditions do the mass media perform which functions in the management of conflict in Cuba?

STRUCTURES AND FUNCTIONS OF THE CUBAN MASS MEDIA

All Cuban mass media are owned, operated, and financed by the government, the PCC, or their constituent organizations. Radio and television are the most important media for mass integration, education, and mobilization. Castro effectively used Radio Rebelde, a clandestine radio station, during the guerrilla war, and in the early days of the new government he appeared on national radio and television, often daily, to explain revolutionary goals and encourage popular participation.[9] Owing largely to this early success, the Cuban leadership has continued to invest heavily in and rely on the national broadcasting system. Consequently, the organization and control of Cuban broadcasting is highly centralized. All broadcasting media are administered by the Cuban Institute of Radio and Television (ICRT), which in turn is directly supervised by one of the most influential vice presidents of the Council of Ministers, José R. Fernández Alvarez.[10]

In contrast, the print media are not centrally administered. More than 100 newspapers, magazines, and specialized journals are published in Cuba by most mass organizations and divisions of the party or government. Major national newspapers are: *Granma,* the official voice of the PCC; *Juventud Rebelde,* published by the Union of Young Communists; and *Los Trabajadores,* published by the Central Union of Cuban Workers. Examples of major Cuban magazines and journals are: *Verde Olivo,* Revolutionary Armed Forces; *El Deporte,* National Institute of Sports; *Politica Internacional,* Ministry of Foreign Relations; and *Mujeres,* Cuban Federation of Women. Each organization has primary responsibility for staffing, operations, and editorial policy; however, party officials have coordinating powers and considerable influence in matters of policy. Nonetheless, there is no information ministry that administers all or most of the nation's mass communication activities.

Because of the diverse organization of the print media and the indirect, decentralized control by party and government (*Granma* would be one of several notable exceptions), any variation in the content of Cuban media would most likely be found among newspapers and magazines. This is not to imply that any Cuban publications criticize or oppose stated national goals; however, the organizational structure of the print media allow them to attach different agendas to national needs and policies by emphasizing matters of greatest concern to the sectors they represent. To the extent that these publications set different agendas by discussing different topics, drawing on different sources of information and using different styles and interpretations, they are serving a feedback control function.

This chapter will argue that the degree to which the Cuban media serve a feedback control function in addition to the distribution control function is related to four interrelated factors: ideology, economic and technological constraints, social differentiation, and social conflict.

Ideology

Marxist-Leninist ideology, which views the press as a purposive tool of the state to further revolutionary goals, began to play a central role in the development of the Cuban mass media on June 4, 1963, when Castro went on national radio and television to report on his recent visit to Moscow. Prominent among the topics he discussed was *Pravda,* the official newspaper of the Central Committee of the Communist Party of the Soviet Union. Castro complimented the newspaper's physical format, content, and editorial leadership and called on the Cuban press to use *Pravda* as a model.[11] In just over two years, *Hoy* and *Revolución,* Havana's two major dailies, each representing rival factions within the new revolutionary government, were merged to form *Granma,* the single, official voice of the Central Committee of the newly reorganized Communist Party of Cuba. *Granma* is radically different from its parent newspapers, *Hoy* and *Revolución,* both of which were an uneasy mixture of revolutionary ideology and prerevolutionary style, organization, and format, and it is remarkably similar to *Pravda,* with the exception that it is slightly more flamboyant in its use of color and special graphics.

The foundation upon which *Pravda,* the rest of the Soviet press, and, by extension, the Cuban press are built is a quote from Lenin describing the functions of a newspaper as collective propagandist, agitator, and organizer.[12] Although not specifically mentioned in his famous quote, Lenin also assigned great significance to a fourth function of the press—self-criticism.[13] A summary of Inkeles's description of these four functions, adapted to the Cuban press, follows:[14]

Agitator. Contrary to the capitalist press, the communist press makes no pretense of independence in operation or objectivity in reporting. The media are intended to transmit, explain, and interpret the important actions of the government to the mass population. In the case of Cuba, *Granma* preserves and extends Castro's words by publishing lengthy verbatim transcripts of his speeches. Government decrees and party policy papers are also published frequently. In addition, the press is responsible for justifying and advocating those official pronouncements. Lenin especially emphasized the responsibility of the press in educating the masses on topics of applied economics, a philosophy that Castro has practiced throughout the Cuban revolution.[15] In fulfilling this mission, the communist press must emphasize social processes rather than dwelling on current events and people—the main topics of most Western news stories.

Propagandist. Communist propaganda, not pejorative in this context, is the means of educating party cadres about

Marxist-Leninist theory. In this capacity, the press is the vehicle for ideological education for a specialized audience, the rank-and-file party workers. With periodic indoctrination about the theoretical underpinning of government actions, party officials throughout the country are believed to perform their jobs more effectively. The entire second page of the usual six pages in *Granma* is often devoted to such ideological lessons.

Organizer. The communist press is also an official gazette for organizing the administrative operations of the complex government and party bureaucracy. *Granma* is mandatory reading for provincial and local party officials who seek the latest directives from Havana and instructions on how to implement them. By the same token, the magazines and journals of the different government divisions and mass organizations explain technical information to specialists in the field or publicize the techniques and experiences of the best workers. As in the propaganda function, the press serves the organizing function for a small, specialized segment of the total audience.

Self-critic. As the Soviet government grew highly bureaucratic under the weight of numerous layers and complex regulations, the leadership discovered that it was impossible for supervisors to check more than a small portion of government operations. Consequently, the Soviet leadership implemented Lenin's fourth press function. By encouraging the general public to expose and criticize operational deficiencies and ideological deviations through the press, the leadership established a means through which the effectiveness of the bureaucracy could be checked without relying on the bureaucracy and, at the same time, created a controlled channel through which the public could express its grievances directly to the policymakers. These grievances, however, must be confined to the tactical operations of government and not deal with revolutionary philosophy or question decisions already made by the central government, in accordance with the principle of democratic centralism. For decades, the Soviet government has attempted to accomplish the self-criticism function in two main ways. First, tens of thousands of worker-peasant correspondents were recruited to write articles about their local or workplace conditions. This network of volunteer correspondents is expected to bring the perspective of the masses to the attention of the leadership. Second, Soviet newspapers, especially local newspapers, run many letters-to-the-editor, articles by ordinary citizens, and other forms of citizen feedback. Together, these devices are intended to create a channel for releasing public tension and aggression and a source of information used to regulate government operations so that they are neither too far ahead of mass thinking nor too far behind. This press function is probably the most delicate to implement and maintain.

The Cuban press has been relatively slow in serving the self-criticism function. Although Cuban leaders and editors frequently mentioned the need for more self-criticism, a regular letters-to-the-editor column and other forms of substantive citizen feedback did not appear in *Granma* and other newspapers until the mid-1970s. Most of the self-criticism is top-down, from the leadership to lower levels of government and the public, rather than bottom-up, from the masses to the leadership. Nonetheless, some citizen feedback by voluntary correspondents and ordinary citizens does appear in the Cuban press, and statements by the leadership indicate that greater emphasis will be placed on it in the future. At the Fourth Congress of the Union of Cuban Journalists, held in March 1980, First Vice President Raúl Castro delivered a strongly worded speech calling for more press criticism. "Criticize all you want! The Party is behind you!" he shouted to the delegates as he was leaving the stage.[16]

Although we probably will never know for sure if Fidel Castro was a committed Marxist-Leninist before the insurrection, his brand of communism is better described as an attribute of the revolution rather than its essence. Ideology has frequently been compromised to accommodate unique local conditions and evolving opportunities. Castro is, according to Herbert Matthews, "pragmatic and opportunistic, not dogmatic."

Matthews added:

> Fidel Castro, like Mao Tse-tung, is an activist, not a theorist.
> He does all sorts of things and calls them Marxist-Leninist. As
> Raul Castro said to me some years ago, "After all, Marxism is a
> flexible concept; it allows for development and change."[17]

Clearly, the acceptance of Marxist-Leninist ideology has had
a major impact on the Cuban press since the mid-1960s and
will continue to affect the operations and functions of the press
into the 1980s. But the effect of ideology is not all-encompassing or even primary in explaining the mass communication
process in Cuba. This chapter argues below that other factors,
especially structural conditions in the Cuban social system,
are more important in understanding the activities of the press.
This conclusion contradicts writers who view the press as a
captive of a few men and their political ideology.

Economic and Technological Constraints

Development of the Cuban mass media has been and will be
limited by what is economically and technologically possible.
For ideological and practical reasons, Cuba has made a strong
commitment to national and international communication;
however, it is faced with the dilemma of being a technologically
isolated country committed to a technologically advanced
field. In the more than two decades of the Cuban revolution,
there has been an explosion in technology in both the print and
broadcast media. Not only have the Cuban media been unable
to keep pace with the developments, but in some sectors, Cuba
has made no improvement in media equipment at all.[18]
    The Cuban television system best demonstrates this prob-
lem. Information gathered during tours of Cuban studios and
interviews with ICRT officials clearly indicates that the equipment problem has become acute and that it is nearing the point
where repairs and cannibalization will no longer keep the
antique equipment in operation. A Cuban broadcasting official
claims that Cuban television equipment is the oldest in

operation in the world.[19] When Cuban television started in 1952, second-hand equipment from the United States was used. That same basic equipment, supplemented with a patchwork of replacement parts and new equipment, was still in use in 1981.

The problem is compounded by the lack of technological compatibility between the U.S.-built television system and the systems of Cuba's Soviet and Eastern European allies; the trade embargo on compatible replacement parts from the United States; and foreign exchange and credit difficulties with nonsocialist suppliers of compatible equipment, e.g., Japan. The 625-line television sets manufactured by the Soviet Union for itself and its socialist trading partners cannot be used on Cuba's 525-line system. Consequently, Cuba was forced to spend an unusually large amount to meet its first five-year plan (1976-1980) for importing a half million TV sets specially made in the USSR for sale in Cuba.[20] And, according to Gilberto Díaz, vice president of JUCEPLAN, Cuba hopes to supplement the Soviet imports by manufacturing TV sets domestically during the next five-year plan.[21] Even if Cuba had the economic wherewithal to junk its U.S.-built TV system and replace it with a Soviet system, Cuban policymakers apparently are not inclined to do so. ICRT officials expressed a strong desire to remain on the 525-line system, despite all the problems, because while that equipment is incompatible with the East-bloc, it is compatible with virtually all of the television systems in Latin America.[22]

Given Cuba's other economic problems, the allocation of scarce foreign exchange to purchase television equipment (to say nothing of the costs of manufacturing or importing radio equipment, newsprint, ink, printing presses, and so forth) probably has contributed to widespread shortages of essential consumer items. In the 1976-80 economic period, the number of TV sets in electrified homes increased by more than 124 percent,[23] but during the same period, the output of many basic commodities, including food and clothing, increased only a small amount or in some cases actually declined.[24] In a zero or minus sum economic game, the heavy investment in the mass media probably requires that Cubans postpone other development projects and make additional economic sacrifices.

The economic constraints also have an impact on the content of the media, and again, especially television. Although Castro claimed in 1980 that 60 percent of all Cuban TV programming was domestically produced,[25] interviews with ICRT officials in the previous year indicate that the actual percentage is much lower.[26] Regardless of the correct figures, the fact remains that a large percentage of the programming is produced abroad. Cheap, prepackaged programs such as cultural shows from Eastern Europe, vintage movies from the United States, and documentaries from the Televisa system in Mexico are commonplace on Cuban television. The innovative use of archaic technology and the creative use of limited air time by Cuban producers notwithstanding, the content of Cuban television is tightly constrained by the Cuban economy.

Social Differentiation

Because the mass media are part and parcel of the social system in which they operate, the media's function would be expected to be different in different types of social systems and to change as the social system changes. Data collected by Tichenor et al. on the functions on newspapers in large cities and small communities in the United States support the hypothesis that the less complex and less differentiated the community, the more likely the local newspaper is to serve mostly the distribution control function. These small-town newspapers tended to avoid local conflict and to build a local consensus as a defense against outside threats. In one study of the research program, 59 percent of the weekly newspapers in small, homogeneous communities reported no local government conflict of any kind during a one-month period. The researchers argue that the smaller, less complex communities have fewer means of protecting the social order from collapsing in an uncontrolled public debate and were capable of solving most clashes between the relatively few sectors by interpersonal means rather than through the community newspaper.[27]

Their data also support the related hypothesis that the larger, more complex and more differentiated the community, the more likely the city newspaper is to serve a feedback control function in addition to the distribution control function. In these communities, the press initiates social action and maintains political discourse. In contrast to the small town, 80 percent of the metro daily newspapers reported at least some city government conflict during the same one-month period. The researchers argue that the larger cities are more diverse, have a greater number of power bases, but are unable to solve conflicts between them by the interpersonal means characteristic of small towns. Consequently, the big city newspapers would be expected to serve as a channel for resolving debates. However, the researchers conclude that distribution control is, by a large margin, the most frequently performed of the two functions in both large and small towns.

Several descriptive studies of the media in socialist and revolutionary societies around the world support the hypothesis of Tichenor et al. at a national level—the more complex and differentiated a national system, the more likely that the nation's media will perform a feedback control function in addition to distribution control. For example, Liu and others reported that in China during the Great Leap Forward, the press was tightly controlled by the Party Central Committee, published no criticism, and performed solely a distribution control function. A few years later, during the power struggle of the Cultural Revolution, the established party press performed a feedback control function, which included thinly veiled attacks on Mao himself. The Red Guard responded with their own attacks printed on small, crude news sheets and, more commonly, with *tatzepao* (big character wall posters).[28] When the power struggle was settled, Mao had the people's right to display wall posters guaranteed by the Chinese Constitution, but the media returned to rigid distribution control.[29] In the late 1970s, following the death of Mao, highly critical wall posters (e.g., Democracy Wall), underground journals, and other forms of feedback control reappeared as

power-contenders maneuvered to control the government and
again were forcefully ended when the political battle was
resolved.[30] Similar phenomena in which the media performed
a critical or feedback control function during periods of
revolution or increased differentiation of power were reported
for example by Pierce[31] and Schiller[32] in Chile, Zeman[33] in
Czechoslovakia, Mowlana[34] in Iran, and Seaton and Pimlott[35]
in Portugal.

Conversely, considerable research has documented that in
times of strict centralization of power, the feedback control
function of the media virtually disappears.[36] For example,
content analysis of *Pravda* and *Izvestiya* (the official organ of
the Supreme Soviet) conducted by Inkeles during the Stalin
period revealed virtually no differences in the domestic and
foreign news agendas set by the two newspapers. Even the
Marxist-Leninist principle of self-criticism was limited during
the oppressive Stalin period, according to Inkeles. Stalin condemned the "vulgarization" of public criticism of government
officials and effectively allowed only criticism that clearly
strengthened party rule.[37]

The conventional wisdom in many journalistic writings and
some academic works[38] that the Cuban government is a
monolith controlled by one man is not supported by the bulk of
academic literature. Azicri, Casal, Domínguez, Gonzalez,
LeoGrande, Mesa-Lago, Valdés, and others have documented
a period of growing complexity in the Cuban government.[39]
During the late 1970s, political power became more differentiated, an expanding bureaucracy contributed more to making and enforcing rules, and means of public representation in
decision making were increased.

To accommodate those structural changes, the function of
the Cuban mass media would also be expected to change.
However, only limited evidence supports the hypothesis that
coupled with the process of institutionalization, the Cuban
press increased its feedback control function. Using secondary
data analysis, interviews with Cuban media policymakers, and
other descriptive evidence, a recent monograph argued that a

corresponding increase in criticism and other forms of feedback control appeared in the Cuban press in the late 1970s.[40]
Two useful content analyses of *Granma* during the institutionalization period identify manifestations of feedback control,
but neither study collected data from other time periods for
comparison. Rodríguez described the type and level of criticism
in the letters-to-the-editor column, "By Return Mail," from
1974 to 1976 and inferred the possible causes and effects.[41]
An unpublished content analysis by the U.S. government
meticulously recorded topics, country references, and an
evaluation of positive and negative interpretations for entire
issues for most dates from January 1976 through December
1978.[42] Further, Domínguez, using descriptive methods, cor-
relates the increased public participation in local government
in the 1970s with the appearance of critical letters-to-the-
editor and a modest amount of investigative reporting.[43]

Tichenor et al. conclude:

> As an integral part of the community, the newspaper reflects
> the concerns of the dominant power groupings. The term
> *reflects* is appropriate in the sense that it is neither a total nor an
> undistorted reproduction of current events and institutions.
> Newspapers reflect selectively, in ways determined not by
> editorial idiosyncrasy but by the structure and distribution of
> social power in the community. A newspaper in a one-industry
> town is unlikely to report that industry in a critical way. It will
> reflect community consensus about that industry through
> reporting socially noncontroversial aspects of that industry and
> generally avoiding reports that would question it.[44]

Clearly, Cuba is a one-industry town governed by a strong
chairman of the board, but within that context, differences
between the divisions of the industry and social groups in the
community continue to exist. Although the differences are less
pronounced than in a larger, modern, more complex society,
significant increases or decreases in the differentiation of
Cuban society could translate into changing functions of the
mass media.

Social Conflict

The level and type of conflict or tension in society are essential to the understanding of the mass media and closely related to social differentiation. Tichenor et al. believe that social conflict is the natural and often healthy product of a complex social system. As different social groups within the social system seek to achieve competing or countervailing goals, tension among them is likely to exist. Social systems that are in the process of change resulting in shifting linkages between power-contenders are even more likely to generate conflict. In many circumstances, the conflict can help solidify and revitalize old norms, stimulate citizen participation, or strengthen internal cohesion within the social system. At other times, conflict may negatively affect the social system by destabilizing the relationships between the social groups or impeding the existing social processes.[45]

To a large extent, the mass media in modern social systems exist to manage conflict. In times of relatively low tension, the mass media may contribute to the maintenance of the social system by increasing intensity and widening the scope of conflicts. For example, Cuban newspaper reports of debates at local CDR meetings in the late 1970s may have encouraged citizen participation in the expanded legislative structures in Cuba. In periods of relatively high tension, the mass media may attempt to suppress the tension and build consensus within the system. For example, during economic downturns in Cuba during the early 1970s and early 1980s, newspaper appeals to nationalism and attempts to focus attention on matters of domestic agreement or common enemies—usually foreign—may have quelled unrest.

Tichenor et al. found strong correlations between type and level of community conflict and amount of coverage of those issues in the local newspaper.[46] A longitudinal pilot study of the "bad" news in Tennessee newspapers reported by Haskins tends to support the conclusion that the level of systemic tension is related to the type of news that is reported. The content analysis of front pages found great fluctuations in the ratio of bad news to good news between 1893 and 1973. Bad news declined to its lowest point during the Depression in 1933.[47] "There is a relationship between the physical and material health of society and the incidence of bad news," Haskins concluded. "In really bad times, there is a need for good news and an effort is made to seek it out. Conversely, when things are good, we focus on the bad."[48] Similarly, Domínguez documented significant and rapid social change during the Cuban revolution, concluded that it had caused varying levels of psychological strain for individual Cubans and structural tension for the total social system, and predicted that the changes would continue to lead to conflict.[49] However, no systematic research has related the shifts in types and level of conflict in Cuba to the functions its mass media play for society.

This chapter argues that contrary to conventional wisdom, the Cuban press is not a monolith responding solely to the ideological dictates of a single ruler. Rather, it is an integral part of the total national system and tends to respond to the changing economic, political, and social conditions in Cuba and around the world. In sum, the functions that the press performs for society to some extent transcend political ideology.

THE STUDY

Methodology

A content analysis of Cuban publications was designed to test the general proposition that the Cuban press performs a feedback control function in addition to a distribution control function and that the extent to which it performs the feedback control function is related to the degree of social differentiation and level of social conflict in Cuba. A purposive sample of six major Cuban newspapers and magazines was selected for analysis. Five of the publications represent different sectors of the national power structure or cater to a segmented audience within a sector. They are: *Granma,* the official newspaper of

the Central Committee; *Juventud Rebelde,* a newspaper published by the Communist Youth Union for younger audiences;
Vanguardia, party daily of the province of Santa Clara;
Trabajadores, national newspaper of the Central Union of
Cuban Workers; and *Verde Olivo,* weekly magazine of the
Revolutionary Armed Forces. In addition, *Bohemia,* a general
interest, mass circulation magazine that represents no particular government division or social sector, was used as a bench-
mark. The issues of the publications were randomly selected;
however, in numerous cases, the randomly selected issues
were not readily available, and the next closest date was
studied. In the case of *Trabajadores,* a relatively complete,
systematic sample could not be obtained, and the publication
was dropped from the study.

The entire issues for the selected dates were analyzed by
Spanish-speaking graduate students or seniors from the Latin
American Studies Program or Department of Spanish at The
Pennsylvania State University.[50] Each discrete item in the
publications (including contiguous headlines, artwork, photos,
and graphs) was coded into several objective and subjective
categories. The major categories were: size of the item,
prominence of display, author, main and secondary topic,
geographic emphasis and dateline, editorial style or treatment,
main actor in the item, and an evaluation of positive or
negative interpretation.[51]

Because most of the categories were objectively defined or
clearly delineated, periodic intercoder and intracoder reliability checks indicated considerable agreement among the coders.
The median reliability score for all categories was 88 percent.
The only category in which the coders consistently dropped
below 85 percent agreement was the evaluation of positive or
negative interpretation. The lowest intercoder check for the
positive-negative scale was 66 percent. With the exception of
the positive-negative scale, most of the disagreement among
coders was due to clerical errors randomly distributed throughout the sample rather than to differences in judgment. Further,
the coders' work was scattered throughout the sample; thus, it

is highly unlikely that the small amount of coder disagreement could account for the differences in the publications' content.

Time Periods

The Cuban publications were studied in three time periods that, according to the Cuban studies literature, experienced different levels of social conflict and degrees of social differentiation.

1970. The focus of the Guevarist mass mobilization of the 1960s was to harvest a phenomenal 10 million tons of sugar in 1970. The attempt to reach this unrealistic goal not only failed but seriously damaged the neglected portion of the economy. The resulting production declines meant that the already dissatisfied masses would face even greater austerity in coming years. The government was nearly bankrupt, absenteeism among workers was widespread, and public discontent was high. The internal tension was compounded by foreign pressures. Relations with the Soviet Union, although slightly improved since 1968, were relatively cool, and relations with the United States were hostile. The architects of the 1970 failure were a small inbred group of military men closely supervised by Castro himself. Military influence pervaded virtually every facet of society, and the party, unions, and other mass organizations stagnated.[52] In effect, 1970 was a period of high social conflict and low social differentiation.

1975. From the ashes of the 1970 debacle, Cuba built a government structure that differed markedly from that of 1970. By 1975, the process of institutionalization was in full swing. The party and mass organizations had been strengthened, Castro had delegated some of his power, and local governments were experimenting with popular representation in a pilot of "poder popular." In addition, Cuba had reestablished rapport with the Soviet Union, eased tensions with the United States, and with the help of higher sugar prices, stabilized (although not solved) some of the grim economic problems.[53] Therefore, 1975 was a period of increased social differentiation and reduced social tension.

1980. A new stage of the revolution seemed to be evolving as Cuba entered the 1980s. Severe economic problems returned, resulting mostly from the failure of the sugar and tobacco harvests and the financial drain of supporting Cuban troops in Africa. Increased absenteeism, black market activity, corruption, shortages of basic products, and general unrest were reported in the country.[54] Castro's response was an administrative reorganization resulting in greater centralization of control of important government divisions, such as the Ministry of Interior.[55] And in the spring of 1980, Cuban officials opened the port of Mariel, precipitating a disorderly boat exodus of more than 125,000 Cubans to the United States. That, Cuba's African involvement, and the election of Ronald Reagan soured the apparent trend toward normalization with the United States. In sum, 1980 was a year of slightly decreased differentiation and increased conflict.

Hypotheses

Between those time periods, variations within and among publications are operational indicators of feedback control. As the feedback control function increases, the publications should assign new and different agendas of the primary topics, geographic emphasis, and main actors. Further, a wider variety of news sources for the publications and a greater amount of citizen feedback and negative interpretation of domestic affairs should also signal an increase in the feedback control function. In sum, divergence of media agendas indicates an increase in feedback control and convergence of media agendas indicates a decrease in feedback control.

In 1970, a period of greater conflict and less social differentiation, a lower level of feedback control would be expected. In 1975, a period of less conflict and more social differentiation, a higher level of feedback control is hypothesized. And finally, in 1980, a period of greater conflict and a constant (or slightly lower) level of social differentiation, a slightly lower level of feedback control would be expected.

FINDINGS AND DISCUSSION

In general, the data support the conclusion that the Cuban press is not monolithic in content and that significant differences exist within and between publications. Rank order correlations range widely from perfect agreement between some publications on some categories to low levels of agreement and, in some cases, substantial disagreement between other publications on other categories. Even in the cases of high levels of agreement between Cuban publications, the levels of agreement do not appear to be consistently greater than for similar studies of non-Communist media systems.[56]

There is also limited support in some categories for the hypothesis that Cuban media content converges and diverges in relationship to structural changes in the Cuban social system. The less than unequivocal support for the latter hypothesis is due, at least in part, to the crude operational measurements of the dependent and independent variables. The findings will be discussed in greater detail below and supplemented with additional evidence from secondary research and interviews with Cuban editors and other media policymakers in 1977 and 1979.

Sources

Analysis of the sources or authors of information in Cuban publications supports the hypothesis of changing levels of feedback control. Although rank order correlations for news sources (see Table 2.1) are relatively high in all three time periods, the level of agreement dipped in 1975 and increased in 1980, as predicted. Table 2.2, which details the sources for all sampled publications except *Vanguardia,* for which data were not available in all three time periods, also supports the hypothesis.

Reflecting Cuba's increased international involvement and improved relations with the Soviet Union between 1970 and 1975, Cuban publications increased their use of foreign news agencies, primarily TASS. In all three time periods, the publications carried a small amount of wire copy from non-

TABLE 2.1   News Sources

Spearman (r) Correlation Coefficients*

	1970					1975					1980				
	GR	JR	VO	BH	VN	GR	JR	VO	BH	VN	GR	JR	VO	BH	VN
1970															
Granma															
Juventud Rebelde	.96														
Verde Olivo	.75	.73													
Bohemia	.81	.75	.71												
Vanguardia	—	—	—	—											
1975															
Granma	.72														
Juventud Rebelde		.63				.88									
Verde Olivo			.44			.51	.63								
Bohemia				.78		.78	.63	.62							
Vanguardia					—	.85	.86	.63	.51						
1980															
Granma	.65					.94									
Juventud Rebelde		.62					.89				.80				
Verde Olivo			.89					.63			.60	.65			
Bohemia				.57					.74		.67	.75	.90		
Vanguardia					—					.79	.66	.85	.71	.92	

*+1 = perfect agreement between ranked categories for the two publications; -1 = perfect disagreement between ranks. Categories listed in Table 2.2.

	Agreement Among All Publications (except Vanguardia)		
Kendall Coefficient	1970	1975	1980
of Concordance (W)**	.82	.74	.79

**W can assume a value of 0 (perfect disagreement) to 1 (perfect agreement).

socialist Western news agencies, such as Agence France Presse (AFP). Cuban publications also used a modicum of copy from two U.S.-based international news agencies— Associated Press and United Press International. After a series of stinging oral attacks by Castro in 1969, the Havana bureaus of AP and UPI were closed down, the correspondents expelled, and all formal exchanges terminated; however, late in 1979, both AP and UPI signed contracts in which they agreed to formal exchanges with Prensa Latina. The data in

TABLE 2.2   Sources of Total Items by Year

% rank	1970	1975	1980
publications' own correspondents	49.0 (1)	53.6 (1)	45.7 (1)
Prensa Latina	21.4 (2)	19.0 (2)	20.5 (2)
unknown or other	19.7 (3)	15.0 (3)	19.2 (3)
foreign news agency	3.1 (4)	4.5 (4)	3.4 (5)
AFP (France)	2.1	1.1	.6
TASS (USSR)	.5	1.6	1.0
PAP (Poland)	.1	0	0
ADN (East Germany)	.1	0	.1
AP (USA)	0	.3	.2
Novosti (USSR)	.3	.4	.3
UPI (USA)	0	.2	0
Other	0	.9	.9
other foreign media	2.3 (5)	.3 (10)	.3 (11)
official documents	1.8 (6.5)	.9 (8)	1.8 (7)
ordinary citizens	1.8 (6.5)	2.3 (5)	3.0 (6)
volunteer correspondents	.4 (8)	1.5 (7)	1.3 (8)
government or party official	.3 (9.5)	.7 (9)	.6 (9)
other Cuban medium	.3 (9.5)	.1 (11)	.5 (10)
Agencia de Información Nacional	0 (11)	2.2 (6)	3.7 (4)
decentralized sources*	56.9	62.3	54.2
centralized sources*	23.5	20.6	22.9
N	1629	1504	1646

NOTE: All publications except Vanguardia
*Prensa Latina (the official Cuban news agency), official documents (including speech transcripts), and government and party officials are classified as centralized information sources in this analysis. All other categories, except Agencia de Información Nacional (AIN) and unknown sources, are defined as decentralized. Because AIN was founded in 1974 and therefore does not have comparable data in all three time periods, it was excluded from the analysis of centralized and decentralized sources.

Table 2.2 do not adequately reflect Cuba's active participation in the Non-Aligned News Agency Pool beginning in the late 1970s.[57] The foreign language weekly editions of *Granma* make heavy use of dispatches from the non-aligned pool, but few are used in domestic editions.

In 1974, Cuba added a domestic complement to Prensa Latina. The new news agency, Agencia de Información Nacional (AIN), has its own staff and transmission facilities and is primarily charged with carrying news and commentaries to and from the provinces.[58] AIN would have accounted for a greater percentage of the total content, if *Vanguardia,* a provincial newspaper, had been included in Table 2.2. Nearly 10 percent (second rank) in 1975 and 5 percent (third rank) in 1980 of *Vanguardia's* content came from AIN. Unfortunately, little more is known about the organization, resources, control, and mission of the new news agency.

The small dip in the use of official documents and the small peak in letters and other materials written by ordinary citizens and volunteer correspondents in 1975 indicate support for the hypothesized relationship between feedback control and changes in structural conditions. Because of the small cell sizes, these changes might not be meaningful when viewed individually; however, the relationship holds up when Table 2.2 is collapsed into decentralized and centralized sources of information. As predicted, the percentage of decentralized sources increased in 1975, a period of greater social differentiation and less social conflict, and decreased in 1980, a period of greater conflict and consolidation.

Not examined in this study, but important for the total Cuban communication milieu, are alternative sources of information. A large (although unknown) number of Cubans frequently listen to Miami radio stations on standard medium wave receivers. Castro and other Cuban officials have argued that the commercial lure of Miami radio was a major cause of the Cuban exodus in 1980.[59] A rise in underground pamphlets and news sheets in Cuba has been rumored in the conservative foreign press but not independently confirmed.[60] The existence of alternative media cannot help but affect the policy and content of the official media. Fidel Castro's main report to the Second Party Congress, Raúl Castro's speech to the Fourth Congress of the Union of Cuban Journalists in 1980, the Central Committee's 1979 policy statement on the Cuban media, and numerous other recent statements by Cuban officials implicitly or explicitly call for new and creative sources of official information to combat the influence of "bourgeois ideology" from the alternative media.[61]

TABLE 2.3   Main Topic

Spearman (r) Correlation Coefficients*

	1970					1975					1980				
	GR	JR	VO	BH	VN	GR	JR	VO	BH	VN	GR	JR	VO	BH	VN
1970															
Granma															
Juventud Rebelde	.73														
Verde Olivo	.26	.64													
Bohemia	.17	.55	.78												
Vanguardia	—	—	—	—											
1975															
Granma	.61														
Juventud Rebelde		.83				.73									
Verde Olivo			.76			.35	.48								
Bohemia				.73		.57	.54	.64							
Vanguardia					—	.57	.81	.56	.54						
1980															
Granma	.63					.89									
Juventud Rebelde		.62					.70				.74				
Verde Olivo			.83					.70			.58	.35			
Bohemia				.61					.80		.57	.55	.61		
Vanguardia					—						.89	.74	.73	.54	.66

*+1 = perfect agreement between ranked categories for the two publications; -1 = perfect disagreement between ranks. Categories listed in Table 2.4.

	Agreement Among All Publications (except Vanguardia)		
	1970	1975	1980
Kendall Coefficient of Concordance (W)**	.71	.67	.67

**W can assume a value of 0 (perfect disagreement) to 1 (perfect agreement).

Content

Overall rank order correlations of main topics in the Cuban publications (Table 2.3) remain relatively steady between 1970 and 1980 and therefore do not support the hypothesized trend in feedback control. However, changes in specific content categories in Table 2.4 lend some support to the hypothesis and clearly demonstrate that the Cuban press is not a monolith.

TABLE 2.4 Main Topic of Total Items by Year—Percentage (rank)

	1970					1975					1980				
	Granma	Juventud Rebelde	Verde Olivio	Bohemia	Vangardia	Granma	Juventud Rebelde	Verde Olivio	Bohemia	Vangardia	Granma	Juventud Rebelde	Verde Olivio	Bohemia	Vangardia
military	14.4 (1)	14.4 (2)	8.4 (4)	2.7 (10)	—	9.6 (6)	9.5 (5)	12.5 (2)	3.8 (9.5)	3.7 (9)	11.4 (4)	2.7 (11.5)	9.6 (2.5)	6.6 (5)	2.6 (9)
domestic economics	12.9 (2)	6.1 (6.5)	2.0 (10)	10.0 (3.5)	—	10.1 (5)	11.6 (3)	5.4 (6.5)	8.1 (4)	17.8 (1)	9.7 (5)	9.9 (4)	6.8 (4.5)	8.7 (4)	10.9 (4)
sports	10.8 (3)	12.5 (3)	6.4 (6)	2.4 (11.5)	—	11.9 (2)	13.1 (1)	5.4 (6.5)	3.8 (9.5)	14.3 (3)	12.2 (3)	13.1 (3)	5.7 (6.5)	4.2 (9)	20.8 (1)
foreign relations, political	10.3 (4)	8.0 (5)	0.8 (13.5)	2.4 (11.5)	—	22.0 (1)	12.0 (2)	1.2 (12)	4.9 (7)	4.0 (8)	18.4 (1)	13.4 (2)	2.1 (10)	9.6 (3)	10.1 (5)
culture, entertainment, media	8.0 (5)	15.9 (1)	34.5 (1)	28.0 (1)	—	10.9 (3)	10.2 (4)	43.5 (1)	27.5 (1)	17.5 (2)	13.8 (2)	23.6 (1)	40.9 (1)	25.1 (1)	14.8 (2)
accidents, disasters	6.6 (6)	2.1 (14)	0.8 (13.5)	0.4 (15.5)	—	0.8 (15)	0 (16)	0.6 (14.5)	0.4 (16)	1.1 (13)	1.4 (15)	0.6 (15)	0 (16)	1.3 (15)	0 (16)
human and social interest	5.8 (7)	11.3 (4)	10.8 (3)	15.8 (2)	—	3.3 (9)	9.1 (6.5)	6.5 (3.5)	13.2 (2)	8.3 (5)	2.7 (11)	6.3 (6)	6.8 (4.5)	11.9 (2)	8.6 (6)
ideology and history	5.6 (8)	2.8 (11)	8.0 (5)	5.3 (6)	—	5.7 (7)	1.8 (13.5)	6.0 (5)	6.5 (6)	2.3 (10.5)	2.9 (9)	3.0 (9.5)	5.7 (6.5)	2.8 (13)	2.3 (10.5)
domestic government political	5.1 (9)	5.8 (8)	2.4 (8.5)	4.2 (7.5)	—	10.7 (4)	9.1 (6.5)	3.0 (9.5)	7.8 (5)	11.5 (4)	9.3 (6)	8.7 (5)	3.6 (9)	5.9 (7)	5.7 (7)
agriculture & natural resources	4.8 (10)	6.1 (6.5)	2.4 (8.5)	6.4 (5)	—	2.3 (11)	3.3 (9.5)	0.6 (14.5)	1.1 (15)	5.4 (7)	4.1 (7)	2.7 (11.5)	4.6 (8)	3.0 (12)	13.5 (3)
education	3.0 (11)	4.9 (9)	1.2 (11)	3.1 (9)	—	1.6 (14)	3.3 (9.5)	6.5 (3.5)	3.1 (11)	8.0 (6)	2.5 (13)	4.8 (7)	0.7 (13.5)	4.2 (9)	3.4 (8)
health and medicine	2.8 (12.5)	1.8 (15)	0.8 (13.5)	2.2 (13.5)	—	0.2 (16)	2.2 (12)	1.2 (12)	1.6 (13.5)	1.7 (12)	1.1 (16)	2.4 (13)	1.8 (11)	1.9 (14)	1.3 (13.5)
other	2.8 (12.5)	2.4 (12.5)	3.2 (7)	4.2 (7.5)	—	2.1 (12)	8.7 (8)	3.0 (9.5)	9.6 (3)	2.3 (10.5)	1.6 (14)	0.3 (16)	0.7 (13.5)	6.4 (6)	2.3 (10.5)
judicial, crime, corruption	2.7 (14)	2.4 (12.5)	0.8 (13.5)	0.4 (15.5)	—	1.8 (13)	2.9 (11)	1.2 (12)	1.6 (13.5)	0.9 (14)	3.6 (8)	3.0 (9.5)	1.1 (12)	3.2 (11)	2.1 (12)
foreign trade	2.3 (15)	0.3 (16)	0.4 (16)	2.2 (13.5)	—	4.1 (8)	1.5 (15)	0 (16)	2.7 (12)	0.6 (15.5)	2.7 (11)	3.9 (8)	0.4 (15)	1.1 (16)	0.3 (15)
science and technology	2.0 (16)	3.1 (10)	16.9 (2)	10.0 (3.5)	—	2.9 (10)	1.8 (13.5)	3.6 (8)	4.5 (8)	0.6 (15.5)	2.7 (11)	1.8 (14)	9.6 (2.5)	4.2 (9)	1.3 (13.5)
N	603	327	249	450	—	614	275	168	447	349	559	335	281	471	385

For example, *Granma* (the official voice of the party) and *Verde Olivo* (official voice of the military) tend to emphasize different topics, and changes in those emphases were most pronounced between 1970 and 1975. LeoGrande reported that after the 1970 sugar harvest debacle, the basic institutional relationship between the military and the party began to shift. The military withdrew from political and administrative tasks not related to national security, and the party grew stronger in cohesion and power and larger in size. LeoGrande concluded that the party developed into the dominant political force during the 1970s.[62] This important differentiation of power bases seems to be manifested in a divergence of the publications' attention to certain topics between 1970 and 1975. The percentage and rank of military news in *Granma* decreased markedly during this time period, while domestic politics, foreign relations, and foreign trade increased in *Granma*. In comparison, the percentage and rank of military news in *Verde Olivo* increased substantially during the same time period; however, *Verde Olivo's* coverage of domestic politics, foreign relations, and foreign trade remained relatively constant.

Contrasts in main topics between *Juventud Rebelde* and *Vanguardia* also exemplify the different functions of Cuban publications. Although both are publications of the party, *Juventud Rebelde* is a relatively lively newspaper intended, in part, to wean Cuban youth from potentially threatening alternative sources of information, and *Vanguardia* is the official voice of the party in the fertile agricultural province of Santa Clara. How their differing missions affect content is best seen in their agricultural coverage. *Juventud Rebelde* expressed little interest in agriculture during the boom period of high sugar prices in 1975, and its interest declined even further during the crop failures in 1980. During the same period, the percentage of agricultural content in *Vanguardia* more than doubled. Similarly, the percentage of cultural and entertainment content in *Juventud Rebelde* more than doubled between 1975 and 1980, while the same type of content slightly declined in *Vanguardia*.

Correlations for main actor in domestic news items (Table 2.5) are high and do not vary in the predicted direction,

TABLE 2.5   Main Actor in Domestic News

Spearman (r) Correlation
Coefficients*

	1970					1975					1980				
	GR	JR	VO	BH	VN	GR	JR	VO	BH	VN	GR	JR	VO	BH	VN
1970															
Granma															
Juventud Rebelde	.72														
Verde Olivo	.88	.85													
Bohemia	.77	.74	.64												
Vanguardia	—	—	—	—											
1975															
Granma	.79														
Juventud Rebelde		.45				.86									
Verde Olivo			.87			.65	.65								
Bohemia				.82		.86	.93	.84							
Vanguardia					—	.39	.61	.40	.61						
1980															
Granma	.76					.89									
Juventud Rebelde		.63					.64				.29				
Verde Olivo			.68					.55			.57	.71			
Bohemia				.90					.85		.59	.85	.85		
Vanguardia					—						.82	.43	.64	.68	.56

*+1 = perfect agreement between ranked categories for the two publications;
-1 = perfect disagreement between ranks. Categories: Fidel Castro, high government or party official, middle-level government or party official, low-level government or party official, celebrities, ordinary people or citizens, no main actor, or other.

	Agreement Among All Publications (except Vanguardia)		
Kendall Coefficient	1970	1975	1980
of Concordance (W)**	.81	.84	.73

**W can assume a value of 0 (perfect disagreement) to 1 (perfect agreement).

particularly when *Vanguardia* is excluded from the analysis. (*Vanguardia* is a provincial newspaper and would be expected to give low-level government and party officials greater attention than the national publications in the sample.) However, these data should be interpreted with caution. In keeping with Marxist-Leninist ideology, the largest percentage of content dealt with abstract ideas and issues and did not focus on individual people; consequently, relatively few main actors

TABLE 2.6   Geographic Emphasis

Spearman (r) Correlation Coefficients*

	1970					1975					1980				
	GR	JR	VO	BH	VN	GR	JR	VO	BH	VN	GR	JR	VO	BH	VN
1970															
Granma															
Juventud Rebelde	.23														
Verde Olivo	.41	.77													
Bohemia	.20	.77	.89												
Vanguardia	—	—	—	—											
1975															
Granma	.63														
Juventud Rebelde		.60				-.41									
Verde Olivo			.70			-.74	.84								
Bohemia				.55		-.72	.81	.90							
Vanguardia					—	-.70	.43	.70	.75						
1980															
Granma	.81					.78									
Juventud Rebelde		-.37					-.09				.94				
Verde Olivo			.77					.75			.03	.09			
Bohemia				.77					.52		.03	-.14	.60		
Vanguardia					—					.83	-.31	-.43	-.09	.03	

*+1 = perfect agreement between ranked categories for the two publications;
-1 = perfect disagreement between ranks. Categories: Cuban national news, Cuban local news, Cuban foreign news, domestic news from foreign countries, non-Cuban foreign news, and other.

	Agreement Among All Publications (except Vanguardia)		
Kendall Coefficient	1970	1975	1980
of Concordance (W)**	.65	.37	.44

**W can assume a value of 0 (perfect disagreement) to 1 (perfect agreement).

were coded and cell sizes for this measurement are small (sometimes less than 200).

Strong support for the hypotheses appears in Table 2.6. In 1970, a modest level of agreement in geographic focus existed between the Cuban publications, but in 1975, as Cuba came out of isolation into the international arena, the geographic emphases of the publications diverged substantially. The level of correlation declined and the range of correlations increased in 1975, indicating the hypothesized increase in feedback

TABLE 2.7   Dateline

Spearman (r) Correlation Coefficients*

	1970					1975					1980				
	GR	JR	VO	BH	VN	GR	JR	VO	BH	VN	GR	JR	VO	BH	VN
1970															
Granma															
Juventud Rebelde	.86														
Verde Olivo	.39	.26													
Bohemia	.82	.82	.33												
Vanguardia	—	—	—	—											
1975															
Granma	.96														
Juventud Rebelde		.79				1.0									
Verde Olivo			1.0			.43	.43								
Bohemia				.96		.96	.96	.43							
Vanguardia					—	.96	.96	.39	.93						
1980															
Granma	.92					.96									
Juventud Rebelde		.86					.96				1.0				
Verde Olivo			.86					.86			.72	.72			
Bohemia				.64					.54		.54	.54	.41		
Vanguardia					—						.93	.89	.89	.67	.54

*+1 = perfect agreement between ranked categories for the two publications;
-1 = perfect disagreement between ranks. Categories: Cuba, USSR and Eastern Europe, U.S. and Western Europe, Latin America, Middle East, other Third World, other.

	Agreement Among All Publications (except Vanguardia)		
Kendall Coefficient	1970	1975	1980
of Concordance (W)**	.66	.75	.74

**W can assume a value of 0 (perfect disagreement) to 1 (perfect agreement).

control. In 1980, the correlations increased slightly overall and the range decreased, indicating the predicted convergence. However, the same pattern of support did not exist in comparing specific country datelines (Table 2.7) appearing in the publications. When the data are collapsed into clusters of countries, the correlations between publications are high and increase in the latter time periods. The differences in the findings in Tables 2.6 and 2.7 may be because the specific dateline within the foreign news categories is more the product of the unpre-

TABLE 2.8   Percentage of Publications' Total Number of Items

	citizen feedback			official information		
	1970	1975	1980	1970	1975	1980
Granma	0	0.7	0	2.6	1.5	2.5
Juventud Rebelde	0	0	2.7	0	0.7	0.6
Verde Olivo	3.2	1.2	3.9	1.2	0.6	1.1
Bohemia	1.1	3.8	3.4	1.3	2.6	1.9
Vanguardia	—	0	2.1	—	0	1.0
all publications	0.8	1.2	2.2	1.5	1.3	1.6
N	1629	1853	2031	1629	1853	2031

NOTE: Citizen feedback = Letters-to-editor, essays, and so forth written by readers, ordinary citizens, and others desiring to comment on public matters. Official information = Verbatim transcripts of speeches, reprints of government or party documents, decrees, policy papers, minutes of meetings, and so forth.

dictable nature of news and less the product of editorial decisions that are subject to social control.

A comparison of citizen feedback, such as letters-to-the-editor, and official information, such as party documents or speech transcripts, across the three time periods appears in Table 2.8. Because the percentages in the table are small, modest differences should be interpreted cautiously in isolation; however, the results, when interpreted in context with other findings in this study, seem to reinforce the conclusion that different Cuban publications tend to perform different functions for different audiences under different social conditions. Of particular interest is the disappearance of citizen feedback in *Granma* during 1980, the same time period in which citizen feedback first appears in *Vanguardia*. The same trend appears in Table 2.9, which lists the percentage of publications' content that is negative to the state. Negative coverage disappears from *Granma* in 1980 and appears in *Vanguardia* for the first time in the same year. The cell sizes in Table 2.9 are also small and should be interpreted with caution.

Domínguez believes that the passing of the feedback and criticism functions from the national party daily to a provincial party daily is an intentional trend. He argues that because most

102   CUBA

TABLE 2.9   Percentage of Items Negative to State

	1970	1975	1980
Granma	0.7	0.3	0
Juventud Rebelde	0	0.4	0.9
Verde Olivo	0	0	0
Bohemia	0.4	1.1	0.4
Vanguardia	—	0	1.6
all publications	0.4	0.4	0.5
N	1629	1853	2031

NOTE: Negative to state = Negative to state, its bureaucracy and services, or to economy in general, reaction against public outputs, and so forth. Does not include items negative to national, ideological, or political theme or items negative to personal and particular Cuban behavior or person-to-person and social relations.

of the criticism is about local matters such as poor bus service, local media can better handle the feedback function. Further, he says that by handling a complaint in the fragmented environment of the municipality, the government prevents a snowball effect of complaints that might occur if it appeared in the national media.[63]

In addition, the findings in Tables 2.8 and 2.9 for *Bohemia,* the general circulation and general interest magazine, most closely agree with the hypothesis that the feedback control function should increase in 1975 and slightly decrease in 1980. The findings for the other publications, which are more specialized in content, audience, or editorial control, do not follow the hypothesized trend as closely, and in the case of *Verde Olivo,* the most specialized of the publications owing to its role as the voice of military, changes in citizen feedback are the opposite of those predicted.

Indicators in Tables 2.8 and 2.9 of some participatory and critical journalism are consistent with repeated statements by Castro, other Cuban leaders, and media policymakers. "One of the factors that contributed to a certain degree of laxity in socioeconomic activity was that frequently people were not as critical and self-critical as necessary," Castro said in the main report to the Second Party Congress. He repeated his mandate from the First Party Congress that the Union of Cuban Journalists should redouble its commitment to constructive criticism of the revolution.[64] Several months before, Raúl Castro had sounded the same theme in his speech to the Union's Fourth Congress. "It is imperative that our work . . . delve deeper into basic problems and place greater emphasis on questions that really define the progress being made in the construction of socialism," he said. "Criticism within our ranks is a political duty and social responsibility."[65]

In November 1979, the Ninth Joint Session of the Party's Central Committee issued what appears to be the definitive document on Cuban mass media policy and content. The document, titled "Concerning the Strengthening of the Exercise of Criticism in the Mass Media," made the following main points:

— Criticism is a constitutionally guaranteed right for all citizens and a "method inseparable from the life of the Party."
— Criticism is an essential weapon for both identifying and solving problems that impede the development of democratic socialism.
— Effective criticism should be fraternal in spirit, constructive in objectives, and precise in target.
— The mere process of criticism is educational for the masses and stimulates public participation in solving problems.
— Authority is not weakened by criticism; rather, it is enhanced.
— Officials are cautioned against superficial, evasive, or self-serving responses to reporters' questions and criticisms.
— Party officials are directed to "(a)ct energetically in the presence of any attempt to muzzle such criticism, just as with reprisals that may be tried to be carried out against journalists, functionaires or workers who give information about errors and defects."
— Criticism in the media should be systematized, and permanent sections of critical content, such as letters-to-the-editor columns, should be established.
— Media content should emphasize problems preventing the development of socialism, especially economic problems.
— Journalistic style should be less mechanical and more creative. The use of humor as a creaive tool for making media messages more readable and convincing was specifically mentioned.[66]

The policy paper by the Central Committee and the statements by both Castros are merely the capstone of the most persistent theme in the discussion of the Cuban media in the past half-dozen years, and to some extent the Cuban press has responded. In 1974, *Granma* began publishing a letters-to-the-editor column titled "By Return Mail," through which citizens could register their complaints about the tactical operations of the government. Rodríguez found that the majority of the letters in the *Granma* column from 1974 to 1976 were neutral in tone; however, the percentage of negative letters exceeded positive letters. The vast majority of the negative letters criticized state operations, and none dealt with ideological matters.[67] Other publications, such as *Juventud Rebelde, Bohemia,* and most of the provincial dailies added similar columns shortly afterward. Radio stations, such as *Radio Rebelde,* read letters over the air, and ICRT established a Department of Complaints to handle citizen feedback.[68] Stylistic changes were also noted. In 1979, the Institute of Internal Demand launched *Opina,* a mass audience monthly which publishes letters, self-help items, comic strips, and other entertainment, consumer advice mixed in with serious commentary and subtle criticism. The style is relatively lively and often humorous. The magazine also carries large special supplements of classified advertising—a unique addition to domestic Cuban media. In 1980, *Opina* had the largest circulation among Cuban magazines—approximately 300,000-500,000 copies per issue.[69]

Channels

"The mass media have made major gains in reporting on our socioeconomic developments and ideological confrontation with imperialism in this period," Castro told the Second Party Congress. Castro cited substantial growth of print and broadcast channels and "considerable technological improvements in both media," and he called for additional advances in the next five-year plan.[70] Indeed, the Cuban mass media have grown significantly between 1975 and 1980 in many respects.

In broadcasting, the number of receivers and transmitters increased markedly. The number of radio receivers increased from 15.4 per 100 persons in 1975 to 20 per 100 in 1980, and the number of TV sets increased from 6.6 per 100 to 8.1 per 100 during the same period. Dozens of new transmitters were built during the five years. In print, the national circulation of newspapers increased from 924,500 in 1975 to 1.2 million in 1980, thereby increasing the number of copies per 100 people from 10.7 to 12.2.[71]

Despite these impressive advances, the pattern of growth does not indicate a divergence of media channels or content. According to secondary analysis of published media statistics, the increase in channels merely extended the reach of the same voices. For example, the growth in radio (a medium that Castro specifically cited for its advances) in the last five-year plan was concentrated in the national channels. Between 1970 and 1975, the number of radio transmitters increased from 94 to 101. Two of the new channels were originating stations located outside of Havana. The remaining were repeaters for existing stations, only one of which was a repeater for a Havana-based station. Between 1975 and 1980, the number of radio transmitters increased from 101 to 122. However, with the exception of one new originating channel in Havana, all the new transmitters were repeaters for existing Havana stations. In fact, the number of repeaters for stations outside of Havana actually declined during this period.[72] Therefore, the growth in radio between 1970 and 1975 was somewhat decentralized, but between 1975 and 1980, it was highly centralized.

The pattern was similar in the television and print media. Between 1975 and 1980, the Santiago television station, the only local channel in Cuba, was merged into one of the two national channels. During the same period, the number of repeaters for the national channels more than doubled. And despite the increases in circulations announced by Castro, few new magazines or newspapers were published during the five-year period. *Somos Jóvenes* (a monthly youth magazine started in 1977), *Opina,* and a new newspaper for the Island of Youth are notable exceptions.[73]

SUMMARY AND CONCLUSIONS

Most previous research on the Cuban mass media has concentrated on political control and often concluded that the
media are simply a conveyor belt of information from the
leadership to the masses and that all operations and functions
of the media are determined solely by political fiat. This
chapter argues that Cuban media functions are also the
product of economic and technological constraints and especially social conditions that to a large extent transcend
political ideology. Using a systems perspective, the Cuban
mass media are viewed as an interdependent part of a complex
social system that cannot be understood apart from a nexus of
social forces within the system. The media have the power to
control, and in turn are controlled by, other subsystems with
which they are intertwined. Under these conditions, no single
social subsystem (much less one individual) could maintain
exclusive control over any other subsystem, including the
mass media.

According to this perspective, all media systems—communist or capitalist—perform a feedback control function by
which the media apply corrective pressure on the system itself
or on subsystems that are out of functional balance with the
total system. The media can serve this regulatory function by
reporting debates of official bodies, conveying citizen com
plaints about the operation of the government, or by setting
new and perhaps competing agendas for public discussion.

The extent to which two social conditions affect the feedback
control function of the Cuban mass media is the focus of this
research. The two social conditions are: (1) social differentiation—the condition characteristic of larger, more complex
social systems in which power bases become more numerous,
diverse, and articulated. To accommodate these changes, the
media would be expected to serve as a channel for regulating
debates between power bases; and (2) social conflict—tension
that results from social groups seeking to achieve countervailing goals or from shifting linkages between power-contenders.
The mass media in part exist to manage social conflict. In

times of relatively low tension, the mass media may revitalize a stagnating social system by increasing the intensity and widening the scope of conflicts. In times of relatively high tension, the mass media may attempt to quell unrest and build consensus within the social system.

To test the proposition that the extent to which Cuban media perform a feedback control function is related to the degree of social differentiation and inversely related to the level of social conflict in Cuba, a content analysis of five Cuban publications was conducted. An increase in feedback control was operationally measured as divergence of the publications' agendas in content categories such as main topic, geographic emphasis, and main actor, and as a greater amount of citizen feedback content or negative interpretation of domestic affairs in the publications. Randomly selected issues of each publication were studied in three time periods characterized by different degrees of social differentiation and levels of social conflict.

The data yield limited support for the conclusion that the feedback control function in the mass media is related to structural conditions in the Cuban social system. The Cuban print media have set different agendas in some content areas (particularly geographic emphasis), and these agendas tend to vary in relation to the degree of social differentiation and in inverse relation to the level of social conflict. The data contradict the conventional wisdom that the Cuban press is monolithic in content and functions and strongly indicate that substantial changes have occurred in the Cuban media between 1970 and 1980. In sum, Cuban publications serve different functions for different readers at different times.

If this relationship between media functions and social conditions is confirmed in other studies, researchers will be able to cautiously project those findings into the 1980s. Consequently, international communicators and policymakers will have evidence about the likely behavior of the Cuban media under certain social conditions, which should assist in making strategy decisions. In any case, this research should contribute a more complete description of the Cuban mass media and establish additional criteria for comparing the media systems of the world and for better understanding the functions performed by the mass media in generating and resolving social conflict.

NOTES

1. Herbert L. Matthews, *Revolution in Cuba: An Essay in Understanding* (New York: Scribner, 1975), p. 126.

2. John Spicer Nichols, "Republic of Cuba," in George Kurian, ed., *World Press Encyclopedia* (New York: Facts on File, 1982).

3. Jorge I. Domínguez, *Cuba: Order and Revolution* (Cambridge, MA: Harvard University Press, 1978), p. 319.

4. John Spicer Nichols, *Organization, Control and Functions of the Cuban Mass Media, Journalism Monographs* (Lexington, KY: Association for Education in Journalism, 1982).

5. "Fidel's main report to the 2nd Congress," *Granma Weekly Review,* 28 December 1980, pp. 6-16; "Sobre el fortalecimiento del ejercicio de la critica en los medios de difusion masiva," *UPEC* 1, 1980, pp. 5-15; "Discurso de clausura pronunciado por Antonio Pérez Herrero en el acto para el décimo aniversario de Granma," Granma 6 October 1975, p. 2; "Raúl Castro: excerpts from the closing speech at the 4th Congress of the journalists union," *Cuba Update,* June 1980, p. 10.

6. Phillip J. Tichenor, George A. Donohue, and Clarice N. Olien, *Community Conflict and the Press* (Beverly Hills, CA: Sage, 1980).

7. Ibid., p. 85.

8. Ibid., p. 137.

9. Robert N. Pierce in collaboration with John Spicer Nichols, *Keeping the Flame: Media and Government in Latin America* (New York: Hastings House, 1979), pp. 80-85.

10. Interview with José R. Fernández Alvarez, Havana, November 17, 1977; "Decree," Granma Weekly Review, 20 January 1980, p. 5; Elizabeth Mahan and Jorge Reina Schement, "Broadcasting in Cuba and the United States: systems, structures, and practices." Presented at the XXX Annual Conference of the International Communication Association, Acapulco, Mexico, 20 May 1980.

11. Maurice Halperin, *The Rise and Fall of Fidel Castro—An Essay in Contemporary History* (Berkeley, CA: University of California Press, 1972), pp. 228-230.

12. Vladimir Ilyich Lenin, *Collected Works* (London: Martin Lawrence, 1927), p. 114.

13. Alex Inkeles, *Public Opinion in Soviet Russia: A Study in Mass Persuasion* (Cambridge, MA: Harvard University Press, 1958), p. 194.

14. Ibid., pp. 164-174, 194-222.

15. Fidel Castro, *The Press Has the Great Task of Orienting the People* (La Habana: Ministerio de Relaciones Exteriores, 1961); Ernesto Vera, "The press and

the ideological struggle in Cuba," *The Democratic Journalist* (11-12, 1978), pp. 18-23; "Fidel's main report," Granma Weekly Review, p. 13.

16. "Journalists' union holds 4th Congress: March 27-29, 1980," *Cuba Update,* June 1980, p. 10.

17. Matthews, *Revolution in Cuba,* pp. 236-237.

18. This section is an elaboration of an argument developed by my colleague and friend Jorge Reina Schement of the University of Southern California; however, he is not responsible for any errors or misinterpretation.

19. Interview with Leslie Rodríguez Aguilera, director of Directorate of Television, Cuban Institute of Radio and Television (ICRT), Havana, April 7, 1979.

20. Interview with Marcelo Fernández Font, former minister of foreign trade, Havana, November 16, 1977.

21. Ana María Radaelli, "Deep-seated change in the structure of our economy," Granma Weekly Review, 9 November 1980, p. 2.

22. Interview with Rodríguez.

23. Banco Nacional de Cuba, *Highlights of Cuban Economic and Social Development 1976-80 and Main Targets for 1981-85: A Preliminary Report,* January 1981, p. 20.

24. See Carmelo Mesa-Lago, ch. 4, Table 2, "Physical output of selected products in Cuba."

25. "Fidel's main report," Granma Weekly Review, p. 13.

26. Interview with Rodríguez and other ICRT officials.

27. Tichenor et al., *Conflict and Press,* pp. 77-108.

28. Alan P.L. Liu, *Communications and National Integration in Communist China* (Berkeley: University of California Press, 1971), pp. 135-146. Also see Godwin C. Chu, ed., *Popular Media in China* (Honolulu: University Press of Hawaii, 1978) and Frederick T.C. Yu, *Mass Persuasion in Communist China* (New York: Praeger, 1964).

29. Godwin C. Chu, *The Roles of Tatzepao in the Cultural Revolution: A Structural-Functional Analysis* (Carbondale: Southern Illinois University, 1972).

30. See, for example, Fox Butterfield, "Peking's poster warriors are not just paper tigers," The New York Times, 26 November 1978, p. E3; Butterfield, "Freer expression typifies a new dynamism in China," The New York Times, 14 January 1979, pp. 1, 12; Butterfield, "China backs poster as citizens' forum," The New York Times, 4 January 1979, pp. 1, 8; Butterfield, "Editor of underground journal speaks out in Peking," The New York Times, 7 October 1979, p. 3; Butterfield, "Chinese remove wall posters and activists condemn policy changes," The New York Times, 2 April 1979, p. A11; "Goodbye, wall of democracy," The New York Times, 5 April 1979, p. A22; "Chinese to withdraw guarantee of wall poster right in charter," 18 January 1980, p. A2.

31. Pierce with Nichols, *Keeping the Flame,* pp. 59-69.

32. Herbert I. Schiller, *Communication and Cultural Domination* (White Plain, NY: M. E. Sharpe, 1976), pp. 99-100.

33. Z.A.B. Zeman, *Prague Spring* (New York: Hill and Wang), pp. 46-49.

34. Hamid Mowlana, "Technology versus tradition: communication in the Iranian revolution," *Journal of Communication* 29 (Spring 1979), pp. 107-112.

35. Jean Seaton and Ben Pimlott, "The role of the media in the Portuguese

revolution," in Anthony Smith, ed., *Newspapers and Democracy* (Cambridge, MA: The MIT Press, 1980), pp. 174-199.

36. Frederick S. Siebert, *Freedom of the Press in England 1476-1776* (Urbana: University of Illinois Press, 1965).

37. Inkeles, *Public Opinion in Russia,* pp. 198-220.

38. For example, see Raymond D. Gastil, *Freedom in the World: Political Rights and Civil Liberties* (New York: Freedom House, 1979), pp. 225-226.

39. "Forum on institutionalization," *Cuban Studies/Estudios Cubanos* 9 (July 1979), pp. 63-90; Max Azicri, "The institutionalization of the Cuban state: a political perspective," *Journal of Interamerican Studies and World Affairs* 23 (August 1980), pp. 315-344; Lourdes Casal, "On popular power: the organization of the Cuban state during the period of transition," *Latin American Perspectives* 2 (4, 1975), pp. 78-88; Jorge I. Domínguez, "Sectoral clashes in Cuban politics and development," *Latin American Research Review* 6 (Fall 1971), pp. 61-87; Edward Gonzalez, "Complexities of Cuban foreign policy," *Problems in Communism* 26 (November-December 1977), pp. 1-15; William M. LeoGrande, "Continuity and change in the Cuban political elite," *Cuban Studies/Estudios Cubanos* 8 (July 1978), pp. 1-13; Carmelo Mesa-Lago, *Cuba in the 1970s: Pragmatism and Institutionalization* (Albuquerque: University of New Mexico Press, 1974); Nelson P. Valdés, "Revolution and institutionalization in Cuba," *Cuban Studies/Estudios Cubanos* 6 (January 1976), pp. 1-37.

40. Nichols, *Cuban Mass Media.*

41. Ernesto E. Rodríguez, "Public opinion and the press in Cuba," *Cuban Studies/Estudios Cubanos* 8 (July 1978), pp. 51-65.

42. Unattributable source. No intercoder reliability checks were conducted in this study.

43. Domínguez, *Cuba,* pp. 408-410.

44. Tichenor et al., *Conflict and Press,* pp. 219-220.

45. Ibid., pp. 77-108.

46. Ibid., p. 144.

47. Jack B. Haskins, "The trouble with bad news," *Newspaper Research Journal* 2 (January 1981), p. 6.

48. Evelyn Lauter, "Bad news is good news—to some," *The Quill,* February 1981, p. 17.

49. Domínguez, *Cuba,* pp. 504-511.

50. The author wishes to thank Professor Martin S. Stabb, head, Department of Spanish, Italian, and Portuguese, Penn State, and the coders, Kelli Adams, James Hardman, Susan T. Rogers, and Tamara Williams.

51. The positive-negative scale is an adaptation of Rodríguez, "Public Opinion in Cuba." Code sheets and other methodological details are available from the author at 215 Carnegie Building, University Park, PA 16802.

52. Mesa-Lago, *Cuba in the 1970s,* pp. 8-9.

53. Ibid.

54. For example, see Jorge I. Domínguez, Chapter 1, this volume.

55. "Decree," *Granma Weekly Review.*

56. For example, see Paul J. Deutschmann, *News-page Content of Twelve Metropolitan Dailies* (Cincinnati: Scripps-Howard Research, 1959), cited in Guido

H. Stemple, III and Bruce H. Westley, eds., *Research Methods in Mass Communication* (Englewood Cliffs, NJ: Prentice-Hall, 1981), pp. 139-140.

57. Edward T. Pinch, "The Third World and the Fourth Estate: a look at the Non-Aligned News Agencies Pool," Senior Seminar in Foreign Policy, Department of State, April 1977.

58. Ernesto Vera, "Mass media in Cuba," *The Democratic Journalist,* November 1979, p. 16.

59. Interviews with ICRT officials, Havana, April 1979; also see "Fidel's main report," Granma Weekly Review, pp. 6, 13.

60. For example, see Brian Vine, "The decline of Castroism," Daily Express (London), 8 April 1980; reprinted in *World Press Review,* June 1980, p. 51; and "Cubans raid shop printing illegal flyers," The Times of the Americas (Washington), 30 January 1980, p. 3.

61. Ibid.; "Raúl Castro," *Cuba Update,* p. 10; "El fortalecimiento del ejercicio de la critica," *UPEC.*

62. William M. LeoGrande, "Party development in revolutionary Cuba," *Journal of Interamerican Studies and World Affairs* 21 (November 1979), pp. 457-480.

63. Jorge I. Domínguez, personal communication, April 15, 1981.

64. "Fidel's main report," Granma Weekly Review, pp. 11, 13.

65. "Raúl Castro," *Cuba Update.*

66. "El fortalecimiento del ejercicio de la critica," *UPEC.*

67. Rodríguez, "Public opinion in Cuba," p. 63.

68. Interview with Luis Mas Martin, director, Radio Rebelde, Havana, April 7, 1979 and Rodríguez.

69. "Criticism and the mass media," *Cuba Update,* April 1980, pp. 6-7.

70. "Fidel's main report," Granma Weekly Review, p. 13.

71. Data in this section are from J. M. Frost, ed., *World Radio TV Handbook* (London: Billboard, 1971, 1974, 1976, 1981); Unesco, *World Communication* (Paris: The Unesco Press, 1975); Tullio Camilglieri, "Cuba: :a Radrodiffusione Oggi (Cuba: Broadcasting Today)," *Milleconali,* November 1978, p. 43; Vera, "Mass media in Cuba," *Democratic Journalist,* "Fidel's main report," *Granma Weekly Review,* p. 13.

72. Cuban media statistics are not audited and often unreliable. Listings in the *World Radio TV Handbook,* while usually reliable, are based on its ability to identify stations rather than their actual existence.

73. "Fidel's main report," Granma Weekly Review.

3

The Economy

Caution, Frugality, and Resilient Ideology

CARMELO MESA-LAGO

At the beginning of the year 1979, the Cuban economy entered its third decade under the Revolution. At the end of 1980, the Second Congress of the Cuban Communist party was held and guidelines for the Cuban economy in the next quinquennium and until the year 2000 were elaborated. In April 1981 there was another important celebration: the twentieth anniversary of the proclamation of the socialist nature of the revolutionary process. The socialist economy of the largest island of the Caribbean has reached adulthood, and a fresh review of its current situation and its future outlook is in order. I have recently examined Cuba's socioeconomic performance in the first two decades of the Revolution (1959-78) and this chapter will not duplicate that work.[1] And yet vital statistics and documents published in 1980, plus the time perspective, now allow a thorough evaluation of the first five-year plan (1976-80), a task I could not fully accomplish before. This chapter will appraise the fulfillment/unfulfillment of the 1976-80 plan and analyze the reasons behind its success/failure; it will also study the second five-year plan (1981-85) and the feasibility of its major goals and will discuss some of the conflicts that the Cuban economy will face in the 1980s.

TABLE 3.1   Selected Cuban Socioeconomic Indicators: Actual
             Performance and Goals 1971-1985

	Actual Performance		Planned Goals	
	1971-75	1976-80	1976-80	1981-85
Macroeconomic Indicators				
Global Social Product[a]	13.7	4.0	6.0	5.1
Investment (billion pesos)	7.5	13.2	15.0	15.2-15.8
Labor productivity[a]	9.0	4.0	7.0	3.3
Foreign Trade Indicators				
Exports[a]	29.4	6.6	—	7.0
Imports[a]	21.3	6.5	—	6.8[d]
Cumulative deficit (billion pesos)	1.4	1.6	—	1.5[d]
Percent of trade with:				
USSR[c]	46	63	—	65[d]
All socialist[c]	65	76	—	69[d]
Increment of trade with:				
USSR[b]	66	173	40-50	50
All socialist[b]	56	143	—	30
Social Indicators				
Enrollment middle schools (thousands)[e]	338	825	873	895[d]
Inhabitants per physician[e]	1,008	626	750-790	500-550
Housing[f]	79,685	82,934	150,000	200,000
Day-care centers[e]	658	825	1,050	950[d]

a. Annual average growth rate.
b. Total percentage increase over previous period.
c. Average for the period.
d. Estimate.
e. Figures in the year at the end of the period.
f. Total number built in the period.

SOURCES: C. Mesa-Lago, *The Economy of Socialist Cuba: A Two Decade Appraisal*
(Albuquerque: University of New Mexico Press, 1981); Comité Estatal de Estadísticas, *Cuba en
Cifras 1979* (La Habana, 1980); Banco Nacional de Cuba, *Highlights of Cuban Economic
Development 1976-1980 and Main Targets for 1981-1985* (Havana, 1981); *Proyecto de
Lineamientos Económicos y Sociales para el Quinquenio 1981-1985* (La Habana, 1980);
Bohemia, January 2, 1981, pp. 56-57; and *Guía Estadística 1980.*

THE FIRST FIVE-YEAR PLAN:
SUCCESS OR FAILURE?

In spite of the fact that Cuba has elaborated two five-year
plans, one four-year plan (1962-65), and at least a dozen
annual plans, a very small number of quantitative targets have
been made known. Thus, the evaluation of the overall success
or failure of the 1976-80 plan is not an easy task. Table 3.1
contrasts actual performance in 1971-75 (first period) and

1976-80 (second period) and the published goals for 1976-80 in three crucial economic areas: macroeconomic, foreign trade, and social indicators.

Both the macroeconomic and foreign trade data, given in Cuban pesos, are affected by inflation in an unknown magnitude. Cuban officials claim that these data are in practice given in constant pesos, but I have argued elsewhere that they are partly affected by "socialist inflation" and hence are in current pesos. My crude evaluation is that inflation was significantly reduced in 1971-75 but increased in 1976-80; hence figures for the second period are somewhat inflated. The average growth rate of GSP declined by more than two-thirds in the second period (4 percent) over the first period (13.7 percent); also, the 1976-80 growth goal was unfulfilled by one-third. On the other hand, investment increased by 75 percent in the second period but still fell 12 percent short of the target (more on this later). Labor productivity in the second period was less than one-half the rate of the first period and fell 43 percent short of the goal. In the second period, the average growth rate of exports declined by 78 percent and that of imports by 70 percent, while the cumulative deficit grew slightly. Trade-partner concentration with the USSR (and socialist countries) sharply increased in 1976-80. There are no data to evaluate goal performance on trade. In general, the two combined sets of economic indicators clearly show (with the exception of investment) a severe deterioration in the second period and a very significant unfulfillment of plan goals. It should be taken into account, however, that the period 1966-70 was one of serious economic decline; hence the high rates of 1971-75 were in part a recuperation of lost economic growth. Conversely, it was difficult to maintain in 1976-80 the high growth rates achieved in the previous period.

Performance in the social sphere was better, but mixed. The principal health indicator shows that the target was overfulfilled; the number of inhabitants per physician in 1980 was reduced further than planned. The 1980 goal of enrollment in middle schools was unfulfilled, but only by 5.5 percent. On the other hand, although the total number of dwellings built in 1976-80 was slightly higher than in the previous period, the plan target was unfulfilled by almost one-half. The target of day-care center construction was also unfulfilled by 22 percent. Unfortunately, we do not have official aggregate data available on consumption per capita, although various analyses conducted outside of Cuba suggest that the distribution of basic consumer goods peaked in the first half of the 1970s, mostly in 1975-76 (more on this later).

Table 3.2 presents data on the physical output of 22 products important both for domestic consumption and exports. Production in 1980 was higher than in 1975 for 13 products, while it was smaller for 7 products and practically stagnant for 2. This was a deterioration in relation to the performance in the previous period; in 1975, production was higher than in 1970 for 18 products, was stagnant for 2, and declined for only 2. A comparison between actual output in 1980 and sixteen output targets available for 1980 shows that fourteen of the targets were unfulfilled and only two were fulfilled. Furthermore, for seven of the unfulfilled targets, actual output was from 42 to 92 percent below the target, while for the other seven the degree of unfulfillment fluctuated from 12 to 35 percent; overfulfillment of the two targets was 10 and 16 percent.

In summary, Tables 3.1 and 3.2 show that: the Cuban economy performed much worse in 1976-80 than in 1971-75; the dynamism of foreign trade slowed down and the degree of trade-partner concentration worsened in the second period; there was an overwhelming percentage of unfulfilled output targets in the 1976-80 plan and the degree of unfulfillment was extremely high; in the social sector there was continued improvement and fulfillment/overfulfillment in education and health, but housing and day-care center building targets were unfulfilled. Thus we may conclude that the 1976-80 plan was a dismal failure in economic terms and had mixed results in social terms.

There were nine reasons behind the economic failure of the 1976-80 plan: (1) the sharp decline in the value of Cuban exports (mostly of sugar) and an increase in the value of imports, which at the outset affected the feasibility of the plan; (2) plan targets were too ambitious and investment, although apparently high, had a low efficiency; (3) natural phenomena like pests and hurricanes afflicted agriculture; (4) the plan to mechanize sugar cane cutting and expand mill capacity lagged behind; (5) in the nonsugar sector, two key lines of production, nickel and fishing, encountered serious difficulties; (6) the introduction of the new management and planning system suffered significant delays and complications; (7) the distribution of consumer goods deteriorated in 1979-80, and the visit of Cuban exiles made the scarcities more evident; (8) the labor force was affected by lack of discipline, low productivity, and unemployment; and (9) the African campaigns resulted in economic losses. An analysis of these problems follows.

Deterioration in the Terms of Trade

Sugar remains the single most important product of the Cuban economy, and in the second half of the 1970s made up 86 percent of the value of Cuba's exports. Fidel Castro recently said: "We must admit that our economy today revolves around the sugar industry ... Other [economic] branches are growing ... but nothing can be compared to the thousands of millions of pesos in foreign exchange that the sugar industry contributes."[2] The guidelines for the 1981-86 plan state: "The nation exports fundamentally a semi-elaborated product: raw sugar. The other exports still have a minor importance."[3] Asked why, 21 years after the Revolution, Cuba was still "absolutely dependent on sugar," the Vice President of the Central Planning Board (JUCEPLAN) referred to the percentage of Cuba's exports generated by sugar and acknowledged: "Seen from that angle, we continue to be to a large extent dependent on sugar. ... There is no other branch of the Cuban economy that can compete with sugar. [It] would be a terrible mistake ... to give sugar up just so as not to be labeled a monoexporting country."[4]

TABLE 3.2 Physical Output of Selected Products in Cuba: 1960-1980, and 1980 and 1985 Goals (in thousand metric tons unless specified)

Products	ACTUAL OUTPUT									GOALS	
	1960	1965	1970	1975	1976	1977	1978	1979	1980	1980	1985
Sugar	5943	6156	8538	6314	6155	6485	7350	7992	6787	8-8700	9.5-10
Tobacco	45	43	32	41	51	46	40	33	5	60	55
Citrus fruits	73	160[d]	124[f]	182	199	177	198	191	357[h]	550	1300
Coffee	42	24	20	18	19	16	13	22	24	—	46
Eggs (MU)	430	920	1509	1851	1829	1846	1924	2018	2326	2000	2300
Rice	323	50	291	338	335	334	344	390	—	600	630-640
Beans	37	11	5	5	3	2	2	2	2[g]	—	35
Pork	38	48	15	43	52	58	61	60	57	80	85
Milk	767	575	380	591	682	722	783	791	889[h]	1000	1000-1300
Fish	31	40	106	143	193	184	211	155	186	350	300
Nickel	13	28	37	37	37	37	35	32	38	100	69
Salt	59	106	89	157	151	129	130	122	131	—	600

Electricity (Mkwh)	2981	3387	4888	6583	7192	7707	8481	9403	9895	9000	15000
Steel	63	36	140	298	250	330	324	328	304	440	1800-2000
Cement	813	801	742	2083	2501	2656	2711	2613	2840	5000	4900
Fertilizers	438[c]	860[e]	577	749	798	863	946	873	1059	—	1250
Textiles (Mm^2)	116[c]	96	78	144	139	152	156	151	157	260-280	325
Shoes (M)	14	16	16	23	21	35	18	16	15[g]	35	29
Soap	34[c]	37	33	41	43	35	38	34	38	—	—
Refrigerators (TU)	0	12	6	50	44	46	45	55	25	100	—
Radios (TU)	0	82	19	113	92	120	121	143	200	300	500
Cigars (MU)	591[a]	657	364	383	359	352	354	295	166	—	360[g]

a. 1959
b. 1961
c. 1963
d. 1966
e. 1969
f. 1971
g. estimate based on official data
h. doubtful

M = millions T = thousands U = units H = hectolitres m^2 = square meters kwh = kilowats/hour

SOURCES: Output from *Boletín Estadístico de Cuba 1968-1971, Anuario Estadístico de Cuba 1972-1979, Cuba en Cifras 1979, Guía Estadística 1980,* and Fidel Castro, "Main report to the 2nd Congress of the Communist Party of Cuba," Granma Weekly Review, December 28, 1980, pp. 6-16. Goals for 1980 from Comité Central del PCC, *Directivas para el Desarrollo Económico y Social del País en el Quinquenio 1976-1980: Tesis Resolución* (La Habana, 1976). Goals for 1985 from *Proyecto de los Lineamientos Económicos y Sociales para el Quinquenio 1981-1985* (La Habana, 1980); Castro, pp. 6-16; and Banco Nacional de Cuba, *Highlights of Cuban Economic Development 1976-80 and Main Targets for 1981-85* (Havana, January 1981).

TABLE 3.3   Sugar Prices in the International Market and the
            USSR-Cuban Agreement: 1970-1981
            (in U.S. cents per pound)

Years	International market price[a]	Soviet price paid to Cuba	Difference
1970	3.75	6.11	+ 2.36
1971	4.53	6.11	+ 1.58
1972	7.43	6.11	- 1.32
1973	9.63	12.02	+ 2.39
1974	29.96	19.64	-10.32
1975	20.50	30.40	+ 9.90
1976	11.57	30.95	+19.38
1977	8.10	35.73	+27.63
1978	7.81	40.78	+32.97
1979	9.65	44.00	+34.35
1980	28.66	—	—
1981[b]	18.43	—	—

a. Free market price (f.o.b.) Caribbean ports.
b. First three-quarters.

SOURCES: International market price, IMF, *International Finance Statistics* (1970-1981) and New York Times, January-December 1981. Soviet price from *Boletín Estadístico de Cuba 1970-71, Anuario Estadístico de Cuba 1972-1978,* and CEPAL, "Cuba: Notas para el estudio económico de América Latina 1980," MEX/1044/9 Abril 1981, pp. 23-24.

Although the USSR has paid considerably more (from 27 to 421 percent) for Cuban sugar imports than the international market price (see Table 3.3), Cuba still exports about 28 percent of its sugar to the world market and hence is affected by its fluctuations. In 1974, when Cuban planners had almost completed the first five-year plan, the price of sugar in the international market had reached an historical height of almost 30 cents per pound and, in November of that year, the price peaked at 65 cents. In 1975, when the plan was already being discussed in the central ministries, the price of sugar began to decline, but the average for the year was still more than 20 cents per pound. Eugenio R. Balari, Director of Cuba's Institute of Domestic Demand, told me in 1979 that the planners had prepared three variants of the plan—optimistic, fair, and pessimistic—according to "possible" sugar price fluctuations; they had to choose the worst variant and still, because prices declined more than expected, 22 investment projects were hurt.[5] Fidel Castro has complained that according to "all the experts," the price of sugar "would never drop

TABLE 3.4   Foreign Trade of Cuba: 1974-1980

| | In Million Pesos | | | | Percentage of | | | |
Years	Exports (f.o.b.)	Imports (c.i.f.)	Total Transactions	Trade Balance	Total Trade with Other USSR	Socialist	Trade Deficit with Other USSR	Socialist
1974	2,236	2,226	4,462	+ 11	41	18	100	0
1975	2,947	3,113	6,060	-166	48	12	0	0
1976	2,692	3,180	5,872	-488	53	14	0	0
1977	2,918	3,461	6,379	-543	62	13	0	13
1978	3,417	3,558	6,974	-141	69	13	0	33
1979	3,500	3,687	7,187	-187	68	18	82	0
1980*	3,977	4,246	8,223	-269	56	17	47	53

*January-November; preliminary.
SOURCES: *Anuario Estadístico de Cuba 1976-1979;* statistics supplied by the State Committee on Statistics to the author in July 1979; Banco Nacional de Cuba, *Highlights of Cuban Economic Development 1976-1980 and Main Targets for 1981-1985* (Havana, 1981); and *Guía Estadística 1980.*

below 16 to 17 cents per pound," but it actually declined to 9 cents per pound by the end of 1976. Hence, in the first year of the plan the sugar sector generated one-half of what was expected.

The value of Cuban exports in 1976 declined and, in spite of significant suspension in contracted imports, the latter increased slightly. Thus the trade deficit almost tripled and, in 1977, became the second highest in history (see Table 3.4). By September 1976, Castro warned that the plan goals would not be met. Although the price of sugar in the international market increased again in the second half of 1979 and reached a second historical height (36 cents per pound) in the fourth quarter of 1980, the price of imports skyrocketed as did freight and rental fees for merchant vessels. Thus, large trade deficits continued, although at lower levels than in 1976-77. To cope with this problem, in 1977-78, Cuba had to negotiate short-term loans in the capitalist market for "hundreds of millions" of dollars, which in turn forced a substantial increase in debt service payments. In 1979, however, only $40 million could be raised, and most of it had to be used to pay the debt service.[6]

Table 3.4 shows Cuba's increasing trade dependency on the USSR in the second half of the 1970s: while in 1974 only 41 percent of Cuba's trade was with the USSR, that proportion steadily grew, reaching 69 percent in 1978-79. This was the result of the decline in sugar prices in the international market and the parallel increase of Soviet subsidies to Cuban sugar imports. (But in 1980, when sugar prices in the international market began to rise, the proportion of Cuba's trade with the USSR declined.) In 1975, the USSR introduced an adjustment trade mechanism in its trade with Cuba, increasing the price of sugar imports (with a minimum of 500 rubles per ton) proportionally to the increase in prices of a group of Soviet exports (e.g., steel, oil, foodstuffs, machinery). While in 1974 100 percent of Cuba's trade deficit was with the USSR, in 1975-78, as a result of the adjustment mechanism, the deficit disappeared entirely. Surprisingly, in 1979 the USSR again held the majority of Cuba's trade deficit (82 percent), and in 1980 the totality of that deficit was with the USSR (47 percent) and other socialist countries (53 percent). The Economic Commission for Latin America (ECLA) has reported that the reappearance of the huge deficit with the USSR "was due to the increase in [Cuba's] imports and the decline in the value of exports." This explanation is not satisfactory, since the adjustment mechanism should have taken care of precisely that and because the value of sugar exports actually increased in 1979-80. ECLA adds, however, that while in 1975-77 Cuba's terms of trade with the USSR were constant, they deteriorated in 1979 due, among other reasons, to a "substantial modification of the contractual base which served to establish the adjustment mechanism, by disconnecting the price paid for sugar from Soviet exports to Cuba."[7] Unfortunately, this is the only information we have on this crucial arrangement; if true, it means that the generous conditions provided by the USSR in 1975-78 have been suspended, or at least substantially modified.

Ambitious Targets and Investment Inefficiency

The previous discussion shows that a substantial part of the resources Cuba expected in 1976-80 did not materialize, and this in turn made impossible the acquisition of equipment and inputs necessary to fulfill many of the plan's targets. But, as Table 3.2 suggests, a good number of the targets were set too high to begin with. A top Cuban planner said in 1980 that the statistical base for the first five-year plan was "not very reliable in many cases," and this was compounded with "errors of subjectivism"; thus, as reality became evident, JUCEPLAN had to adjust the targets downward in successive annual plans.[8]

According to Castro, investment in 1976-80 totaled 13.2 billion pesos and was only 12 percent short of the initial target of 15 billion. The National Bank of Cuba has provided disaggregated annual investment data (1976 = 2.37 billion pesos, 1977 = 2.54, 1978 = 2.7, 1979 = 2.85, and 1980-target = 2.65) whose total is similar to Castro's figure.[9] If the total investment figure is correct, it means that in the recession period of 1976-80 there was an increase of 76 percent of investment over the boom period of 1971-75. (Such high investment for 1976-80 seems incompatible with Balari's report, quoted above, that the worst variant of the investment plan was selected, and still 22 investment projects were cut.) The annual investment figures indicate that in 1976-79 the growth of investment surpassed that of the GMP and that the investment ratio (over GMP) was a constant 27 percent, the highest in Cuban socialist history, except perhaps for 1968, the dreary year of the Revolutionary Offensive. This suggests that consumption must have been significantly reduced in the second half of the 1970s.

Another resemblance to the Mao-Guevarist years of high capital accumulation was the dispersion of investments among too many projects, as a Vice President of JUCEPLAN has acknowledged: "We started many projects of [large] magnitude at the same time [and this] prevented us from finishing some of them on time. . . . Many projects begun in this five-year period [1976-80] will be completed in the next."[10] Other practices reducing investment efficiency were: absence of a research basis for the investment plan; excessive centralization of investment but very poor coordination; failure to assure all needed elements and technological imports; lack of a policy of depreciation and replacement; scarcity of investment-project specialists; and poor objective evaluation of investment efficiency.[11] In spite of some administrative decentralization introduced in the 1970s, investment is still basically financed by the state budget. The original SDPE included a "development fund" fed by part of the enterprise profits and used for reinvestment in its expansion. Eventually the fund was discarded; therefore, investment is not currently made according to enterprise profitability but by central decision according to national needs and priorities.[12]

Hurricanes and Agricultural Plagues

Two hurricanes and three devastating pests seriously affected agricultural output in 1979-80. Hurricane Frederick struck Cuba in 1979, and its heavy rains generated losses of 120 million pesos; mainly afflicted were plantations of citrus fruits, tubers, vegetables, rice, and cacao. Floods harmed the extraction of salt, damaged the largest textile factory and one electric plant, and paralyzed work in quarries, which in turn provoked a cut in cement output.[13] Hurricane Allen hit the Isle of Youth in August 1980 and, among other things, blew 25,400 tons of grapefruit off the trees.[14] This makes it hard to believe the officially reported 87 percent increase in citrus production in that year (see Table 3.2).

Sugar cane plantations were shattered at the end of 1979 and through 1980 by an epidemic of *roya* (cane smut or rust). This blight is caused by a parasitic fungus housed in the roots of the cane, which dries its leaves and paralyzes the growth of the plant. The epidemic mostly attacked the variety of sugar cane with the highest yield and adaptability, "Barbados 43-62" (developed in Barbados in 1943 and introduced in Cuba in 1962), which was planted on one-third of sugar cane land. However, only about one million tons of sugar were lost in the 1980 harvest, because most of the infected cane was ground and sugar produced, although at a very low yield. The infected cane seed had to be extracted, all fields disinfected, and rust-resistant cane varieties planted.[15] Castro and other Cuban officials have suggested that the epidemic was not naturally induced but U.S.-"planted."[16] And yet Cuba's top scientific agricultural journal has reported that the blight began in Africa in 1977, particularly in Angola, and was also observed in the Dominican Republic. From there it spread in 1978-79 to ten countries in the Caribbean Basin (including Cuba) and to Florida. The journal acknowledged that the combination of high temperature and humidity present in Cuba in 1978 contributed "to the high incidence of the disease."[17]

Another type of parasitic fungus, "blue mold" (because of the bluish color the leaves take), struck tobacco plantations at the end of the 1978-79 harvest and destroyed from 20 to 27 percent of the crop, causing a loss of 100 million pesos. In the following year (1979-80), the epidemic wiped out 95 percent of the crop, with losses reaching 400 million pesos. At the end of 1979, Cuba had to import 300,000 tons of tobacco from Spain; in 1980 the harvest declined to one-eighth of the 1978 harvest, all tobacco factories were shut down, 26,000 workers were laid off, exports of tobacco products were suspended, and the rationing of cigars and cigarettes was tightened.[18] The fungus was resistant to known fungicides. Eventually, a new fungicide from Switzerland proved to be effective, but it was in short supply, very expensive, and time-consuming, complex, and costly in its application. It had to be used in specified quantities to avoid the gradual adaptation of the fungus to it; it had to be applied by hand to the entire plant (badly contaminated plants had to be burned); nursery seeds also had to be sprayed and humidity controlled; and tobacco planted for self-consumption had to be banned because, being outside of pest control, it could become a permanent focus of infection for commercial plantations. As with the sugar rust, Cuban officials insinuated deliberate U.S. "planting" of the disease, but this was contradicted by the director of Cuba's Plant Sanitation, Ministry of Agriculture, who reported that: the fungus had been endemic in Cuba for the last 20 or 30 years (in 1957-60 it became active and harmed three consecutive harvests); the wind blows the spores, which can travel as far as 200 miles by air or can be carried in people's clothing or by birds; the epidemic afflicted the Caribbean, Canada, and the United States, causing the latter $250 million in losses; Cuba requested and received help from a U.S. Department of Agriculture technician, and a Cuban specialist was allowed to consult with U.S. experts at the tobacco research center in Lexington, Kentucky; and climatic factors (high temperature, heavy rains, and humidity) determined the rapid spread of the disease in Cuba.[19]

An epidemic of porcine colera or African swine fever wiped out hogs in the province of Guantánamo and infected pigs in two other eastern provinces. As with the sugar and tobacco pests, insinuations of deliberate infection were soon dismissed when it was reported that Haitian immigrants carrying live pigs in their boats introduced the disease to Cuba.[20] The supply of meat to the population was also affected by a 7 percent decrease in the cattle population, due mainly to a significant reduction of cattle raised by private farmers. To compound the problem, poultry imports from a socialist country did not materialize and forced the slaughtering of underweight cattle.[21]

Delays in the Mechanization of the Sugar Harvest and Expansion of Mill Capacity

The mechanization of the sugar harvest has advanced fastest in lifting the cut cane: 97 percent in 1980 vis-à-vis a goal of 100 percent. A close second is plowing: 90 percent in 1980 vis-à-vis a goal of 100 percent. Cleaning the cane of leaves and the pinnacle is done in "conditioning centers." In 1970 there were some 300 of these centers which mechanically cleaned 25 percent of all cane cut; in 1980, 511 centers were reported and, if they had the same capacity, possibly cleaned 53 percent of the cane. The last operation to be mechanized has been the cutting of the sugar cane: in 1971-76, the proportion of mechanized cutting rapidly increased from 2 to 33 percent at an annual average of 6 percentage points, but by 1980 mechanization had risen to only 45 percent, a significant slowdown in the process of mechanization (at half the rate of growth of 1971-76) and considerably below the 1980 goal of 60 to 80 percent.[22] Most surprising is that in 1977-80, the mechanization of cane cutting was expected to receive a big push with the inauguration in Holguín, in 1977, of a factory that would turn out 600 KTP harvesters annually. One-and-one-half years after its inauguration, the factory had only produced 195 units, and output was 360 units in 1979 and 500 in 1980; thus the KTP factory has produced about half of what was originally planned.

There is no official explanation for this problem; it might have been caused by nondelivery of vital KTP harvester components produced in the USSR (e.g., the engine, the hydraulic pump, the wheels) or by technical problems in the factory itself.[22a] Additional problems in the sugar harvest were the delay in the delivery of 300 Japanese tractors and interruptions caused by mechanization, because heavy machines are paralyzed when it rains. The slowdown in cane cutting mechanization has reversed the 1971-76 declining trend in the number of cane cutters; in 1978 there were 143,000 cane cutters, and their number jumped to 190,000 in 1980 despite a goal to reduce them to 50,000.[23]

The 1976-80 plan envisaged the construction of four new sugar mills to expand installed capacity by 500,000 tons and the rebuilding and modernization of at least 21 of the existing mills to boost capacity by another one million tons. The first new sugar mill was completed in the spring of 1980 and the second later that year, with a combined 200,000-ton capacity; the other two sugar mills were reported near completion toward the end of 1980. Therefore, none of the four new sugar mills could contribute to the sugar harvests during the 1976-80 plan.[24] Concrete information has not been provided on the modernization program; however, Castro reported in the fall of 1980 that frequent breakdowns in the old mills had become a "real headache" and that 10 percent of the work schedule was lost due to those breakdowns. He also related difficulties with centrifuges imported from Poland, delays in the supply of spare parts, interruptions in the cane supply to the sugar mills created by workers weekend rest, and uncontrolled burning of the cane causing sugar loss.[25] To cope with some of these problems, the grinding period gradually increased from 99 days in 1975 to 118 days in 1979. At the same time, the industrial sugar yield fell dramatically from 12.44 in 1975 to 10.82 in 1980.[26]

Difficulties in the Nickel and Fishing Industries

After three consecutive years of steady nickel output at 37,000 tons, there was a decline in 1978 and a further decrease in 1979 to 32,000 tons (the lowest output in eleven years), but in 1980 the previous output level had recuperated (see Table 3.2). (Contrary to claims from some Cuban officials, nickel's total output in 1976-80 was equal to the 1971-75 total.)[27] The official explanation for the 1978-79 decline in output was the renovation of the twenty-year-old plant at Moa.[28] The initial nickel output goal for 1980 was 100,000 tons, but this was later reduced to 47,000 tons. The latter was to materialize by raising the actual capacity of the two nickel plants (Moa and the older Nicaro), something which did not happen. Original expectations that the first stage of the new nickel plant in Punta Gorda would start operations by 1980 (producing 10,000 tons) were soon discarded due to considerable building delays. The plant was promised by the Soviets as early as 1972, but apparently they had to use hard currency to acquire the equipment and this prompted the stall.

A crucial question is whether the Punta Gorda plant will use the same technology as the old plants or a more fuel-efficient technology. Cuba's nickel deposits are laterite ores with low nickel content which, because of high energy consumption associated with extraction, are eight to ten times more costly to process than sulfides (which use flotation rather than thermal energy). In the 1940s and 1950s, when the first two Cuban nickel plants were built by the United States, oil was relatively cheap and extraction was profitable.[29] But, as Castro has acknowledged, the nickel industry is now "ruined" due to its obsolete technology. While nickel prices had increased 40 percent by 1979, oil prices had jumped fifteenfold.[30] Because of Soviet subsidies to the price of nickel imported from Cuba and of oil exported to Cuba, the latter profits from its selling of nickel to the USSR but not so with the rest of the world. Still, because of the oil subsidy, Cuba has an advantage over other countries which use the same technology. Thus, in 1980, the oil component of total production costs in Cuba was 19 percent as opposed to 34 percent in the Dominican Republic. But Cuba is at a serious disadvantage with those countries which either have sulfide ores or use a more fuel-efficient technology.[31]

According to Lawrence Theriot, a specialist on Cuba in the U.S. Dept. of Commerce, in late 1977 the Soviets approached Western engineering firms to acquire the more efficient technology for the Punta Gorda plant, but due to the high hard currency expenditure involved, they apparently "decided to replicate the existing twenty-year-old nickel plant [technology]." Later, Theriot had a meeting with Cuban nickel technicians in which they assured him that they had obtained a technology similar to the one used in Australia.[32] I have been unable to obtain such a clear-cut answer from Cuban officials. Castro has recently stated somewhat ambiguously that: "In mining, the most efficient methods *must* [instead of *will*] be used to extract full value from existing mineral deposits on the basis of low energy technologies."[33] Finally, the U.N. Economic Commission for Latin America, in its 1980 report on the Cuban economy, suggested that Punta Gorda would use the old technology: "When the new nickel plant is operating at full capacity it will require a higher supply of oil at subsidized prices unless the increase in the price of nickel in the international market makes its production profitable."[34]

Fishing was a continuous success story of the Revolution until the second half of the 1970s; production grew steadily and by 1974 it was 194,000 tons, 7.5 times that of 1958. The first decline (13 percent) occurred in 1975, there was a recuperation in 1976 and a new decline in 1977, then in 1978 the highest production ever was followed in the next year by a sharp drop (27 percent). In 1980, output, although increased, was below the 1976 level (see Table 3.2). In 1971-75, the total fishing catch jumped by more than 100 percent over the previous period, but in 1976-80 growth slowed to 29 percent. The principal reason for the output oscillations and slowdown in the second half of the 1970s has been the universalization of the 200-mile fishing limit, which has restricted the Cuban fishing fleet's access to traditional fishing waters and forced its transfer to farther zones. In addition, there has been a deficient utilization of available resources; fishing vessels were probably used to transport Cuban troops to Angola; in 1979, Peru canceled a profitable fishing agreement with Cuba; the largest seafood nursery (in San Antonio) was destroyed in 1979 by the pollution caused by an oil tanker which sank close to it; and the U.S.-Cuban fishing agreement which had been informally in operation since 1978 was rejected in 1980 by the U.S. Senate.[35]

Complications in the Implementation of the SDPE

In an interview I had in mid-1979 with two top Cuban planners, they assured me that all elements of the new system of economic management and planning (SDPE) which began to be introduced in 1976 would be fully in force nationally by the end of 1980, including economic calculation, self-financing, contracts among enterprises, labor norms (or output quotas), collective incentive funds, and price reforms.[36] A few months before our conversation, JUCEPLAN had released the results of a national survey checking the implementation of twenty different aspects of the SDPE in all enterprises of the pilot plan. The survey found that numerous enterprises did not apply or violated the new system in terms of accounting, costs, capital amortization, labor norms, inventories, and so forth, while revealing that half of their administrators had not been trained in management schools.[37] In 1980 it became obvious that none of the elements of the SDPE would be in operation at the end of that year. Although 95 percent of enterprises were using "principal elements" of economic calculation, its full implementation was postponed until 1981, and the same was said of self-financing and contracting among enterprises; labor norms were functioning in only 59 percent of the enterprises (covering 75 percent of their workers) and full coverage was not expected until 1982; the collective incentive fund was being applied to only 7 percent of the enterprises, and national implementation was delayed until 1981-85; and the reform of wholesale prices was deferred for 1981, that of retail prices for 1981-85, and the entire price system for 1986-90.[38]

A new national survey on the SDPE, done in February 1980, made a thorough analysis of the serious difficulties encountered in the four-year implementation of the system.[39] The report is one of the longest, most complex, and boring Cuban documents I have ever read, but if one has the necessary background and is armed with the patience of Job, it is quite revealing. Its description of the problems confronted by the SDPE is appalling, while the list of recommendations is not only long but of such magnitude that it becomes utopian, lacking any guidelines in terms of priorities. The overall impression conveyed by the document is that too many reforms were introduced simultaneously, lacking sufficient material and human basis, and with excessively centralized control but ineffective coordination.[40]

Some of the overall deficiencies listed were: lack of, obsolete, or frequent breakdown of equipment; insufficiently qualified and stable personnel; poor discipline in enforcing the plan and applying its methodology; deficient, inconsistent, and delayed data; constant changes, serious incompatibilities, and lack of coordination between goals and allocated inputs; excessive centralization and inflexibility in decision making and insufficient input from lower echelons; too aggregated targets which are difficult to implement; and a very high volume of administrative work. Some astronomical figures can better illustrate the latter: the planners released 102,047 rules on consumption, 334 volumes to partly cover wholesale prices, 10,428 labor-organization measures, and 1,282 material balances. It was also reported that 43 percent of the data requested from enterprises were unnecessary, hence increasing their burden and taking time from vital chores.

It is impossible in this chapter to cover the entire SDPE report; hence I have chosen only a few of its important aspects for illustration: *Credit:* in 1979, 20 percent of loans taken by state enterprises from the National Bank were 45 to 90 days behind payment deadlines; the proportion increased to 26 percent in 1980 for a total of 1.4 billion pesos in unpaid loans. *Inventories:* 39 percent of the enterprises did not report inventories and 49 percent did not submit lists of unused inventories; as a result, some enterprises were shut down for lack of supplies which sat idle in other enterprises. *Prices:* inspections revealed that there was a very high incidence of violations of state-fixed prices, 500 cases were in court, and a good number of violators had been fined or imprisoned. On the other hand, due to price rigidities, out-of-fashion merchandise was stockpiled in inventories and perishable goods were lost. *Contracts:* unfulfillment of contracts among enterprises was widespread, largely because of no application of sanctions to violators; this resulted in no deliveries, delays, or deficient products, causing a chain reaction of bottlenecks. *Quality Controls:* 30 percent of the enterprises lacked controls altogether, and inspections revealed that 90 percent of the products did not meet the quality norms. *Training:* 30 percent of directors of central agencies had not received training in management schools, and in some key agencies the proportion was even higher, e.g., 41 percent in the sugar industry.

Deterioration in the Supply and Quality of Consumer Goods

In a previous work I have compared rationing quotas in Cuba in 1962-79, finding that there was a significant reduction of quotas in the late 1960s, a noticeable improvement through most of the 1970s, but a deterioration in 1978-79 (and possibly in 1980). In spite of the temporary improvement in the 1970s, rationing in 1978-79 was tougher than in 1962: quotas of fourteen (out of nineteen products compared) were lower, two were stagnant, and only three were higher.[41] Another comparison, conducted by the Swedish economist Brundenius, on the per capita consumption of 42 food and beverage products in 1963-78, shows that consumption of two-thirds of those products peaked in 1972-76, with a high concentration in 1975.[42] The CIA has recently published a similar study based on Cuban data comparing official per capita distribution of five major food groups and eight major staples in 1965-78; it shows that distribution of 75 percent of the products peaked in 1971-76, and 25 percent in 1965-70, while none peaked in 1977-78.[43] Unfortunately, these studies do not cover the recession years of 1979-80 in which distribution of consumer goods must have deteriorated due to the agricultural plagues, the decline in fishing output, the cut in imports of foodstuffs from market economies (e.g., powdered milk, beans), and the delays or suspension of deliveries of some foodstuffs from socialist countries (e.g., poultry).[44] Table 3.2 shows that in 1979, output of more than half of the products declined, and there were declines in one-third of the products in 1980. The increase in investment in the second half of the 1970s at higher growth rates than GSP also confirms our conclusion that consumption had deteriorated, particularly at the end of the decade.

Cuban leaders have tried to compensate for the meager distribution of rationed consumer goods with a series of market mechanisms such as the parallel market (where consumer goods produced in excess of the amount needed for rationed supply are sold at state-fixed prices which approximate the market price) and free peasant markets (in which agricultural products—except beef, coffee, and tobacco—are sold at free market prices). These markets provide important incentives for the higher income brackets, but prices of products sold on such markets are not affordable by the majority of the population.

One of the most interesting interviews recently transmitted by Cuban TV was with the Minister of Food Industry in the fall of 1980. Prior to the program, there were more than 1,000 calls to the station, and a survey was also conducted on consumer dissatisfaction. Several journalists asking the questions said that "a large part of the population" had "expressed concern" over the supply or quality of consumer goods such as milk, meat, bread, refreshments, beer, cigarettes, and matches. Specific complaints were voiced on: the high price of powdered milk; the suspension of the fresh milk quota to children when they reach seven years of age, while fresh milk is sold in the parallel market at 3 pesos per gallon; delays and uncertainty in the distribution of rationed beef, cheating in the weight of meat, and scarcity of poultry; stale or burnt bread being sold, and a scarcity of crackers and cookies outside of Havana; problems in the distribution of refreshments due to insufficient bottles and caps; low quality, uncleanliness, lack of pasteurization, and "foreign objects" inside bottles of beer (thousands of cases of beer had to be recalled, and still 1,000 reached consumers); quality of cigarettes seriously affected and sticks found in them; and so forth.[45]

An external factor, the visit of 125,000 Cuban exiles in 1979 and early 1980, aggravated the situation. The exiles arrived at a time when the economy had deteriorated, and they made things worse with their phenomenal demonstration effect of the consumer society. The visitors brought expensive gifts to relatives and friends (or bought them at exorbitant prices in state tourist shops), showed photos of their homes, cars, and other consumer goods, and described with Latin zeal their "good life" in the United States. Thus Cubans suffering from twenty years of scarcity contrasted first-hand their frugal existence with that of their relatives and friends living abroad. Cuban officials who have referred to this problem have tried to reduce its importance. Carlos Rafael Rodríguez has said that "some people think we did not foresee" that the influx of

Cubans from abroad "would create problems." Acknowledging that a negative effect of the visits had been "the erroneous stimulation of hopes of the U.S. way of living," he nevertheless claimed that only a minority of the population had been influenced.[46] The impact should have been wider, as the 1980 exodus of 125,000 Cubans suggested; afterwards, visits of exiles declined significantly.

"Softening," Low Labor Productivity, and Unemployment

As in many other societies, the severe economic deterioration in Cuba was accompanied by an increase in crime. By the end of 1979, Castro reported that many employees were stealing from their enterprises, and delinquent attitudes had also spread to the masses: From 20 to 30 percent of the bus ridership did not pay their fares, and 90,000 illegal wires had been connected to steal electricity. At the same time, officials in high positions were taking advantage of their jobs to get privileges, and this created irritation and set a bad example. To combat crime and corruption, Castro asked for 4,000 more policemen, 1,100 patrol cars, and new prisons.[47] The SDPE report also revealed that enterprise revenues often were not deposited on time, thus facilitating "illegal appropriation of funds."[48]

Labor productivity steadily declined in 1977-79, reaching 0.8 percent in the latter year. Raúl Castro bitterly complained that "problems of indiscipline, lack of control, irresponsibility, complacency and negligence [aggravated our] notorious lack of efficiency." He reported labor absenteeism, deliberate slowdowns to avoid overfulfilling already low labor norms (work quotas), deals among foremen and workers to meet the norm in half a day, or fulfillment of two or three work quotas in a single day in order to have free days in which to do nothing or to do something else that brought in more money.[49] In spite of tough measures and appeals, in the first half of 1980, 26 percent of the enterprises under SDPE had suffered a decline in productivity over the previous year.[50]

The best description of the situation in 1979-80 has been given by Fidel Castro:

> A number of bad habits were spreading. . . . Perhaps it was felt that [the reforms of the 1970s would] perform miracles and that everything would get much better automatically. . . . There were increasing signs that the spirit of austerity was flagging, that a softening up process was going on in which some people tended to let things slide, pursue privileges, make accommodations, while work discipline dropped. Our worst enemies could not have done us more damage. Was our Revolution beginning to degenerate? . . . We must deal firmly with the first signs of petit bourgeois accommodation or undisciplined attitudes and even the slightest evidence of corruption.[51]

Aggravating these problems, there was an increase in unemployment at the end of the 1970s as the demand for labor decreased while the labor supply bulged due to the entrance into the labor market of the baby boom of 1959-65 (birth rates climbed from 2.8 to 3.5 percent in that period, and thereafter declined, reaching 1.7 percent in 1978).[52] The SDPE put emphasis on the reduction of labor costs, and labor organization measures were to result in a cut of 55,232 workers.[53] In addition, the SDPE collective incentive fund was expected to make managers and workers more interested in manpower reduction in order to save and increase profits (more on this later). At the end of 1980, a new system of "free labor contracting" was introduced, allowing managers to promptly fire unneeded or troublesome workers (something that previously took considerable time and effort) and be free to hire the most qualified manpower.[54] The economic deterioration of 1979-80 induced a cut in investment, while postponement of imports of equipment and inputs for factories provoked shutdowns and slowdowns. The 1976-80 plan had originally envisaged an expansion of construction activities, but the lack of resources, exportation of cement (to obtain desperately needed foreign exchange), and delays in imports of construction materials left 60,000 to 70,000 workers jobless.[55] In addition, the blue-mold epidemic resulted in the temporary dismissal of 26,000 tobacco workers. Those left unemployed by conjunctural problems *(interruptos)* did not lose the linkage with their enterprise and were paid 70 percent of their salaries. But placing those permanently left out *(disponibles)* became a difficult task, as they often turned down alternate jobs as being inadequate.[56]

Lack of adequate jobs seems to have been a cause behind the massive exodus of 1980. A sample taken among those sixteen years and older who came to the United States showed that an average of 5 percent were unemployed in Cuba, with a much higher proportion among females (13 percent) than males (4 percent). When these figures were adjusted following U.S. definitions, all the rates increased: total unemployed 6 percent, females 25 percent, and males 5 percent.[57]

The current situation is expected to continue through the next quinquennium, since the labor supply will not decline until late in the decade. The major mechanism to cope with the problem is the exportation of the labor surplus. Some 30,000 to 40,000 jobs were probably available after the great exodus of 1980, and Castro has made clear his interest in an orderly transfer of disenchanted Cubans to the United States. Currently there are some 20,000 Cuban civilians working abroad (e.g., in Algeria, Libya, Iraq, Nicaragua, Grenada) as part of lucrative service contracts which generated 125 million pesos in 1980. On the other hand, the possibility of significantly expanding Cuba's military force abroad is small due to increasing domestic defense needs (real or perceived) and the political and economic costs of foreign military campaigns.[58]

In the 1980s a large number of Cuban workers will go to those COMECON countries which have labor deficits. At the end of 1979 Castro announced that some 10,000 Cubans would be sent to cut timber in Siberia in exchange for wood badly needed on the island. Carlos Rafael Rodríguez has also reported that agreements have been signed with Czechoslovakia, the German Democratic Republic, and Hungary to supply them with low-skilled manpower in exchange for products that Cuba needs.[59] Additional measures have been taken in the domestic market to ease unemployment: thus, the 1981-85 plan foresees that the female share of the labor force will be stagnant.[60] (No wonder the percentage of unemployed females who left in 1980 was so high.) In the sugar industry, extra labor shifts were introduced in the 1980-81 harvest to take advantage of "large labor surpluses" in some provinces (this measure was rejected as wasteful in the early years of the Revolution when there was a manpower deficit). After the harvest is over, the "surplus personnel" are expected to be involved in other agricultural chores.[61] But the most important step is the expansion of the private sector in agriculture and personal services, both to create new jobs and to increase the supply of foodstuffs and services provided by carpenters, mechanics, electricians, tailors, laundresses, and so forth. Private farms and small service shops are now allowed to hire employees directly.

The Economic Cost of the African Involvement

In a well-documented study on this subject, Sergio Roca concludes: "It is incontrovertible that Cuba's involvement in Africa, in both its military dimension and its civilian aspect, has imposed a severe burden on the domestic economy."[62] In 1965, the last year for which we had figures before the state budget was dropped for one decade, military expenditures took 5.2 percent of Cuba's GMP. In the first half of the 1970s, military expenditures probably declined as the U.S. threat against Cuba diminished, but since 1975, with the Cuban involvement in Angola, military expenditures probably increased, and by 1978 had reached 7.2 percent of GMP. In 1965, defense and internal order accounted for 8.4 percent of the total Cuban budget, and again that proportion probably declined in the first half of the 1970s.[63] As Table 3.5 shows, the proportion in 1978 had risen to 8.6 percent and in 1979

TABLE 3.5 Percentage Distribution of Expenditures in the State
Budget in Cuba: 1978-1981

Items in the Budget	1978	1979	1980	1981
Financing of the economy[a]	43.9	41.3	41.7	41.7
Health, education, culture, etc.	29.2	31.1	32.7	29.3
Housing and community services	3.6	4.2	3.8	3.7
Public administration[b]	5.9	5.5	5.1	6.0
Defense and internal order	8.6	8.9	8.5	7.5
Other activities[c]	4.4	4.8	4.7	6.9
Reserve[d]	4.4	4.2	3.5	4.9
TOTAL	100.0	100.0	100.0	100.0

a. Productive activities.
b. State agencies, OPPs and judiciary.
c. In 1962-65, this item was called "Payment of the public debt."
d. For contingencies.
SOURCES: 1978 Granma, December 23, 1977; 1979 Granma Weekly Review, January 21, 1979, p. 3; 1980 Granma Weekly Review, January 6, 1980, p. 3; and 1981 Bohemia, January 2, 1981, p. 58.

increased again to 8.9 percent. There was a decline to 8.5 percent in 1980, but it was still higher than the 1965 proportion. Obviously, scarce resources which could have gone into production or services for the population have been invested in the African military adventures.

The deployment to Africa of administrators, technicians, mechanics, truck drivers, and other qualified personnel has deprived the domestic economy of badly needed cadres. In 1979, the President of JUCEPLAN acknowledged that Cuba's involvement in Africa had negatively affected the implementation of the SDPE "because many valuable technicians have been sent away to those countries thus depriving our internal tasks of their availability and experience."[64] Service contracts involving civilian activities are more difficult to judge, since most of them involve a benefit for Cuba. The question is whether revenue generated by the use abroad of Cuban physicians, dentists, teachers, nurses, and construction workers significantly offsets the diminution of services to the Cuban population. Finally, Cuban military involvement in Africa may have contributed, at least partly, to the suspension, cut, or nonrenewal of economic and technical aid to Cuba in 1976-78 from Sweden, Holland, Norway, West Germany, and Canada.

A VIEW TO THE NEXT QUINQUENNIUM: 1981-85

If two single words could characterize the outlook of the next quinquennium, they would be caution and frugality. The brief euphoria of the mid-1970s boom has been substituted by a much more down-to-earth, Spartan mentality based on the realities of the late 1970s. Castro warned at the end of 1979 that in confronting its problems, Cuba would not turn to radical solutions or move to extremes.[65] In other words, the island will continue in the orthodox Soviet path without deviations to the "left" (Mao-Guevarism) or to the "right" (Titoism). In 1980, when sugar prices began to rise in the international market, Castro quickly admonished that the mistake of the 1970s would not be repeated, that the leaders and the masses should not have illusions of spending more: "There will be no spectacular leap in our people's living standard." And later he said: "[We are] working toward long-range solutions, that we will not be able to provide now nor put into practice until after the next five years."[66] Referring to the fiasco of 1976-80, Castro said that the 1981-85 plan had been drawn based on reliable figures and employing the most realistic criterion possible: "The main idea is to surpass, not fall short of [the plan] goals; to pledge the Party to carry out the possible, not the impossible."[67]

To reduce the risk of unfulfillment of the plan targets for 1985, Cuban planners not only set relatively modest goals but also tried to protect themselves. In a seminar in Havana in 1980, a top official from JUCEPLAN reacted to my skeptical analysis of the feasibility of the 1981-85 targets (based on the official published figures) by saying that he was against fixing concrete production targets but favored, at most, setting the installed output capacity.[68] Some of the original output targets of the plan were significantly reduced at the time of its approval, e.g., 500,000 tons less for sugar, 400,000 tons less for cement, 300,000 tons less for citrus, and 95,000 square meters less for textiles.[69] One of the few modifications introduced into the law on the five-year plan was to suspend the obligation of meeting the plan targets *annually,* so that planners and managers will enjoy more flexibility in the overall fulfillment of the goals.[70]

The cautiousness of the planners becomes apparent when the overall targets for 1981-85 are contrasted with those for 1976-80 (see Table 3.1). Still, it is important to point out that most targets for the first year (1981) of the current five-year plan were set below the annual average for the quinquennium. This suggests either that the planners are expecting a significant recuperation of the economy in the next four years, or that in spite of their apparent cautiousness, they were still taken by the old optimistic spirit (more on this later).

The annual average rate of GSP growth is set at 5.1 percent in 1981-85, lower than the 6 percent target of 1976-80 although higher than the actually accomplished rate of 4 percent; but the target for 1981 is set at 3.9 percent, lower than the annual targets for both five-year plans and actual performance in 1976-80. The same is true of the rate of labor productivity, set at 3.3 percent for 1981-85, less than half the 1976-80 target rate and also smaller than actual performance in the same period; the 1981 target is 3 percent, lower than the average rate set for 1981-85.

Total investment for 1981-85 is only slightly higher than in the previous quinquennium (actually lower if inflation is taken into account). This means that the increase in investment *at current prices* in 1981-85 will be from 15 to 20 percent, compared with an increase of 76 percent in 1976-80 over 1971-75. The investment target for 1981 is set at 2.8 billion pesos, 300 million below the average annual investment target for 1981-85. Although capital accumulation, in constant dollars, will be smaller in the current quinquennium, there seems to be a commitment to increase the efficiency of investment by avoiding its excessive spread among too many projects and concentrating it in a small number of important projects, completing investment projects initiated in 1976-80 before starting new ones, and by reducing the period of maturation of investment.[71] This investment policy is similar to the one practiced in 1971-75 and, if truly enforced, it should pay dividends. Investment efficiency may be negatively affected, however, by several problems: the leadership's decision not to introduce the "development fund" (based on enterprise profitability) and its replacement by centralized allocation (based on other criteria) compounded with poor central coordination; the high percentage of state enterprises that do not repay loans on time; current price distortions (to continue through 1981-85 due to the delay in price reform) which impede an objective evaluation among alternative investment projects; and the lack of a policy of depreciation and replacement.

Table 3.2 provides additional evidence of the planners' circumspection in setting output targets for the current quinquennium. Out of fifteen output targets which are comparable in 1981-85 over 1976-80, five are smaller in 1981-85—from 20 to 31 percent (nickel, tobacco, cement, fish, and shoes); three are stagnant or slightly higher—from 0 to 6 percent (milk, rice, and pork); three are moderately higher—from 14 to 16 percent (sugar, eggs, and textiles); and four are substantially higher—from 33 to 300 percent (citrus, electricity, steel, and radios).

We lack data on the 1976-80 and 1981-85 targets for foreign trade, and hence goal comparisons are impossible. However, the 1981-85 targets, when contrasted with actual performance in the previous period, indicate a slight rise in the rate of exports and imports, with an increased trade-partner concentration with the USSR (from 63 to 65 percent) and reduction of trade with other socialist countries (from 13 to 4 percent). The most surprising figure is the increase of trade with the USSR, projected as 50 percent for 1981-85, similar to the 1976-80 target but considerably below the actual increase of 173 percent in 1976-80 and also below the increase of 66 percent in 1971-75 (see Table 3.1).

All projected increases in social indicators for 1981-85 (except for housing) are quite modest. The target for day-care center construction in 1985 is smaller than the target for 1980. The 1985 goal for enrollment in middle schools involves a minor increase (about 3 percent), compared with a jump of 157 percent in 1980 over 1975, but this may be the result of an approximation to universal coverage in secondary education. The reduction of the ratio of inhabitants per physician projected for 1985 is also quite modest, but the ratio in 1980 was already one of the lowest in the Western Hemisphere. Conversely, the housing-construction target for 1981-85 is an anomaly in the overall planning picture for the quinquennium: an increase of 141 percent over the actual number of dwellings built in 1976-80. However, the goal for 1976-80 was also overoptimistic and eventually unfulfilled by almost one-half. The target in the 1981 plan—20,000 dwellings—is more realistic at half of the annual average set by the five-year plan and only 5,000 more than the dwellings actually built in 1980. Even this modest increase does not seem to be supported by the proportion of state budget expenditures allocated to housing. Table 3.5 shows that such a proportion in 1981 is smaller than those in 1980 and 1979.

The budget distribution clearly indicates that in 1981, proportionally fewer resources will go to social services. Thus, in addition to the cut in the share of housing, the share of health, education, and culture is reduced by 3.4 percentage points. All this is consistent with the policy, which began in the 1970s, of changing the emphasis in distribution from one based on need (typical of the 1966-70 Mao-Guevarist period) to one based on work. In 1979, Castro announced that "social consumption" (i.e., social services and goods provided free by the state based on the idealistic distribution according to need) would be reduced in 1981-85.[72] The SDPE envisages the continuous elimination of "unnecessary gratuities" (free social services and goods), and to that effect a list has been compiled of those services and goods now provided free which may be susceptible to a charge.[73] It is foreseen that by 1985 the overall distribution of consumption will be 80 percent individual and 20 percent social.[74]

The overall economic performance in the next quinquennium is going to depend on the amount and efficiency of investment (already discussed), the performance of key productive sectors such as sugar and nickel (both in output and prices), the economic aid provided by the USSR, and labor productivity which is tightly connected with incentives. An analysis of the last three factors follows.

Evaluation of the Feasibility of Output Targets

The sugar industry will maintain its predominant role in the Cuban economy. The Vice President of JUCEPLAN has affirmed that the dependency on sugar will continue into the future and that the sugar sector will be the principal source of capital accumulation in 1981-85. Furthermore, "according to plans that have been outlined for the development strategy up to the year 2000, one of the bases of Cuba's industrialization will be the sugar industry."[75] The original sugar output target for 1981-85 set an increase of 30 percent over 1976-80, for an annual average output of 9.1 million tons and a 1985 target of 10 to 10.5 million tons.[76] Later on, the target was scaled down to an increase of from 20 to 25 percent in the period, for an annual average output of from 8.3 to 8.7 million tons, and a 1985 target of 9.5 to 10 million tons.[77] In order to reach such a reduced target, several premises will have to materialize, and I have serious doubts about many of them. All the rust-infected sugar cane was scheduled to be replanted by the spring of 1981, about 350,000 hectares; in November 1980, 160,000 hectares should have been replanted, but due to heavy rains, only 100,000 actually were. Even before this delay (in August 1980), it was forecast that sugar cane yields in 1981 would be only 28 to 33 percent of the average of 1976-79. Toward the end of 1980, it was acknowledged that the recuperation of the 1978-79 sugar output levels would be difficult to achieve and that the 1981 and 1982 harvests would still be affected by the epidemic.[78] The number of cane conditioning centers planned for 1985 is also insufficient: they should be able to mechanically clean only from 46 to 49 percent of the target harvest of 9.5 to

10 million tons, a reduction in relation to 1980 when the centers cleaned 53 percent of the cane.[79] I have already explained that the mechanization of cane cutting was well behind schedule in 1980 (45 percent versus an initial target of 80 percent, later reduced to 60 percent). The target for 1985 is 50 percent (only 5 percentage points more than in 1980); thus, the increment in sugar output planned for 1985 (from 42 to 50 percent more than in 1980) will have to be achieved with a substantial addition in manpower—not an easy task, indeed.

Finally, crucial to achieving the output goal of 9.5 to 10 million tons for 1985 is the completion of eight new sugar mills in 1981-85 (an additional seven mills are also planned to be started in this period), each with a grinding capacity of 100,000 tons, plus the enlargement of nine other mills and the modernization of another fourteen.[80] In order to evaluate the feasibility of this task, one must recall that the 1976-80 plan contemplated the construction of four new mills. However, only two were finished by mid-1980, and two were reported "near completion" by the end of that year, but none was operational during the plan. In 1979, Cuba's installed milling capacity was close to 8 million tons; hence, the addition of all twelve mills could increase capacity to 9.2 million. The additional 300,000 to 800,000 tons required to reach the output goal must then be produced in the nine enlarged mills. Notice that some of this "added" capacity only compensates for the destruction and deterioration of old mills. Thus, while in 1959 there were 161 mills, this number decreased to 152 in 1969 and to 148 in 1979. In summary, even if all of the above premises are fulfilled, it will be practically impossible to achieve the 1985 sugar goal unless Cuba launches a gigantic mobilization similar to that of 1970, and that may also turn out to be a Pyrrhic victory. Without such mobilization, output will probably be between 8.6 and 8.8 million tons.

The nickel output target for 1985 (69,500 tons) is to be achieved with an expansion of 32,500 tons over existent capacity according to the schedule shown in Table 3.6. Initially, the total output now planned for 1986-90 was

TABLE 3.6   Increase in Nickel Output Planned for 1981-1990

Years	Installed Capacity (in thousand tons)				
	Nicaro	Moa	Punta Gorda	CAME I Camarioca	TOTAL
1981	18.0	19	0	0	37.0
1982	22.5[a]	19	0	0	41.5
1983	22.5	24[a]	0	0	46.5
1984	22.5	24	23[b]	0	69.5
1986-90	22.5	24	30[c]	30	106.5

a. Overhauling and expansion of existing plants.
b. Stage one (11,000) and two (12,000) of new plant become operational.
c. Stage three (7,000) becomes operational.
SOURCES: *Proyecto de Lineamientos...*, p. 14; Banco Nacional de Cuba, *Highlights of Cuban Economic Development...*, p. 12; and Quesada, August 1980.

expected to be achieved in 1976-80; hence, one must be cautious as to the feasibility of the 1985 target. The probability of reaching 46.5 tons is high, but the completion of the first two stages of the Punta Gorda plant by 1984 is less probable. Even if the new plant is completed, there is the question of whether or not it will have a more fuel-efficient technology.

The overall increase in fishing output for 1981-85 is planned to be 1,249,000 tons, for a boost of 33.9 percent over the previous five years, higher even than the 28.7 increment of 1976-80 over 1971-75. However, in view of the difficulties experienced during the previous quinquennium in fishing in territorial waters which were accessible prior to 1975, the current quinquennium target is somewhat optimistic. Since part of the fishing fleet has been transferred to more distant new zones, its operation is probably more costly and its return less predictable. Future investment in the expansion of the fleet must be made according to accessibility to closer and more profitable fishing zones.[81] Castro has predicted an annual rate of increase of 10 percent in fishing output in 1981-85.[82] I do believe that output in the current quinquennium will be as erratic as in the previous one, that the overall target for 1981-85 will not be fulfilled, and that the probability of reaching 300,000 tons in 1985 is not high; a target of 250,000 to 260,000 tons seems more feasible in view of the 1960-80 trend.

In spite of the blue-mold epidemic, the 1985 output target of 55,000 tons of tobacco is not too unrealistic. In 1976, the tobacco harvest yielded 51,000 tons; after a decline of output to 40,000 tons in 1978, due to low state prices, Cuba significantly raised the *acopio* price to private farmers who produce 79 percent of the total tobacco output. Unfortuntely, the blight hit the next two harvests and the impact of the new incentives was lost. But the epidemic now seems to be under control, tobacco (unlike sugar cane) is an annual cultivation (66,000 hectares of tobacco were reportedly planted in 1980), and a good harvest is expected for 1981.[83] On the other hand, the recuperation of the traditional quality of the Havanas will require at least three years, since it takes a blend of tobacco from three or four crops to produce the best cigars. The quantity target of cigars to be produced in 1985 is remarkably modest (similar to that of 1976-78, prior to the epidemic), and hence will probably be overfulfilled.

Economic incentives, such as credit facilities and higher prices to private farmers, and increased wages to workers on state plantations also seem to have worked well in coffee. The private sector produced 82 percent of the coffee crop in 1967 but only 45 percent in 1978, and output declined accordingly from 34,000 to 13,000 tons. With the new incentives, private farm output increased to 60 percent of total output in 1980, and production vigorously recuperated in 1979-80. Still, the 1985 target appears too high.

In the industrial sector, the target for electrical output in 1985 (15,000 Mkwh) is quite ambitious. At the end of 1980, total installed capacity was 850 Mw; new thermal plants under construction total 325 Mw, with 100 Mw in Mariel, 100 Mw in Santiago, and 125 Mw in Nuevitas. If other thermal plants are to be started in 1981-85, it is doubtful that they will be completed during that period, and the "Jaraguá" nuclear plant will not enter into operation until 1986-90 because of delays caused when Cuban geologists discovered that the plant was being built in a seismic zone.[84] The expanded capacity in thermal plants will be 38 percent over 1980 capacity, and yet the planned output increase is more than 48 percent. Even if we assume that Cuba will get all the needed oil to operate these plants and that the frequent breakdowns are kept at a minimum, a target of less than 14,000 Mkwh seems to be the maximum achievable.

The remarkable boost in cement output planned for 1985 (an increase of 70 percent for 4.9 million tons) is to be reached with the construction of two cement plants, both provided by the German Democratic Republic. The first plant is being built in Cienfuegos, with a total capacity of 1.65 million tons. Its first unit became operative in 1980, while the second and third units should begin production in 1981-85. When all three units are in full production, Cuba's total cement output should be 4.3 million tons.[85] It should be noted, however, that although te first unit began its production in 1980, it added only some 130,000 tons over the output of 1978 (the year 1979 is not taken as a base due to the decline in output caused by Hurricane Frederick), perhaps because that unit will not be fully operative until 1981. The second cement plant, with a projected capacity of 1.4 million tons, is to be built in Mariel; although we have practically no information on this plant, my educated guess (based precisely on the lack of data) is that it will not be fully operational by 1985, and thus cement output should be between 3.7 and 4.3 million tons.

The 1985 output target for textiles also appears quite ambitious: 325 Mm^2, a more than twofold increase over the 1980 output. The new plant, "Desembarco del Granma," with a 60 Mm^2 capacity, was reported open by the end of 1980, but obviously did not increase the stagnant textile output of 1977-79 (at 152 Mm^2). A second plant, to be supplied by the USSR, will be built in Santiago, with an 80 Mm^2 capacity, and the old plant in Ariguanabo is to be expanded by 25 to 35 Mm^2.[86] If all these ambitious projects materialize, the 1985 target will be fulfilled, but the chances are that it will not be by a significant margin.

Other pretentious industrial output targets are in steel and fertilizers. To achieve a 450 percent increase in steel output, the existing steel plant, "Antillana de Acero," will be expanded and a new steel mill built in Holguín. My prediction is that the goal will be grossly underfulfilled. The Cubans had serious problems with the nitrogenous fertilizer plant of Cienfuegos and the Soviets had to give them a hand, but there is a new plant being built in Nuevitas and the target increase of 32 percent seems feasible.[87]

In the "productive service" sector, tourism is the major source of foreign exchange. The number of foreign tourists in 1971-75 increased from about 2,000 to 38,000, and the number kept climbing in 1976-78, so that in the latter year 96,652 tourists visited the island. In 1979, with the governmental opening of doors to Cuban exiles, the number of all foreign tourists probably reached its height under the Revolution: an estimated 196,000 visitors. But the incidents in the spring of 1980 both cooled the desire of exiles to return to the fatherland and made the Cuban government more selective about visas. Therefore, the total number of tourists apparently declined to 125,000 or less, significantly below the 300,000 tourist goal set for that year. The screening of Cuban exiles significantly increased in 1981, and the Reagan administration's strong position against Cuba probably discouraged some U.S. tourists; thus, less than 100,000 tourists were expected to visit Cuba in that year. Playing it safe, the planners have not set a goal for 1985, although thirteen new hotels are scheduled to be built in 1981-85, about half the number constructed in the previous quinquennium.[88]

The analysis of the feasibility of output targets for 1981-85 suggests that, in spite of my initial impression of planners' caution, most of the goals are too optimistic. Out of the twenty targets for 1985 shown in Table 3.2, I estimate that twelve will be unfulfilled by a significant degree (sugar, nickel, citrus, steel, cement, textiles, electricity, radios, fishing, beans, rice, and salt); six will be close to fulfillment (tobacco and coffee—if private incentives continue—milk, fertilizers, shoes, and pork); and two will be overfulfilled (eggs and cigars).

Foreign Trade and Economic Aid

The guidelines for the 1981-85 plan state that Cuba's economic development will depend greatly on foreign trade and the generation of external credits: "Cuba needs external financing to give a push to output in key economic branches." The guidelines prescribed greater integration with the USSR and other socialist economies and less dependence on trade with market economies.[89] In spite of this, although the five-year plan forecasts that Cuba's trade with the USSR will increase from 63 to 65 percent, it indicates that trade with other socialist countries should decline from 13 to 4 percent, while trade with market economies should increase from 23 to 31 percent (see Tables 3.1 and 3.4).

At the end of October 1980, after five months of negotiation—well beyond the expected deadline—Soviet and Cuban representatives signed the 1981-85 trade agreement in Moscow. It provides for an increase of 50 percent in trade between both countries, a modest target when compared with the 173 percent increase of 1976-80.[90] The protocol for the Soviet-Cuban agreement on credit and economic cooperation for 1981-85 was not signed until April 1981, when the annual plan was already in effect.

According to the brief Cuban press release, the agreement covers the "largest investment made so far in Cuban-Soviet cooperation, and will practically *double* [in 1981-85] Soviet cooperation with Cuba in 1976-80."[91] However, total Soviet-Cuban economic cooperation in 1976-80 increased by 154 percent over 1971-75, a much larger increment than the one projected for the current quinquennium. It may be that the nature of that cooperation will be different, with more being provided by the USSR in development credits, which are repayable, and less in nonrepayable trade subsidies. The total cumulative Soviet economic aid given to Cuba in 1960-79 amounted to $16.7 billion, about one-third in repayable loans and two-thirds in nonrepayable subsidies. (In 1979 alone, Cuba received $3.1 billion in Soviet economic aid—$8.5 million daily—equal to $315 per capita and one-fifth of Cuba's GSP in that year.) However, the distribution of that aid changed drastically through the last decade, greatly benefiting Cuba. In 1971-75, 57 percent was in loans and 43 percent in subsidies, while in 1976-80, 13 percent was in loans and 87 percent in subsidies.[92] The increasing Cuban trade deficit with the USSR in 1979-80, and the possibility that the adjustment mechanism introduced in 1975 has been substantially modified, suggest a reversal in the distribution of Soviet economic aid. Another important innovation in the 1980s is that Cuba is placing emphasis on obtaining external financing, especially from the USSR, with amortization based on the transfer of part of the output of the plant built with foreign credit. Thus, one-half of the output of the Punta Gorda nickel plant is scheduled to be transferred to the USSR.[93]

As mentioned above, trade with other socialist countries is expected to decline not only in relative but also in absolute terms. Based on official Cuban targets and figures, I have estimated that Cuban trade with socialist countries (other than the USSR) is planned to be 1.7 billion pesos in 1981-85, about one-third of the amount in 1976-80 and the lowest volume of trade with that group of nations in any five-year period since 1966. Cuban trade with those socialist countries increased by 34 percent in 1971-75 and by 61 percent in 1976-80, but seems to be scheduled to decline by -64 percent in 1981-85. A U.S. specialist on East-West trade has reported that Soviet pressure on Eastern European countries to share the Cuban burden has been unsuccessful, and that these countries are increasingly dissatisfied with the heavy Soviet subsidies provided to Cuba.[94] Castro's complaints, at the end of 1979, of problems with imports from Poland and other unidentified socialist countries, and the SDPE report's reference to "import uncertainty" of countries that supply Cuba and do not "stick to delivery schedules"[95] are indications of potential mutual dissatisfaction between Cuba and other socialist countries.

The trade deficit planned by Cuba for 1981-85 is about 1.5 billion pesos, similar to the deficits in the previous two quinquenniums (see Table 3.1). Since Cuba is planning to increase its trade with the USSR (and if the 1979-80 trend continues), most of that deficit will be with the Soviets. The planned increase in trade with market economies is probably based on the expectation of high sugar prices and surplus or balanced trade with the West. This would be extremely important for Cuba, because by 1979 its debt with Western countries was about $3 billion, resulting in an annual payment of $150 million in debt service.[96] In the 1981 Cuban budget, the line which shows the highest rise over 1980 is "other activities," with a 2.2 percentage point increment (that line was previously called "payment of the public debt"). Another line experiencing an unusual jump (1.4 percentage points) is the suspicious "reserve" (see Table 3.5). I have already discussed the significant decline in loans provided by Western banks to Cuba at the end of the 1970s; in 1980, Switzerland canceled a loan of 30 million Swiss francs, and in 1981, Credit Lyonnais also canceled a loan for 150 million DM. The escalation in debt service payments may force the USSR to come to the rescue of Cuba with hard currency if sugar prices deteriorate in 1981-85.

Vital for Cuba's economic development in the next five years is the supply of oil, practically all of which is imported from the USSR, taking from 11 to 13 percent of Soviet deliveries to all COMECON countries. According to Castro, the USSR has indeed guaranteed 97 percent of the oil supply in the next quinquennium, but he has reported a planned increase of 10 to 15 percent of available fuel in 1981-85, or 2 to 3 percent annually.[97] This appears to be a significantly lower rate than that of the 1970s; imports of all fuels increased at an average annual rate of 5 percent in 1971-75 and 6.6 percent in 1976-79, while oil consumption in 1976-80 rose at a rate of 6.9 percent.[98] This apparent slowdown in oil supply must affect industrial expansion (particularly electricity) and economic development in general. In 1980, Venezuela suspended the annual supply of 3 million barrels of oil that had been initiated in 1978 as a result of an agreement with the USSR. On the other hand, in 1981 Mexico and Cuba signed an agreement by which Mexico's state oil corporation (PEMEX) will explore oil and gas deposits in Cuba, sell 10,000 metric tons of liquid gas plus an unspecified amount of lubricants, rebuild an old gas liquefication plant, and expand an oil refinery in Cuba. In April 1981, it was announced that the PEMEX technicians had discovered oil deposits on Cuba's northern coast close to Havana; however, PEMEX has refused to confirm or deny this reported discovery.[99] Even more important, in May it was reported that Mexico and the USSR have agreed that the former should supply most Cuban oil needs, while the USSR would supply oil to such Mexican oil importers as India, Yugoslavia, and Spain. Although this exchange agreement still maintains the burden of the subsidies on Soviet shoulders, it would free Soviet oil tankers and significantly reduce the cost of freight for Cuba.[100]

Still, one of the most important factors shaping the Cuban economy in 1981-85 will be the price of sugar in the international market. As Table 3.3 shows, the price increased in 1979-80, but peaked at 35.7 cents per pound in the last quarter of 1980 and declined through the first three-quarters of 1981, down to 11.6 cents in September. Sugar futures, although higher than current prices, also declined from about 22 cents per pound in March 1981 to 13 cents in December of that year.[101]

The price boom at the turn of the decade was a deviation from a normal ten-year price cycle caused by a sudden sharp decline in world production. The USSR had a terrible sugar beet crop and faced a deficit of at least 3 million tons in 1980-81. Cuba was hit by the sugar rust and lost 1.2 million tons in 1980, which forced an equal reduction of Cuba's exports to several countries, mainly the USSR, and the latter had to increase its purchase of sugar on the international market. Brazil's expected increase in sugar exports (some 300,000 tons more) did not materialize because a large strike of cane cutters affected output, and the Iran-Iraq war forced an increase in its fuel alcohol production from sugar. A serious drought in Peru transformed this country from exporter to importer of sugar. And the same blight that affected Cuban cane plantations spread through the Caribbean, especially hitting the Dominican Republic.[102] By the end of 1980, however, Cuba reported that its harvest that year had been 6.8

million tons (as much as one million tons higher than Western estimates), and that the epidemic was under control. Increasing world sugar output in 1981-82 is expected when several Caribbean countries recuperate previous output levels; and sugar exports from Brazil (in part encouraged by the 1981 world oil glut), Central America, and the Philippines should also increase in response to high prices. In the United States, the world's largest consumer, a decline in sugar consumption is forecast as sugar is replaced by high fructose corn syrup. Still, there is a possibility of some modest increases in prices in the next five years depending on world sugar supply.[103] If Cuba's planned increases in sugar output materialize in 1982-85, they will reduce the world deficit, pushing sugar prices down.

Productivity, Economic Incentives, and Ideological Hangovers

A series of reforms introduced in 1980 have increased incentives to raise productivity among workers and farmers. These reforms are positive, but often the stimuli are not strong enough, and in other cases conflict with politically or ideologically motivated priorities and policies.

Introduction of a general wage reform began in mid-1980 with the objective of increasing productivity, efficiency, and achieving a better distribution of the labor force. When the reform is finally implemented, 600 million pesos will be distributed in wage and salary raises. The old wage scale is now considered inadequate, too egalitarian; hence, the reform will expand wage differentials according to functions and responsibility. Managers should earn a wage higher than that of the most qualified personnel under their supervision; special wage systems are introduced for airplane pilots and ship captains, as well as for highly qualified technicians; and civilians working abroad are paid an extra 20 percent over their regular salaries. In addition to the basic wage, there are extra payments for overtime and work performed under dangerous or strenuous conditions, bonuses for fulfilling and overfulfilling work quotas, and a collective incentive fund connected with enterprise profitability.[104] The latter should create a "vested interest" of the workers in fulfilling the enterprise output targets and reducing costs, because these, in turn, would increase the profit, the fund, and the workers' share.[105] The fund is divided roughly into one-third for collective facilities (e.g., sociocultural activities, clubs, gymnasiums, vacations, or housing—but no more than 60 percent in the latter) and two-thirds in individual monetary shares (which cannot exceed twenty days' wages). When the collective fund was tested in 1979 in 7 percent of Cuban enterprises, less than one-third of them earned a profit and a right to the fund; among those few which qualified, the individual annual share fluctuated from 37 to 103 pesos per capita—not too powerful an incentive, even in Cuba's frugal economy.[106] (The median wage in Cuba is 150 pesos monthly.) Another problem with the wage reform is that it has a ceiling of 450 pesos and, although there are exceptions, if that maximum is thoroughly enforced, it will result in salary cuts for top personnel; thus, the wage pyramid will be truncated, with not enough "legal" incentives at the apex.

A special system of wages and incentives for sugar workers was also introduced at the end of 1980 to increase productivity and output and raise their low living standards in order to attract more manpower to the vital sugar sector. Workers received a 15 percent raise (on top of any other wage-reform increment) plus 10 percent for fulfilling the output quota over a two-week period with 80 percent attendance in the field. New awards in kind include 700 cars to be sold to those with high productivity (400 of them for technicians and 300 for workers), 1,500 motorcycles, 500 air conditioners, and 500 trips to socialist countries. Extra labor shifts have been introduced so that rest is guaranteed to all workers during the harvest. A large number of houses have been promised to sugar workers, as well as a better supply and higher quality of work clothing and equipment, and strengthening of work safety. A final bow to pragmatism: Military service is waived for student graduates who sign for a number of years in the sugar sector.[107]

Incentives to private farmers are geared to increase the output of key crops such as tobacco and coffee; those stimuli include higher prices for *acopio* and better credit facilities. In 1980, free peasant markets were introduced allowing the private farmers to sell their products at the price set by supply and demand; the revenue from these sales cannot be invested in land or heavy equipment but can be spent for consumer goods or deposited in banks.[108] These important incentives, however, are countered with some ideological goals and red tape, such as the creation of a tax on farmers' income, state pressures to merge private farms into cooperatives, and delays in state payments for *acopio* deliveries.[109]

Since the late 1970s, self-employment in services has not only been permitted but encouraged by state authorities. There are few regulations, hiring of workers is now permitted by the new system of free labor contracting, and state enterprises can contract with artisans and the self-employed, providing them with inputs in exchange for 30 percent of their profit. The rapid expansion of this sector can be measured by the phenomenal growth of classified ads published in the magazine *Opina,* the only Cuban publication in which the forces of supply and demand have a free (paid) hand. There are offers of repair work for all types of consumer durables imaginable, as well as for houses and cars; personal services are advertised from magicians and clowns to gardeners and masseurs; and even services to state enterprises are listed, such as studies on productivity and accounting.[110] But the government has imposed a tax on self-employment income (admittedly hard to collect) and has recommended the creation of self-employed cooperatives to facilitate taxation and other types of control.[111]

Overall incentives for the population with higher income include supply of certain consumer goods at dear prices, and the parallel market, in which surplus products are sold at a state-fixed price which reflects supply-and-demand "equilibrium prices." According to a top official of JUCEPLAN, the high prices of these goods are an incentive to improve the population's skills, labor effort, and income. The parallel market is also a mechanism for the gradual elimination of rationing, but to what degree is a matter of controversy. Pragmatists seem to favor a rapid expansion of the parallel market in order to enhance incentives and eliminate rationing; others more ideologically inclined are cautious. The Vice President of JUCEPLAN was asked in a published interview if the continued existence of rationing did not clash with incentive mechanisms for remuneration according to work. He answered positively, adding that those who work harder and earn higher wages should be able to get more goods; thus, to fully implement the principle of payment according to work, rationing must be eliminated. The state, he continued, guarantees stable prices of basic products for lower income brackets of the population even if this means a subsidy to imports so that the low-income consumer does not have to bear the price increase; but this policy affects the higher-income consumer because it reduces the nation's capacity to import expensive products such as TV sets or alcoholic beverages.[112] And the official party newspaper has said:

> Despite inflation the world over, which has a particular effect on such an open economy as Cuba's, retail [rationed] prices of basic items have remained frozen at the levels of the early years of the Revolution. The objective was not to hurt the household economy, but this has meant large state subsidies that go against the necessary equilibrium in internal financing.[113]

The line should be held at the point where the leadership senses political trouble; thus, theoretically, price increases should not exceed the new wage raises. At the end of 1981, the government decreed price increases for 1,510 consumer goods, including most essential foodstuffs and manufactures such as meat, fish, rice, beans, milk, sugar, tubers, vegetables, fats, fruits, coffee, refreshments, cigarettes, textiles, soap, and gasoline. Price increases ranged from 7 to 525 percent, the average increase being 65 percent and the actual increase for the average family about 50 percent (see Table 3.7). In addition to the price hike, several gratuities were eliminated,

TABLE 3.7   Price Increases of Selected Consumer Goods in Cuba: 1981

Product[a]	Percentage Increase Range	Average
Beef	27-36	31
Chicken		8
Fish	12-114	42
Milk	25-50	36
Rice		20
Beans	28-76	50
Tubers	33-114	66
Vegetables	7-575	105
Fats	21-25	23
Fruits	11-140	75
Sugar	45-100	72
Coffee		67
Refreshments		100
Tobacco	40-67	56
Soap and detergent	43-100	70
Fabric	33-54	38
Gasoline	69-78	74

a. Practically all products have varieties by type and quality, e.g., there are seven varieties of fish by species, and two qualities of beef cut. To reduce the table, products have been clustered; the first column shows the range of price increases within the cluster, while the second shows the average increase of the cluster.

SOURCE: Based on Granma, December 14, 1981.

like free meals in workers' cafeterias, school uniforms, and free admittance to museums, zoos, and botanical gardens. The government argued that prices had been frozen since 1962 and that the state subsidized consumption for a total of 1,887 million pesos in 1976-81. Thus the increase attempts to adjust prices of consumer goods to their real cost, although the government estimates that in 1982-85 it will still subsidize consumption for 671 million pesos.[114]

The price increase appears to be considerably higher than the wage raise and (together with the elimination of gratuities) should cut the purchasing power of the population, particularly that of the lower-income strata. To somewhat protect the poor but also provide better incentives to the higher-income strata, prices of low-quality food have been increased less than the prices of top-quality brands; for instance, prices of the worst fish species were raised by 12 percent while those of the best species by 88 and 114 percent. The new price system takes supply and demand into account; hence, the price of out-of-season vegetables and tubers was increased from 2 to 20 times higher than the price of those in season. In other words, the wealthier will be able to buy the best and the rarest while the poorer will have to be content with the most abundant and lowest quality.

Politically speaking, the price increase should result in some popular discontent. But economically, the government was forced to do this and, if the grudging from below does not get out of control, the new price structure should result in substantial savings and improved material incentives. One only wonders about the size of the increase and the fact that it was not introduced gradually but all at once. Whether or not this is an indication of the magnitude of the current economic deterioration and the difficulties which lie ahead in the rest of the current five-year period, it is clear that the pragmatists scored in this battle.

Another conflict between ideology and pragmatism emerges with the use of voluntary labor. Although the latter was drastically curtailed in the 1970s and can now be utilized only when its net productivity is proven beforehand, the leadership still pays rhetorical homage to it. Paradoxically, the use of voluntary labor rewards tricky entrepreneurs who go for an easy peso but penalizes the morally motivated administrator. It happens that under the SDPE, those enterprises which provide volunteers still have to pay their wages, with no production but cost increases, and hence less profits. On the other hand, many enterprises which receive the volunteers do not reimburse the corresponding labor value to the mobilizing agency, thereby increasing their output without a corresponding wage expenditure and thus boosting their profits. To add insult to injury, the time spent in voluntary labor is not technically considered as time worked and hence does not accrue to the collective fund share.[115] It is obvious that with this kind of trouble the terminal defeat of voluntary-labor enthusiasts is just a matter of time.

Last but not least is the conflict of military expenditures versus development and consumption expenditures. This became evident in 1975-80 due to Cuba's military adventures abroad, but has taken a domestic twist with the increased U.S. threat to Cuba under the Reagan administration. To confront the menace from the colossus of the North, the Cuban leadership has resorted to TTM (Territorial Troop Militia), which should double or triple national defense by mobilizing from 150,000 to 300,000 militia who are not members of the armed forces, the reserves, or the civil defense. Castro has stressed that the added military burden will not affect the economy and thus the motto for 1981-85 is "combining production and defense." Members of the militia do not receive any remuneration; they are trained after work hours or during weekends or vacations, and to supply them with weapons a national fund-raising campaign was initiated in early 1981.[116] One of the first contributors was the poet laureate Nicolás Guillén, who donated 50,000 pesos from his royalties (suggesting that in spite of the truncated wage pyramid, the elite is still doing quite well), and on May Day more than 17 million pesos had been collected.[117] In spite of official claims, the new military mobilization involves substantial costs for the population: time taken away from study, rest, and even productive work; resources extracted from the population for training, transportation, clothing, and ammunition; and the permeating spirit of mobilization which was so catastrophic in the 1960s. I have estimated that the annual cost of this mobilization would be from 75 to 150 million pesos. Reiterating that production and development will not be neglected due to the defense effort, Castro exhorted on the twentieth anniversary of the proclamation of the socialist nature of the Cuban Revolution:

We have to make an extra effort. It is true that this takes up a great deal of time . . . and energy . . . and it calls for resources. But our people have the ability of multiplying themselves [and] when circumstances so require, what normally takes two hours to do is done in one, and work goes on as necessary.[118]

This quote summarizes well the Spartan, frugal spirit of the third decade, not too different in this sense from the previous two, with predominant pragmatism and caution but amazing resilience of ideology and romanticism as well.

NOTES

1. Carmelo Mesa-Lago, *The Economy of Socialist Cuba: A Two-Decade Appraisal* (Albuquerque: University of New Mexico Press, 1981).

2. F. Castro, "Speech to close the 16th Congress of the sugar workers trade unions," Granma Weekly Review, November 9, 1980, pp. 2-3.

3. *Proyecto de Lineamientos Económicos y Sociales para el Quinquenio 1981-1985* (La Habana, 1980), p. 6.

4. Gilberto Díaz, interview in Granma Weekly Review, Supplement, November 9, 1980, p. 3.

5. Eugenio R. Balari, Director of Cuban Institute of Internal Demand, conversation in Havana, July 14, 1979.

6. Most of the information comes from F. Castro, "Discurso en la clausura del II período de sesiones de 1979 de la Asamblea Nacional del Poder Popular," Palacio de las Convenciones, December 27, 1979, Departamento de Versiones Taquigráficas, and "Main report to the 2nd Congress of the C.P.C.," Granma Weekly Review, December 28, 1980, p. 6. The Economic Commission for Latin America, contradicting Castro's loan figure of $40 million in 1979, has reported loans for $230 million from nonsocialist sources (France, Japan, and Belgium). See CEPAL, "Cuba: Notas para el estudio económico de América Latina, 1979," México, August 4, 1980, pp. 1, 22, 24.

7. CEPAL, "Cuba: Notas para el estudio de América Latina, 1980," Mexico, April 9, 1981, pp. 4, 28.

8. Felino Quesada, Seminar of the Institute of Cuban Studies, Havana, August 4, 1980.

9. Castro, "Discurso"; and Banco National de Cuba, *Highlights of Cuban Economic Development 1976-1980 and Main Targets for 1981-1985* (Havana, 1981), pp. 5-6, 16-17. Cuban statistical yearbooks have not reported investment figures since 1972.

10. Díaz, p. 2.

11. Comisión Nacional de Implantación del Sistema de Dirección y Planificación de la Economía (SDPE), *Informe Central: Reunión Nacional SDPE* (La Habana, July 1980), pp. 34-35.

12. Quesada, Havana, August 4, 1980.

13. CEPAL, "Cuba . . . 1979," pp. 1, 20.

14. Granma Weekly Review, August 17, 1980, p. 3.

15. Information gathered in a discussion with Cuban sugar technicians in the sugar mill, "30 de Noviembre," Pinar del Río, August 2, 1980.

16. Castro, "Discurso."

17. Isabel Alfonso y J. Sanjurjo, "La roya de la caña de azúcar y su organismo causal en Cuba," *Ciencias de la Agricultura* 5 (1980), pp. 3-7.

18. Virginia Hamill, "Blight snuffs out tobacco crop," Washington Post, March 15, 1980; John Koten, "Fungi attack Cuba's tobacco fields," Wall Street Journal, March 26, 1980; and Castro, "Discurso," and "Main report."

19. Pedro Luis Bernal, "Para controlar el moho azul," *Cuba Tabaco* 2 (April-June 1980), pp. 8-17, and interview with Donn Shannon, "Cuba on mend after disease wrecks crops," Los Angeles Times, May 20, 1981, Business Section, p. 1.

20. There is evidence that the CIA had a role in inducing the previous (1970) epidemic of porcine colera. Castro first reported the 1979 epidemic in "Discurso." The Haitians were first identified as carriers by the Los Angeles Times, February 12, 1980 and by the Washington Post, February 29, 1980. One week later, Castro confirmed the U.S. reports in "Speech at the closing session of the 3rd Congress of FMC," Granma Weekly Review, March 16, 1980, p. 3.

21. Castro, "Discurso" and "Main report," p. 1; also, Banco Nacional de Cuba, p. 14.

22. 1970-1979 actual figures and 1980 goals come from my book, *The Economy of Socialist Cuba,* Table 13. 1980 actual figures are from *Proyecto de Lineamientos,* p. 3, and F. Castro, "Main report," p. 7 and "Speech to close the 16th Congress," pp. 2-4.

22a. KTP is a Russian abbreviation for "sugar cane cutter in one range." Output from KTP factory from *Anuario 1979,* p. 93 and *Guía Estadística 1980,* p. 7. I gratefully acknowledge information on the KTP provided by Claes Croner, "Choice of technique, technological progress and human resources: a case study of Cuban sugar-cane harvesting," Stockholm, September 1981.

23. Same sources as Note 22, and F. Castro, "Speech at the closing of the second session of the National Assembly of People's Power," Granma Weekly Review, January 11, 1981, p. 2. Castro has manipulated the data by stating that the 190,000 sugar cane cutters in 1980 were "75,000 less than in 1971-75" ("Main report," p. 7); if the comparison had been made with 1975-1978, the result would have been an increase in cane cutters.

24. Mesa-Lago, *The Economy of Socialist Cuba,* ch. 4; interview at sugar mill "30 de Noviembre," August 2, 1980; and *Proyecto de Lineamientos,* p. 3.

25. F. Castro, "Speech to close the 16th Congress," pp. 2-4.

26. Mesa-Lago, Table 12; CEPAL, "Cuba . . . 1979," p. 16, and "Cuba . . . 1980," p. 5.

27. Vice President of JUCEPLAN Díaz (p. 2) has stated that "[nickel] production levels have increased over these five years [1976-1980]."

28. Quesada, Havana, August 4, 1980.

29. Mesa-Lago, ch. 4; and Theodore H. Moran, "The international political economy of Cuban nickel development," in *Cuba in the World,* Cole Blasier and C. Mesa-Lago, eds. (Pittsburgh: University of Pittsburgh Press, 1979), pp. 257-272.

30. F. Castro, "Discurso."

31. CEPAL, "Cuba . . . 1980," p. 16.

32. Lawrence H. Theriot et al., "Soviet economic relations with non-European CMEA: Cuba, Vietnam and Mongolia," Joint Economic Committee, *Soviet Economy in Time of Change* (Washington, DC: GPO, Vol. 2, 1979), pp. 562-563; and Theriot information given in Washington, DC, October 24, 1980 and April 9, 1981.

33. F. Castro, "Main report," p. 9.

34. CEPAL, "Cuba . . . 1980," p. 16.

35. F. Castro, "Discurso"; *Proyecto de Lineamientos,* p. 3; Quesada, August 4, 1980; and Sergio Roca, "Economic aspects of Cuban involvement in Africa" and Jorge Pérez-López, "Comment: economic costs and benefits of African involvement," in *Cuba in Africa,* C. Mesa-Lago and June Belkin, eds. (Pittsburgh: Latin American Monograph and Document Series, No. 3, 1982), pp. 161-188.

36. Felino Quesada (director of SDPE implementation) and Francisco Martínez Soler, Havana, July 12, 1979.

37. SDPE, *Plenaria del Chequeo sobre el Sistema de Dirección y Planificación de la Economía* (La Habana: JUCEPLAN, February 16, 1979).

38. *Proyecto de Lineamientos,* pp. 3, 6; Comisión Nacional de Implantación . . . SDPE, pp. 131, 233, 247-248; and F. Castro, "Main report," p. 8.

39. Comisión Nacional de Implantación . . . SDPE, 250 pages. All subsequent references in the text come from this source.

40. In several parts of the report, when problems attributable to the central administration are dealt with, the key paragraph is deleted or appears in a different type than in the rest, e.g., pp. 15, 95, 129.

41. Mesa-Lago, *The Economy of Socialist Cuba,* ch. 7, Table 41.

42. Claes Brundenius, "An assessment of basic needs satisfaction in Cuba, 1958-1978," University of Lund, October 1980, Tables 1A-1C.

43. CIA National Foreign Assessment Center, *The Cuban Economy: A Statistical Review* (Washington, DC, March 1981), Tables 13 and 15. I excluded meat from the comparison due to lack of data for 1965-70.

44. Castro reported some of these problems in his "Discurso."

45. Interview with Alejandro Roca, Minister of Food Industry, *Industria Alimenticia* (November-December 1980), pp. 8-21.

46. Carlos Rafael Rodríguez, interview with Marta Harnecker, "Cuba: Grandes interrogantes," *Areito* 7: 25 (1981), p. 11. Castro also referred to some negative effects of the visit, but pointed out it generated 100 million pesos in foreign exchange ("Discurso").

47. Castro, "Discurso."

48. Comisión Nacional de Implantación . . . SDPE, p. 94.

49. R. Castro, "Speech at the main event to commemorate the 23rd anniversary of the November 30 uprising," Granma Weekly Review, December 9, 1979, p. 2.

50. Comisión Nacional de Implantación . . . SDPE, p. 126.

51. F. Castro, "Main report," p. 13.

52. For a detailed discussion of unemployment in 1959-79, see my *The Economy of Socialist Cuba,* ch. 6.

53. Comisión Nacional de Implantación . . . SDPE, p. 166. The same report (p. 17) states that "there are limitations imposed on the economy which restrict the possibility of creating new jobs."

54. Quesada, August 4, 1980; and *Latin America Weekly Report,* October 31, 1980.

55. F. Castro, "Discurso."

56. Roberto Veiga, "Informe Central al XIV Congreso de la CTC," Granma, November 30, 1978, p. 4.

57. Robert L. Bach et al., "The flotilla entrants: latest and most controversial," *Cuban Studies/Estudios Cubanos* 11: 2 and 12: 1 (July 1981-January 1982).

58. See *Cuba in Africa,* C. Mesa-Lago and June Belkin, eds., ch. 6.

59. Rodríguez, pp. 8-9; and *Proyecto de Lineamientos,* p. 23.

60. *Proyecto de Lineamientos,* p. 10.

61. F. Castro, "Speech to close the 16th Congress," pp. 2-4.

62. Roca, p. 175.

63. SDPE, Plenaria del Chequeo, p. 31.

64. Roca, p. 180; and Pérez-López, pp. 185-186.

65. F. Castro, "Discurso."

66. F. Castro, "Speech at the rally to celebrate the 20th anniversary of the CDRs," Granma Weekly Review, October 5, 1980, p. 3, and "Main report," p. 9.

67. F. Castro, "Main report," p. 6.

68. Quesada, August 4, 1980.

69. Comparison between original targets published in *Proyecto de Lineamientos* and final targets published by Banco Nacional de Cuba, pp. 7-8.

70. "Dictamen del proyecto de ley del plan unico de desarrollo económico-social del estado para el quinquenio 1981-1985," *Granma Resumen Semanal,* January 11, 1981, p. 3.

71. F. Castro, "Main report," p. 9; and Díaz, p. 2.

72. F. Castro, "Discurso."

73. Comisión Nacional de Implantación . . . SDPE, p. 2.

74. Quesada and Martínez Soler, July 12, 1979.

75. Díaz, p. 3. In spite of my efforts, I have been able to obtain only one document on the 1980-2000 plan, and it is not too useful: Humberto Pérez, *Elaboración de los estudios de la estrategia de desarrollo perspectivo económico y social hasta el año 2,000* (La Habana: CICT-JUCEPLAN, No. 3, 1979).

76. *Proyecto de Lineamientos,* p. 12; and Juan Varela Pérez, "The sugar industry," Granma Weekly Review, Supplement, November 9, 1980, pp. 6-7.

77. Banco Nacional de Cuba, pp. 7-8.

78. F. Castro, "Speech at the rally to commemorate the 27th anniversary of the attack on Moncada," Granma Weekly Review, August 3, 1980, p. 3, "Speech to close the 16th Congress," p. 4, and "Main report," p. 9; and Varela, pp. 6-7.

79. Based on my own calculations, assuming that the average capacity per center is 7,000 tons during the harvest, in 1985 for a harvest of 9.5 to 10 million tons, 661 conditioning centers should handle from 46 to 49 percent of the cane.

80. It is not clear whether the eight new mills projected for 1981-85 include the two which were almost completed at the end of 1980. On my visit to the "30 de Noviembre" (Pinar del Río province) mill on August 2, 1980, I was informed that a total of nine new mills will be in operation by 1985: the two already finished (in Pinar del Río and Camaguey provinces), the two to be completed in 1980-81 (in Cienfuegos and Granma provinces), and five more new mills (in Tunas, Villaclara, Matanzas, a second in Granma, and a second in Pinar del Río).

81. Quesada, August 4, 1980.

82. F. Castro, "Main report," p. 9; and Jesús Abascal, "Production of the Cuban fishing industry between 1976 and 1980," Granma Weekly Review, February 15, 1981, pp. 1-2.

83. *Financial Times.* February 3, 1981.

84. Joaquín Oramas, "The electric industry," Granma Weekly Review, Supplement, November 9, 1980, pp. 8-9; F. Castro, "Discurso"; and *Proyecto de Lineamientos,* p. 13.

85. Quesada, August 4 1980; and José Gabriel Gumá, "Industrial construction," Granma Weekly Review, Supplement, November 9, 1980, pp. 12-13.

86. Díaz, p. 2.

87. Ibid.; and Quesada, August 4, 1980.

88. F. Castro, "Discurso" and "Main report," pp. 8, 11, 13; and Banco Nacional de Cuba, p. 15.

89. Proyecto de Lineamientos, pp. 5, 7.

90. The announcement of the trade agreement was made in Granma Weekly Review, November 9, 1980, p. 1. Both Cuban and Soviet planners had been working since 1978 to coordinate their five-year plans, and the trade protocol was expected to be signed much earlier than October. See John E. Cooney, "Cuba loosens some control on economy," Wall Street Journal, October 31, 1980.

91. Granma Weekly Review, April 26, 1981, p. 8.

92. Based on data from the CIA, p. 39, Table 39; and my book, The Economy of Socialist Cuba, ch. 2.

93. Proyecto de Lineamientos, p. 23.

94. Theriot et al., pp. 557, 564.

95. F. Castro, "Discurso"; and Comisión Nacional de Implantación . . . SDPE, p. 200.

96. Theriot, pp. 564-565.

97. F. Castro, "Speech at the rally," p. 3, and "Main report," p. 9.

98. Based on data from the CIA, pp. 9, 23; and Theriot, pp. 558-559.

99. Marlise Simons, "Mexico in broad energy accord with Cuba," Washington Post, February 8, 1981; Alan Robinson, "Pemex reportedly finds oil off Cuba," Journal of Commerce, April 17, 1981; and "Cuban oil find unconfirmed by Pemex," Journal of Commerce, April 20, 1981. The original article on oil discovery was published in Excelsior (Mexico), attributing it to "sources close to the Cuban government."

100. "Central regional role for Mexico is welcomed by Kremlin," Latin America Weekly Report, May 29, 1981, p. 6.

101. New York Times, Financial Section, April-December 1981.

102. Woodhouse, Drake and Carey, Market Report, September 22, 1980; and Latin America Commodity Report, October 10, 1980. The 1980 decline of sugar output in Cuba caused two odd trade operations: the Dominican Republic sold sugar to Cuba, in August 1980, through Czarnikow-Rionda, New York; and Cuba bought a factory of fructose corn syrup from Sweden (Juventud Rebelde, June 17, 1980, p. 1).

103. U.S. Department of Agriculture, Sugar and Sweetener: Outlook and Situation (February 1981); and Robert D. Barry, "The outlook for sugar and other sweeteners: 1981-1985," American Sugarbeet Growers Association, Tucson, February 3, 1981.

104. "General wage reform," Granma Weekly Review, April 6, 1980, pp. 4-5.

105. Díaz, p. 4.

106. Comisión Nacional de Implantación . . . SDPE, p. 233.

107. F. Castro, "Speech to close the 16th Congress," pp. 2-3.

108. Quesada, August 4, 1980.

109. Proyecto de Lineamientos, pp. 5, 8-9; and Comisión Nacional de Implantación . . . SDPE, p. 97.

110. Opina, January 1981, classified ads.

111. *Proyecto de Lineamientos,* p. 9; and Comisión Nacional de Implantación . . . SDPE, p. 75.

112. Díaz, pp. 3, 5.

113. "General wage reform," p. 4.

114. Granma, December 14, 1981.

115. Comisión Nacional de Implantación . . . SDPE, pp. 87, 241.

116. F. Castro, "Speech at the ceremony to set up the territorial troop militia units," Granma Weekly Review, February 1, 1981, pp. 2-3.

117. Granma Weekly Review, February 8, 1981, p. 1; and ibid., May 10, 1981, p. 2.

118. F. Castro, "Speech to commemorate the 20th anniversary of the proclamation of the socialist nature of the Revolution," Granma Weekly Review, April 26, 1981, p. 3.

4

Foreign Policy

The Limits of Success

WILLIAM M. LEOGRANDE

Cuba's revolutionary leadership has long seen itself as a leader and spokesman for the nations of the Third World, and Cuba's policy toward those states has always been an active one. Yet despite the boldness and even stubborn independence that Cuba has exhibited in this aspect of its foreign policy, there is no denying the fact that Cuba's vital national interests have not usually been at stake in its relations with the Third World. In both an economic and a military sense, Cuba's national security has been a function of its relations with the super-powers—its nearly constant relationship of hostility with the United States and its close friendship with the Soviet Union. Any effort to assess Cuban policy toward the Third World must therefore be undertaken within the context of this larger and more important constellation of relations.

Since 1959, the first and foremost objective of all Cuban foreign policy has been the survival of the revolution. There have been other objectives, to be sure, but all have necessarily been subordinate to survival.[1] During the first decade of the revolution, these secondary goals received attention and resources in direct proportion to their contribution toward guaranteeing security. Survival has had both an economic and a military dimension. The deterioration of the U.S.-Cuban relations in the early 1960s, followed by U.S. efforts to strangle the revolution economically and subvert it militarily, left the Cuban leadership no alternative but to seek a strong outside protector.[2] The Soviet Union assumed this role, reluctantly at first but later with relish. Cuban security came to depend upon Soviet economic and military assistance.[3] With the prospect of improved U.S.-Cuban relations remote during the 1960s, it was essential for Cuba to maintain its close relations with the Soviet Union, even though the Cubans sometimes harbored doubts about the trustworthiness of the USSR.[4]

The Cubans' dilemma was well illustrated in the months following the 1962 missile crisis. The Soviet Union's willingness to resolve the crisis without consulting the Cuban leadership, and to resolve it at Cuban expense (i.e., the missiles that Cuba regarded as a deterrent to U.S. attack were withdrawn), damaged Cuban-Soviet relations severely. Cuba's resulting skepticism over Soviet commitment to the island led the Cuban leadership to seek security by escaping its position as a focal point of the Cold War. Cuba began, cautiously, to explore the possibility of rapprochement with the United States. These initiatives aborted after the assassination of President Kennedy, leaving Cuba with no realistic alternative but to repair its connection with the Soviet Union.[5]

Cuba's efforts to cast itself as a leader in the Third World have made an important contribution to Cuba's major foreign policy objective of surviving on the "front-line" of the East-West conflict. Just as Yugoslavia sought Third World leadership as protection from Soviet retribution for Tito's deviation from Marxist-Leninist orthodoxy, Cuba has sought similar prominence as protection from attack by the United States or abandonment by the Soviet Union. Cuba's dependence on the USSR has meant that Cuba's Third World activism could not be "bloc neutral," but by creating a constituency in the Third World, Cuba could nevertheless raise the diplomatic cost to both superpowers for policies unfavorable to Cuba.

To be sure, the ideological convictions of Cuba's leaders, especially Fidel Castro and Ché Guevara, were a key ingredient of Cuba's activism in the Third World. During the 1960s especially, Cuba felt a close affinity for national liberation struggles that resembled the struggled against Batista. Cuba's closest (if not most important) friends have always been progressive, radically nationalist states that came into being as the result of antiimperialist revolutions—e.g., Algeria, Ghana, Vietnam, Angola, Nicaragua—or in the case of Allende's Chile, an antiimperialist regime resulting from electoral triumph. Yet Cuba's identification with such states has *not* been contingent upon their adopting a Marxist-Leninist model of politics and society. In its search for international allies, Cuba, from the outset, cast its net beyond just the members of the socialist camp.

CUBAN INTERNATIONALISM: FROM ROMANTIC TO PRAGMATIC

Initially, Cuba's attitude toward the Third World was embodied in a romantic and relatively unsophisticated policy aimed at expanding the family of revolutionary states among the underdeveloped nations. Cuba provided material as well as political assistance to guerrilla movements in both Africa and Latin America; it sought to create a new revolutionary international at the Tricontinental Conference; and it sought to forge a "third force" (with Vietnam and North Korea) within the socialist camp to promote a more militant strain of proletarian internationalism.[6] These actions produced serious strains in Cuba's relationship with the Soviet Union; Cuba's activism included not-too-veiled criticism of the Soviets' policy of peaceful coexistence, and also complicated the Soviets' efforts to reduce tensions with the United States.

The gap between Cuban and Soviet views of the world was most clearly visible in Cuba's position within the Non-aligned

Movement. At a time when the majority of the non-aligned nations were committed to reducing world tensions, Cuba was denouncing peaceful coexistence as a fraud because it implicitly undercut the legitimacy of aiding national liberation struggles, and because it seemed to sacrifice the interests of small states on the altar of superpower accord. There could be no peaceful coexistence, Cuba argued, between imperialism and its victims, no coexistence or peace between the superpowers alone unless it was matched by coexistence between large states and small ones.[7]

Paradoxically, Cuba's efforts to export revolution in the 1960s were largely defensive in nature. Early in the decade, the United States mounted a successful campaign within the Organization of American States to isolate Cuba economically and diplomatically. Cuba's promotion of revolution in Latin America was primarily an attempt to break out of this isolation by helping to create other revolutionary governments in the Western Hemisphere. Cuba's relations with Mexico demonstrate quite clearly that when Cuba was able to maintain normal state-to-state relations with its neighbors, it was willing to forego efforts to overthrow them.[8]

The insurrectionary efforts of the 1960s met with little success. Few Latin American guerrilla movements proved to be any match for the counterinsurgency forces deployed against them under the security assistance programs of the Alliance for Progress. When Ché Guevara was killed in Bolivia while trying to create a foco for continental guerrilla war, Cuba began to reevaluate the whole foco theory of revolution.[9] By 1969, Cuba had for all practical purposes abandoned the policy of providing material support indiscriminately to any guerrilla movement, no matter how small and ineffectual.

For several years, no new policy emerged to replace the defunct strategy of exporting revolution. From 1968 to 1972, Cuba turned inward, preoccupied with the drive to produce ten million tons of sugar in 1970. This retreat from the foreign involvements of the previous decade was so startling that it led one commentator to describe Cuba's domestic preoccupation as "socialism in one island."[10] When Cuba reemerged on the world scene in 1972, its foreign policy was considerably changed.

Though the guerrilla movements which Cuba had supported had failed to achieve any measure of success through armed struggle, the left in several Latin American countries had made striking advances through unexpected and unorthodox methods which Cuba had always disparaged. In Chile, the Popular Unity electoral coalition of communists and socialists had won the 1970 election; in Peru, the military government appeared to be enacting a revolution from above; and in Argentina, the Peronist left had returned from the political wilderness through the election of Hector Campora. All three of these nations broke the OAS sanctions against Cuba by re-establishing diplomatic and economic ties with the island. They were joined in short order by several of the English-speaking islands in the Caribbean. In the new international climate of détente, even the conservative regimes of Latin America showed a willingness to normalize relations with Cuba. Newly independent nations in the English-speaking Caribbean were also in the forefront of supporting Cuba's reintegration into hemispheric affairs. Not having been targets of Cuba's earlier efforts to export revolution, these states were less fearful of Cuban subversion and historically less politically dependent upon the United States. Indeed, several of the Caribbean states were themselves ruled by left-leaning populist governments which attracted a certain measure of animosity from Washington.[11]

As a consequence of such favorable developments, Cuba adopted a new Hemispheric policy which was much more conciliatory and tolerant of ideological diversity. Rather than seeking to break out of its isolation by revolution, Cuba sought to do so by diplomacy, establishing normal state-to-state relations with whatever governments were willing to do so. Naturally, the success of this strategy precluded Cuba from providing significant amounts of aid to guerrilla movements as it had in the 1960s. While Cuba continued to provide a safe haven for Latin America's revolutionaries, its program of arms assistance came to a virtual halt.[12]

Cuba's conciliatory approach to its neighbors had considerable success initially. The OAS sanctions were eroded by a steady stream of states that restored relations with Cuba, until the sanctions were finally relaxed in 1975. Even Cuba's archenemy, the United States, appeared willing to renew normal diplomatic and economic ties, and secret negotiations between the two states were begun in 1974.[13]

The early 1970s were also successful years for Cuba in its relations with the Soviet Union. In the fields of both domestic and foreign policy, Cuban practice shifted toward the views of the USSR, thus eliminating the major friction points that had strained relations in the previous decade. Outside Latin America, Cuba moved to a position of prominence in the Movement of Non-aligned Nations—in part because of Cuba's willingness to cooperate with even nonrevolutionary members of the Third World on issues of common interest, and in part because the movement itself was becoming more radical, especially in the field of international economics.[14] As Cuba emerged as a leader of the movement, Cuba's value to the Soviet Union as a broker between the Third World and the socialist camp increased tremendously.

In 1975-76, Cuba dispatched some 36,000 combat troops to help the Popular Movement for the Liberation of Angola (MPLA) defeat its rivals and their international allies (Zaire, South Africa, and the United States).[15] There is considerable evidence to suggest that this involvement was first and foremost a Cuban initiative.[16] It is nevertheless clear that Cuba could not have undertaken such a massive foreign military commitment without the logistical support of the Soviet Union. The joint Cuban-Soviet operation in Angola cemented their bilateral relations and led to substantial increases in Soviet economic and military aid to the island.[17] Within the Third World, Cuba's role in Angola was widely hailed as an example of selfless internationalism in defense of a Third World nation under imperialist assault.[18] Shortly thereafter, Cuba was selected as the site for the Sixth Summit of the Non-aligned Nations, and hence as the chairman of the movement from 1979 to 1982.

In 1978, another joint military venture was mounted by Cuba and the USSR, this time in Ethiopia. Once again, nearly 20,000 Cuban troops were deployed to help defend a fraternal government under attack, in this case by Somalia. This time, however, the operation stimulated more concern than praise among Cuba's growing Third World constituency. For many non-aligned states, Cuba's Ethiopian involvement looked too much like a geopolitical favor done for the Soviet Union.

At a meeting of the Organization of African Unity held during the summer of 1978, Nigerian head of state Olusequm Obasanjo warned the Cubans "not to overstay their welcome . . . lest they run the risk of being dubbed a new imperialist presence."[19] Shortly thereafter, moderates and conservatives within the Non-aligned Movement voiced similar criticisms. Yugoslavian President Josef Broz Tito accused Cuba of introducing "new forms of colonial presence or bloc dependence in Africa," and Egypt launched a campaign to move the site of the Sixth Non-aligned Summit away from Cuba on the same grounds.[20]

Though Cuba's critics were harsh, they were few in number. Widespread opposition to Somali aggression among Third World nations made most of them hesitant to attack Cuba openly. Still, it was becoming clear that Cuba's role as broker between the Third World and the socialist camp contained dangers as well as benefits.

In many ways, the Havana Summit of the Non-aligned Movement represented both the apogee of Cuban influence within the Third World and the beginning of its decline. While it marked the beginning of Cuba's term as chairman of the Non-aligned Movement, the Summit itself did not go as well as Cuba had hoped.[21] Two issues dominated the proceedings, and both concerned how closely the Third World was prepared to lean toward the socialist camp. The first was explicit: Would the movement abandon its traditional stance of "bloc neutrality" and adopt instead the thesis of a "natural alliance" between the underdeveloped world and the socialist camp? The natural alliance thesis was advocated by the radical states, led by Cuba, while bloc neutrality was defended by the moderates, led by Egypt and Yugoslavia. This issue was only obliquely addressed at the Summit itself because the Cubans discovered early in the preparatory process that a majority of the member states were opposed to changing the movement's traditional "bloc neutral" stance. Nevertheless, it was the underlying theme in the major addresses given by Cuba's Fidel Castro, Yugoslavia's Josef Tito, and Tanzania's Julius Nyerere.[22] The movement's refusal to adopt the Cuban view of non-alignment's antiimperialist content constituted an important blow to Cuba's authority at the very moment Cuba assumed the chairmanship of the movement.

The second issue taken up at the Summit was more openly divisive: Should the movement recognize the Heng Samrin government of Cambodia even though it had been installed with the aid of Vietnamese troops, or should Pol Pot's representatives retain Cambodia's chair? The credentials fight was bitter, and it was aggravated by the fact that the whole issue of the movement's attitude toward the Soviet Union was implicitly involved in it. Vietnam had ousted the Pol Pot regime with Soviet aid; to the moderates within the Non-aligned Movement, this amounted to bloc interference in the internal affairs of a non-aligned state. Cuba, which had itself recognized the new Cambodian regime, led the battle on this issue as well and used every advantage possible from its position as host of the summit. Nevertheless, the best result which Cuba could obtain was a compromise in which neither the Heng Samrin nor the Pol Pot government would be given Cambodia's seat. This partial victory was won at great cost, as many delegations complained about the Cubans' manipulation of arrangements and began to wonder openly if Cuba could be trusted, as chairman of the movement, to accurately reflect its consensus when it deviated from Cuban preferences.[23]

The deep political cleavage between radical and moderate members of the Non-aligned Movement reached its most explicit expression at the Havana Summit. It was only through the efforts of a middle group (more moderate than Cuba but more radical than Yugoslavia) led by Tanzania that the meeting managed to achieve political compromises which avoided an open schism. Political differences were also mitigated somewhat by the non-aligned nations' virtual unanimity on economic issues. The New International Economic Order (NIEO), devised by the non-aligned states in the early 1970s, had made little progress toward becoming a reality. With little dissent, the Havana Summit placed the blame for this obstruction squarely on the developed Western nations. When Castro addressed the United Nations General Assembly in October, 1979 to report on the results of the Sixth Summit, he was careful to stress the unity of the movement by emphasizing this economic theme rather than focusing on the more divisive political issues. By carefully pledging to carry out the will of the movement as expressed in the Final Declaration, he also sought to allay any fears that Cuba might use the chairmanship to push the movement further to the left than the consensus of the summit would allow.[24]

Overall, the Havana Summit was not the great political victory Cuba had hoped for, but neither was it a clear setback. The Final Declaration was more radical in substance than the declarations of previous summits, but the movement's consensus was still obviously less radical than Cuba would have preferred. The Cubans pushed that consensus right to the limit at the summit, but with only partial success and at the cost of aggravating the suspicions of the moderates.

The Havana Summit highlighted a central dilemma of contemporary Cuban foreign policy. While Cuba successfully bolstered its relations with both the Soviet Union *and* the Third World during the 1970s, it has yet to devise an effective strategy for managing the tension inherent in these two sets of relations. Cuban foreign policy has a dual identity; Cuba sees itself as both a member of the Third World and a member of the socialist camp. Both identities have their roots in the early years of the revolution, but it was not until the 1970s that Cuba's standing with either of these constituencies was sufficiently high to allow it to act as a broker between them—an enviable position. Cuba perceives no inherent contradiction in its dual role, since the leaders of the revolution have long been on record as believing that socialism is a precondition for real development in the Third World, along with the demise of neocolonialism. Cuba's long-term strategy seems to be aimed at reducing the political distance between its two primary constituencies. Witness Cuba's advocacy of the "natural alliance" thesis, which Cuba sees as having potential benefits for each, and which would obviously enhance Cuba's influence with both.

For Cuba, the danger in the brokerage role it has set out for itself lies in the potential for conflict between the non-aligned nations and the socialist camp, particularly the Soviet Union. When such conflicts develop, Cuba is forced, however reluctantly, to take sides. By having to choose between its two constituencies, Cuba inevitably damages its standing with one of them, which then ironically reduces its value to the other. This dangerous dynamic operated most clearly over the issue of Afghanistan.

While the issue of Ethiopia and Cambodia raised some suspicions within the Third World about Cuba's relationship with the Soviet Union, the Soviet invasion of Afghanistan proved devastating for Cuba. Coming within only a few months of the Havana Summit, the invasion demolished the notion that the Soviets were "natural allies" of the Third World; indeed, it was the first unequivocal case of the Soviet Union intervening in a putatively non-aligned nation to defend its own vision of national security. Not surprisingly, the invasion was widely condemned by the Third World. Its first ramification for Cuba was the loss of the United Nations Security Council election, which Cuba had been contesting with Colombia. Led by Nigeria and India, the non-aligned nations themselves engineered a compromise in which Mexico was elected after Cuba's withdrawal.[25]

Cuba tried as best it could not to alienate either the Third World or the Soviet Union over the issue of Afghanistan. The U.N. General Assembly resolution calling for the withdrawal of all foreign (i.e., Soviet) troops, however, forced Cuba to declare itself. Cuba's choice was made all the more painful by the fact that the resolution was authored by a group of non-aligned states. Cuba ultimately voted against the resolution, explaining that it did so because it would never side with imperialism against a member of the socialist camp. But the Cuban representative uttered not a word in defense of the Soviet intervention. It was a full year before Cuba formally endorsed the Soviet action.[26]

In the field of international economics, Cuba's role as broker between the Third World and the socialist camp has been less prone to conflict. Soviet economic relations with the Third World are much less extensive than are those of the Western nations, thus providing less reason for bitter conflict between the Soviets and the underdeveloped states. And rhetorically, at least, the Soviets have been generally supportive of the demands of the NIEO.[27] There are, of course, differences between Soviet international economic policy and the demands of the Third World, and these resulted in some sharp criticism of Soviet policy at the 4th and 5th UNCTAD meetings in 1976 and 1979. But on the whole, these differences have not been irreconcilable, and the Soviets have shown some limited willingness to compromise.[28]

This situation makes Cuba's position as broker ideal. The Cubans have made the most of it by themselves adopting compromise positions between the views of the NIEO advocates and the Soviets, while urging both parties to recognize the importance of cooperation.[29] The only real limitation on Cuban effectiveness in this policy sphere is the fact that the Soviets provide such limited economic aid to the Third World, apart from close allies such as Cuba. The Soviet Union has neither the intention nor the economic capability to add a significant number of countries to the ranks of such preferred recipients. There is, then, a real limit to how economically helpful the Soviet Union can or will be to the Third World, a limit which constrains Cuba's ability to take maximum advantage from its role as broker on these issues. Nevertheless, international economic issues have proven to be laden with fewer pitfalls for Cuba than have political issues.

The same can be said of Cuba's foreign economic assistance programs in contrast to its military aid programs. Throughout the 1970s, but especially in the latter half of the decade, Cuba

allocated increasing resources to economic assistance programs for friendly governments.[30] The bulk of this aid, in the
form of skilled personnel, was targeted to Cuba's closest
allies—Angola, Vietnam, Ethiopia, Manley's Jamaica, Grenada,
and Nicaragua. But smaller programs were established in a
much wider range of nations in both Africa and Latin America.

These aid programs serve a variety of functions. They
presumably improve bilateral relations between Cuba and the
recipient states, thus increasing Cuba's overall standing internationally. They reinforce the importance in principle of
socialist states providing aid to progressive underdeveloped
nations—a principle which is essential to Cuba's own economy
in its relations with the Soviet Union. When the recipients of
Cuban aid are financially strong (e.g., Angola, Iraq, Algeria)
because of petroleum revenues, Cuba receives payment for the
skilled personnel sent abroad—an export of human capital in
exchange for hard currencies, which helps to ease Cuba's trade
imbalance with the West. Finally, Cuba's economic aid
missions presumably open the door to broad trade relations
with the recipients.

This last objective is especially important for Cuba's efforts
to reduce its own economic dependence on the Soviet Union.
Unfortunately, little real diversification of Cuban international
economic relations has resulted. There are both structural and
contextual reasons for this failure. The structural limits are the
obvious ones: Most underdeveloped nations do not produce
the manufactured goods (especially capital goods) which constitute the bulk of Cuban imports. The utility of barter trade is
thus very much restricted. At the same time, most underdeveloped nations face the same hard currency shortages that Cuba
faces and cannot therefore afford to sustain any significant
imbalance in their trade with Cuba any more than Cuba could.
The contextual problems result from Cuba's recent economic
weakness, which has exacerbated the normal scarcity of hard
currency. Internal economic difficulties have produced an
intensified dependence on trade credits and assistance from
the Soviet Union, wiping out most of the gains in diversification
which Cuba made in the mid-1970s.

The upshot of this is that Cuba's economic relations with the Third World remain very marginal, accounting for only 15-20 percent of trade with *non-communist* trading partners in the years since 1975, and a minuscule 4-7 percent of total Cuban trade.[31] Given the formidable obstacles to future diversification, it is unlikely that Cuba's economic assistance programs, however successful, can overcome them.

CUBA IN ITS OWN BACKYARD

Cuba's policy in the Western Hemisphere has had a distinctly different dynamic in recent years than its policies further afield. In the Third World generally and in Africa specifically, Cuba's influence derives largely from the brokerage role described above. In Latin America, however, this brokerage role is of limited value. Latin American states are generally less active than other Third World states in the global institutions of non-alignment, and few of Cuba's neighbors want or need Cuba to act as an intermediary in their bilateral relations with the Soviet Union. Argentina's growing commercial relationship with the USSR is a prime example of Cuba's irrelevance in this regard.

In fact, Cuba's relationship with the Soviet Union is probably a negative factor in its relations with Latin America, for it revives all the old charges of hemispheric penetration by international communism which were used to justify Cuba's isolation in the 1960s. Finally, Cuban policy in "its own backyard" is of limited interest to the Soviet Union, which recognizes that the Western Hemisphere is a U.S. sphere of influence of only marginal geopolitical importance to the USSR. Thus, while Cuba enjoys greater freedom to set its own policy toward Latin America, it can expect only limited help from its Soviet allies.

Cuba's efforts to improve its diplomatic position in the Western Hemisphere began running into setbacks at the same time as Cuba's difficulties within the Non-aligned Movement were escalating. In Latin America, the sight of Cuban soldiers trooping off to Africa rekindled the fears of the late 1960s.

Cuba seemed to be once again willing (and now much more able) to pursue an activist foreign policy of promoting revolution. Though none of the governments of Latin America went so far as to break relations with Cuba as a result of events in Angola or Ethiopia, the process of reintegrating Cuba into the inter-American community slowed perceptibly. The Carter Administration, of course, abandoned its intention to normalize relations after Ethiopia, and resumed a high level of verbal hostility toward Cuba, as epitomized in the 1978 "Shaba II" crisis and the 1979 Soviet "combat brigade" crisis.[32]

Nevertheless, in 1979 Cuba's position in the hemisphere was probably as strong as it had been at any time since the revolution. In the Caribbean, Cuba had managed to expand its influence with several key states, the most important being Jamaica and Guyana. The principal instrument of Cuban policy in the Caribbean was (and continues to be) economic assistance, mostly in the form of human capital—skilled workers and technicians who work in such fields as construction, education, and health. Though Cuban aid is relatively small, it has been effective, both because it fills a resource gap which financial assistance from the developed nations cannot fill, and because it is, at the same time, "people-to-people" aid.[33]

The emergence of "Caribbean socialism" in Jamaica, Guyana, and Grenada gave Cuba a group of states with at least some ideological affinity for Cuba's own development model. These were the states to which most Cuban aid was directed, and Cuba's success in establishing cordial relations with them led to a flurry of concern in the United States that the Cubans were going to turn the Caribbean into a "Red Lake."

The victory of Edward Seaga's Jamaican Labor Party in 1980 was obviously a severe blow to Cuba's efforts to expand its influence in the region. Jamaica had been Cuba's most consistent friend in the Caribbean since the election of Michael Manley in 1972. While Manley's radical populism was a far cry from Cuban Marixism-Leninism, Cuba and Jamaica stood in close agreement on a variety of international issues; Manley took an active role in the Non-aligned Movement, generally siding with Cuba and the other radical states. When Cuba's intervention in Angola led to a cooling of relations with a number of governments in the Hemisphere, Manley declared, "We regard Cuban assistance to Angola as honorable and in the best interests of all those who care for African freedom."[34]

As the largest of the English-speaking islands, Jamaica has historically been a political bellwether for the Caribbean. Manley's move to establish close relations with Cuba was widely regarded as foreshadowing a general increase in Cuban influence, though the actual increase proved to be less dramatic. Seaga's victory over Manley deprives Cuba of its most important Caribbean friend and reflects a new conservative trend in the region which, with the exception of Grenada, has reduced Cuban influence considerably.

The new revolutionary government in Grenada, tiny as it is, now stands as Cuba's one remaining close friend among the English-speaking states. The ouster of Eric Gairy by Maurice Bishop's socialist New Jewel Movement in March 1980 was heralded by Cuba as a revolutionary breakthrough in the region. When Bishop requested military aid to defend the island against any attempt to return Gairy to power, Cuba responded immediately by providing light arms and a few dozen military advisors.[35]

The sudden blossoming of Cuba's relationship with Grenada worried the United States, which warned Bishop that a close relationship with Cuba would prejudice his relations with Washington. The Grenadans reacted acrimoniously, and diplomatic relations with the United States have been deteriorating ever since. The rhetoric of the New Jewel Movement has been staunchly "anti-imperialist," and Grenada has ostentatiously sided with the socialist camp internationally. For example, Grenada was the only nonsocialist country to side with the socialist bloc in opposing the UN resolution condemning the Soviet Union for its intervention in Afghanistan.[36]

Cuba's economic aid program to Grenada has been of far greater concern to Washington than the New Jewel Move-

ment's rhetorical sallies against Washington. Cuba has provided construction workers and heavy equipment to help build
a major airport in Grenada. Bishop's government portrays the
project as a means of stimulating tourism, thus diversifying the
island's spice economy. Washington worries that the airport
has potential military value for the transport of Cuban troops
abroad.[37]

If 1979 marked the peak of Cuban influence in the Caribbean, the situation in Latin America was similar. At the
beginning of the year, Cuba joined with Mexico, Venezuela,
Costa Rica, and Panama to help the Sandinista National
Liberation Front (FSLN) depose the Somoza government in
Nicaragua, despite frantic U.S. efforts to prevent the guerrillas
from triumphing.[38] Cuba had supported the revolutionaries of
the Sandinista Front since the movement's founding in the late
1960s. Not surprisingly, Cuba has enjoyed excellent relations
with the revolutionary government in Nicaragua. Within days
of Somoza's downfall, Cuba pledged to help rebuild Nicaragua's
war-torn economy. Several thousand Cuban advisors and
technicians have been dispatched to Nicaragua to work in the
fields of construction, health, education, economy, and
security.[39]

Perhaps the most interesting aspect of the Cuban-Nicaraguan
relationship has been Fidel Castro's role as advisor to the
National Directorate of the FSLN. As the Nicaraguans search
for a viable political and economic structure, Castro has
cautioned moderation. The Cuban economy paid a heavy price
for its rapid transition to socialism in the early 1960s, a price
which in some ways it has yet to recoup. The exodus of the
technically skilled middle class, the animosity of the United
States, the dependence on the Soviet Union, and the Hemispheric isolation of the island have all contributed to the
current difficulties being experienced by the Cuban economy.
Castro has reportedly been advising the Nicaraguans to avoid
Cuba's mistakes by maintaining a moderate economic policy
that retains a private sector, a cordial relationship with the
United States, and the confidence of the international financial

community.[40] In short, Cuba has urged Nicaragua to avoid becoming a focal point in a new Cold War, thus enmeshing itself in the same dilemmas of international politics that Cuba has been grappling with for the past two decades. But Cuba's advocacy of moderation has apparently not extended to the issue of aiding insurgents in El Salvador.

The Nicaraguan revolution, along with the growing revolutionary movements in El Salvador and Guatemala, have produced a significant shift in Cuba's hemispheric policy. The main reason for Cuba's abandonment of its 1960s policy of "exporting revolution" was the failure of that policy. The inability of Cuban-sponsored guerrillas to gain any major successes in the 1960s convinced the Cubans that Latin America was simply not ripe for revolution. The uprisings in Nicaragua's cities in September 1978, even though they failed to unseat Somoza, were so massive that they persuaded the Cubans to reassess their opinion of Nicaragua's revolutionary potential. Cuba's leaders seemed to conclude that they had underestimated the strength of the left in the northern tier of Central America—in Nicaragua, El Salvador, and Guatemala. In late 1978, Cuba began once again to provide material aid to the guerrilla movements in those countries.[41] The Sandinistas were the first beneficiaries of this new policy.

Nevertheless, Cuban aid to Nicaragua was relatively circumscribed for a number of reasons.[42] Foremost was the fear that a major Cuban involvement would provide the United States with an excuse to intervene on Somoza's side. Cuba was also cautious lest it undo the progress it had made in the 1970s by pursuing a diplomatic strategy to end its Hemispheric isolation. Finally, other Latin American states were willing to provide the bulk of supplies to the FSLN, so there was no pressing need for massive aid from Cuba, although some aid was certainly provided.

A year later, in El Salvador, it was more difficult for Cuba to maintain a low profile on its support for the guerrilla movement. While Somoza had faced nearly universal opposition in Latin America, the civilian-military coalition government in El Salvador was able to maintain considerably more legitimacy.

Only Mexico, Nicaragua, and Cuba were unequivocal in their support for the Salvadoran left. Nevertheless, Cuban aid to the guerrillas during 1979 and early 1980 followed the Nicaraguan precedent quite closely. Cuba's most significant contributions were in the form of political advice rather than arms.

For a variety of reasons, Cuban policy seems to have changed in late 1980. Internationally, Ronald Reagan had won the U.S. presidential elections and was promising to pursue a "hardline" against Cuba and leftist guerrillas in Central America. Within El Salvador, the left was preparing a "final offensive" that would sweep them to victory before Reagan could escalate U.S. military aid to the Salvadoran government. It appears that Cuba, in cooperation with Nicaragua, expanded its material aid to the Salvadoran left in the months after Reagan's election.[43] When the Salvadoran left's "final offensive" in January 1981 failed to topple the government, both Cuba and Nicaragua seemed to return to their earlier strategy of providing mostly political rather than military assistance. The United States has charged that Cuban and Nicaraguan arms transfers to the Salvadoran left increased once again in mid-1981, but both Cuba and Nicaragua have denied the charges.[44]

Cuba's willingness to once again provide significant aid to Latin American guerrillas is not simply a return to the romantic policies of the late 1960s. Cuban aid has been much more selectively targeted since the Nicaraguan revolution, flowing almost exclusively to movements with a strong political base and a realistic opportunity to come to power. (Cuban links to Colombia's M-19 movement is the one possible exception.) Nevertheless, Cuba's renewed activism in Latin America, combined with the Reagan Administration's efforts to reisolate Cuba within the Hemisphere, have damaged Cuban efforts to maintain normal state-to-state relations with its Latin American neighbors. Within the past year, Costa Rica and Colombia have both severed diplomatic ties with Cuba, and its relations with Venezuela, Ecuador, Peru, and Panama have deteriorated. Only Mexico has been willing to extend its relations with Cuba despite U.S. hostility.[45]

A key event in the deterioration of Cuba's relations with several of its neighbors was the occupation of the Peruvian embassy by Cuban refugees in 1980. The crisis was touched off in April when a busful of Cubans crashed their way into the grounds of the Peruvian embassy in Havana to seek political asylum.[46] This was only the latest in a series of such incidents which had already engaged both Venezuela and Peru in a dispute with the Cuban government over their willingness to grant asylum to Cuban refugees breaking into their embassy compounds. Cuba held that such refugees were no more than common criminals, ineligible for asylum. When the incident at the Peruvian embassy resulted in the death of a Cuban security guard, the Cuban government simply withdrew security from the grounds and announced that anyone wishing to leave Cuba should proceed to the embassy. To everyone's surprise, some 10,000 Cubans arrived seeking emigration.

The embarrassment for Cuba was intense, and the negotiations with Peru, Venezuela, and Costa Rica which followed damaged Cuban relations with all three states. Shortly after the embassy incident, Venezuela announced its intention to release several Cuban exiles who were allegedly responsible for the 1976 sabotage of a Cubana airlines flight that exploded after leaving Barbados, killing everyone aboard. Cuba denounced the planned release in terms reminiscent of the 1960s, and Venezuela came close to severing relations.[47] The repercussions of Cuba's antagonism toward Peru and Venezuela were substantial, since it was primarily the Andean states that were among the most vocal advocates during the 1970s of reintegrating Cuba into the inter-American system. The massive exodus of Cubans to the United States via Mariel, which followed in the weeks after the embassy incident, served to further damage Cuban prestige in the hemisphere and to pose yet another sore point in Cuba's relations with the United States.

Cuban Foreign Policy in the 1980s

As the Cuban communist party approached its Second Congress in December 1980, Cuban foreign policy toward the

Third World was markedly more sophisticated and nuanced than it had been a decade before. The instruments of economic aid, military aid, and dipomatic activity were being used in varying configurations in five principal arenas: Africa and the Middle East, Central America, South America, the Caribbean, and the Non-aligned Movement. Yet despite this sophistication and despite the advances made in the 1970s, Cuba was facing serious difficulties in virtually all of these arenas. In Africa, some 30,000 Cuban combat troops were still on the ground in Angola and Ethiopia, with little hope for significant withdrawals in the near future. Despite the Soviet Union's willingness to underwrite much of the cost of these expeditions, they were by no means cost-free for Cuba, either economically or politically.[48] In the Non-aligned Movement, Cuba has been unable to enhance its standing through its performance as chairman. Forced to take a low profile because of its controversial views, Cuba has done little more than try (unsuccessfully) to mediate the Iran-Iraq war.[49] The movement as a whole continues to implicitly repudiate Cuba's policy preferences by calling for the withdrawal of foreign troops from Afghanistan and Cambodia.

The contradictions between the interests of the Third World and those of the Soviet Union have become more acute, thus greatly complicating Cuba's chosen role as broker between these two constituencies and placing a clear (if temporary) limit on Cuba's global prestige. In Latin America, Cuba's disputes with Venezuela, Peru, Colombia, Ecuador, and Costa Rica, combined with the growing hostility of the United States, have ended any hope that Cuba can improve its diplomatic position within the hemisphere in the near future. In the Caribbean, Manley's defeat by Seaga has put a quick end to any prospect for a major increase in Cuban influence within that region. Even in Central America, where the victory of the Nicaraguan revolution has given Cuba a close friend, the war in El Salvador is posing new difficulties for Cuban foreign policy.

As the decade of the 1980s gets underway, Cuban foreign policy faces four principal dilemmas: (1) How can Cuba best guarantee its own security as the Cold War intensifies and as the Reagan administration singles out Cuba as a special target in its campaign against international communism? (2) How can Cuba effectively manage its role as broker between the Soviet Union and the non-aligned countries when the Third World is discovering that it can have sharp differences with the policies of the Soviet Union? (3) How can Cuba continue to aid revolutionaries in Latin America while simultaneously regaining the momentum toward normalization of relations with its Latin neighbors? (4) How can Cuba reconcile its activist foreign policy with the need to concentrate attention and resources on internal economic and political difficulties?

Events of the past year suggest that Cuba may have exhausted its ability to make diplomatic gains in Latin America and the Caribbean through a policy of conciliation. While Cuba can be expected to continue its search for normal state-to-state relations in these regions, it is certainly possible that it may return to a more militant policy in the Western Hemisphere—both as a response to the growing insurrection in Central America and as a calculated decision that the conciliatory strategy has reached the limits of its effectiveness.[50] The prospects for a more militant policy may be enhanced to the extent that Cuba can adopt such a policy while maintaining its cordial relationship with Mexico, a relationship that has tremendously important economic potential for Cuba.[51] Thus far, Mexico has been willing to stand by Cuba's efforts to aid the revolutionary government in Nicaragua and the guerrillas in El Salvador.

In Africa, Cuban troops will remain in Angola and Ethiopia until the security of those regimes can be guaranteed without Cuban military aid, but considering the costs of those involvements, it is extremely unlikely that Cuba would undertake any additional commitments on this scale.

The greatest international challenge to Cuba in the immediate future comes once again from the United States. The election of Ronald Reagan and the resurgence of the Cold War has again placed Cuba at the focal point of East-West conflict. Indeed, it is ironic that Cuba's successes abroad, especially in

Angola and Ethiopia, were in large measure responsible for U.S. disillusionment with détente. The rhetoric of the Reagan administration clearly casts Cuba as the most dangerous "proxy" of the Soviet Union, and the one which the new administration is most intent upon containing.

Whatever the actual intentions of the Reagan administration, Cuba must view it as a profound security threat. On several occasions during the campaign, Reagan suggested a naval blockade of Cuba in retribution for the Soviet Union's intervention in Afghanistan—even though Cuba had not yet even endorsed the intervention. Since the inauguration, the threat of a blockade or some other military action has been repeated as a way to end the insurrection in El Salvador—by "going to the source."[52] No doubt the principal aim of these threats is to intimidate Cuba into reducing its support for revolutionary movements abroad, and perhaps even reducing its general activism in foreign affairs. If this is indeed the Reagan administration's strategy, it has not been well conceived. Cuba is much stronger militarily today than it was in the 1960s, and it has already begun to enhance its defenses in response to U.S. threats. Militias, which were disbanded in the mid-1960s, are being organized once again to defend the island from large-scale attack, and the regular armed forces have been restructured to enable them to better fight a quasi-guerrilla war.[53] While these preparations may seem overdrawn, given the implausibility of an actual U.S. military assault on Cuba, they underline the Cubans' determination to stand firm in the face of threats, serious or not.

Moreover, the historic tendency of the Cuban leadership, and of Fidel Castro especially, has been to respond to threats with defiance. Neither economic nor military sanctions succeeded in the 1960s in persuading the Cubans to abandon their policy of exporting revolution. This tendency was also in evidence at the Second Congress; Castro's report gave the most explicit endorsement of armed struggle in Latin America from a Cuban official in many years.[54]

Nor is Reagan's policy of hostility toward Cuba likely to weaken Cuba's links with the Soviet Union. Quite the contrary.

By portraying Cuba as a Soviet puppet and threatening action against Cuba for events over which Cuba has little or no control, the United States gives Cuba no real incentive to alter its behavior. If Cuba is to be held responsible for Soviet actions half a world away, Cuban security can best be guaranteed if Cuba *moves closer* to the Soviet Union, thereby increasing the likelihood that the Soviets will come to Cuba's defense in times of crisis. This was well illustrated by the fact that Castro, in his report to the Second Party Congress endorsed, for the first time, the Soviet intervention in Afghanistan—precisely the issue over which Reagan had threatened to blockade the island. Castro also offered the Soviets a thinly veiled endorsement, before the fact, of any Soviet intervention in Poland.[55] The quid pro quo was not long in coming. Speaking on the Polish crisis at the Czechoslovakian Party Congress, President Brezhnev went out of his way to warn the United States that Cuba is "an inseparable part" of the Socialist camp.[56]

Given the limits of the possible for Cuba, both in Latin America and beyond, Cuba's response to the Reagan administration's hostility and the new Cold War is unlikely to entail any profound shift in basic Cuban policy. For Cuba, there are no easy gains left to be made abroad, either in Africa or the Western Hemisphere. The advances of the 1970s must still be consolidated (e.g., in Africa and the Non-aligned Movement), and in some cases may erode (e.g., Latin America). Except in Latin America itself (and perhaps even there), the Reagan administration can do little to reverse the successes of the last decade of Cuban foreign policy.

The principal effect of U.S. hostility can only be to shift Cuba's priority once again to its relations with the superpowers. In this realm, U.S. efforts are most likely to be counterproductive, pushing Cuba into ever closer accord with the Soviet Union, even on issues (such as Eritrea and Afghanistan) where differences have persisted. Since the Reagan administration seems intent upon treating Cuba as a Soviet proxy, even on issues that involve little or no Cuban-Soviet cooperation (e.g., Cuban policy in Latin America), it is positively dangerous for Cuba *not* to coordinate its policy even more closely with the Soviet Union. Cuba can no longer afford even minor divergences.

NOTES

1. On the general objectives of Cuban foreign policy, see Carmelo Mesa-Lago, *Cuba in the 1970s* (Albuquerque: University of New Mexico Press); Jorge I. Domínguez, "Cuban foreign policy," *Foreign Affairs* 57, 1 (Summer, 1978), pp. 83-108; Edward Gonzalez, "Complexities of Cuban foreign policy," *Problems of Communism* 26 (November-December 1977), pp. 1-15; and William M. LeoGrande, *Cuba's Policy in Africa, 1959-1980* (Berkeley: Institute of International Studies, 1980).

2. For a detailed discussion of U.S.-Cuban relations in the 1960s, see Lynn D. Bender, *The Politics of Hostility* (Hato Rey: Inter-American University Press, 1975).

3. Jacques Levesque, *The USSR and the Cuban Revolution* (New York: Praeger, 1978) offers the best chronicle of Soviet attitudes toward Cuba.

4. On Cuban doubts about Soviet reliability in the 1960s, see D. Bruce Jackson, *Castro, the Kremlin, and Communism in Latin America* (Baltimore: Johns Hopkins Pres, 1969).

5. On Cuban policy after the missile crisis, see Bender, op. cit. and Andrés Sáurez, *Cuba: Castroism and Communism, 1959-1966* (Cambridge: MIT Press, 1967).

6. On Cuban aid to guerrillas in Latin America, see Ernesto F. Betancourt, "Exporting the revolution to Latin America," in *Revolutionary Change in Cuba,* Carmelo Mesa-Lago, ed., (Pittsburgh: University of Pittsburgh Press, 1974), pp. 105-126; to guerrillas and governments elsewhere, see LeoGrande, op. cit.; William J. Durch, "The Cuban military in Africa and the Middle East," *Studies in Comparative Communism* II (Spring/Summer, 1978), pp. 34-74; and Nelson Valdes, "Revolutionary solidarity in Angola," in *Cuba in the World,* Cole Blasier and Carmelo Mesa-Lago, eds., (Pittsburgh: University of Pittsburgh Press, 1979), pp. 87-118.

7. See the speeches by Cuban representatives to the non-aligned summits of 1961 and 1964 in *The Conference of Heads of State or Government of Non-aligned Countries* (Belgrade, 1961); (Cairo, 1964).

8. On Cuba's willingness to enter into state-to-state relations even during its most militant years, see Jorge I. Domínguez, op. cit.

9. On Cuba's reevaluation of the "export of revolution" strategy, see Jackson, op. cit.

10. James Petras, "Socialism in one island: a decade of Cuban revolutionary government," *Politics and Society* 1, 3 (February 1971), pp. 203-224.

11. On Cuban relations with the Carribean, see Ronald E. Jones, "Cuba and the English-speaking Caribbean," in *Cuba in the World,* Blasier and Mesa-Lago, eds., op. cit., pp. 131-146; and "The new Cuban presence in the Caribbean," *Caribbean Review* 9, 1 (Winter, 1980).

12. "Statement of Wayne Smith, Department of State," *Impact of Cuban-Soviet Ties in the Western Hemisphere: Hearings,* U.S. House of Representatives, Subcommittee on Inter-American Affairs, 95th Congress (Washington, DC: U.S. Government Printing Office, 1978).

13. Mesa-Lago, *Cuba in the 1970s,* op. cit.

14. For a fuller discussion of Cuba's role in the Non-aligned Movement, see William M. LeoGrande, "The evolution of nonalignment," *Problems of Communism* (January-February 1980), pp. 35-52.

15. The figure of 36,000 troops, nearly twice the estimates made by U.S. intelligence, was cited by Fidel Castro in a secret speech to the Cuban National Assembly in December 1979.

16. On the nature of the Cuban-Soviet partnership in Africa, see LeoGrande, *Cuba's Policy in Africa,* op. cit. For a somewhat different view, see Jiri Valenta, "The Cuban-Soviet intervention in Angola, 1975," *Studies in Comparative Communism* 11 (Spring-Summer, 1978), pp. 1-24.

17. "Statement of Martin J. Scheira, Defense Intelligence Agency," *Impact of Cuban-Soviet Ties in the Western Hemisphere: Hearings,* U.S. House of Representatives, Subcommittee on Inter-American Affairs, 96th Congress (Washington, DC: U.S. Government Printing Office, 1980).

18. The final declaration of the 1976 Summit Meeting of Non-aligned Heads of State congratulated Cuba for assisting Angola in "frustrating the expansionist and colonialist strategy of South Africa's racist regime and its allies." Foreign Broadcast Information Service, *Daily Report: Middle East and North Africa* (FBIS: Washington, DC), August 23, 1976.

19. Quoted in The New York Times, July 20, 1978.

20. Coverage of the Non-aligned Ministerial Conference in Belgrade, The New York Times, July 26, 29, 30, and 31, 1978.

21. LeoGrande, "The evolution of nonalignment," op . cit.

22. For the texts, see *Addresses Delivered at the Sixth Conference of Heads of State or Government of Nonaligned Countries* (Havana, 1980).

23. For a summary of complaints on Cuba's handling of the summit, see The New York Times, September 12, 1979.

24. For the text of Castro's speech to the United Nations, see Granma Weekly Review, October, 1979.

25. These maneuvers are described in The Washington Post, January 11, 1980.

26. The New York Times, December 22, 1980.

27. Toby Trister Gati, "The Soviet Union and the north-south dialogue," *Orbis* (Summer 1980), pp. 241-270.

28. Ibid.

29. Compare, for example, the Soviet and NIEO positions summarized by Gati, *ibid.,* and the Cuban position set forth by Castro at the United Nations, op. cit.

30. For an excellent survey of such programs, see Susan Eckstein, "Socialist internationalism, the capitalist world economy and the Cuban Revolution." Prepared for the annual meetings of the International Studies Association, Philadelphia, March 8-21, 1981.

31. National Foreign Assessment Center, *The Cuban Economy: A Statistical Review* (Washington, DC: Central Intelligence Agency, 1981).

32. These crises are reviewed in detail in LeoGrande, *Cuba's Policy in Africa, 1959-1980,* op. cit.

33. For further details on Cuban aid and involvement in the Caribbean, see "The new Cuban presence in the Caribbean," op. cit.; and *The Impact of Cuban-Soviet Ties in the Western Hemisphere: Hearings* (1980), op. cit.

34. Ronald Jones, op. cit.

35. *The Impact of Cuban-Soviet Ties in the Western Hemisphere: Hearings* (1980), op. cit.

36. The Washington Post, September 29, 1980.

37. Ibid.

38. The Washington Post, June 18, 1979.

39. "Statement of Randolph Pherson, Central Intelligence Agency," *Impact of Cuban-Soviet Ties in the Western Hemisphere: Hearings* (1980) op. cit. p. 46.

40. The New York Times, July 6, 1981; The Washington Post, November 2, 1980.

41. "Statement of Martin Scheina, Defense Intelligence Agency," op. cit., pp. 12-13.

42. For a more extended treatment of Cuban aid to the Nicaraguan insurgents, see William M. LeoGrande, "Cuba and Nicaragua: from the Somozas to the Sandinistas," *Caribbean Review* 9, 1 (Winter 1980), pp. 11-15.

43. The equivocal phraseology here is intentional. The celebrated State Department White Paper, "Communist interference in El Salvador," purported to document a massive increase in Cuban arms aid to the Salvadoran left. However, the questionable nature of the White Paper's evidence leaves considerable doubt as to just how extensive Cuban and Nicaraguan aid actually was.

44. The Washington Post, March 12, 1981; The New York Times, December 13, 1981.

45. Cuba's relations with Mexico have been especially good in the past few years. At the conclusion of a meeting between Castro and Mexican President José López Portillo in August 1980, Mexico endorsed Cuba's demands for an end to the U.S. embargo and the withdrawal of U.S. forces from Guantánamo Naval Base (The New York Times August 4, 1980). In February 1981, Mexico and Cuba signed a broad energy agreement (The Washington Post, February 8, 1980) and later that month Portillo described Cuba as the Latin American nation "most dear" to Mexico (The New York Times, February 21, 1981).

46. The Washington Post, April 11, 1980.

47. Ibid.

48. On the costs of Cuban internationalism, see Eckstein, op. cit.; LeoGrande, *Cuba's Policy in Africa, 1959-1980,* op. cit.; and Sergio Roca, "Economic aspects of Cuban involvement in Africa," *Cuban Studies* 10, 2 (July, 1980), pp. 55-79.

49. The Washington Post, November 14, 1980.

50. This sort of a return to militancy was hinted at in Castro's speech to the Second Congress of the Cuban Communist Party, titled *"Main report to the Second Congress"* (New York: Center for Cuban Studies, 1981), pp. 37-45.

51. Ibid.

52. See the interview with White House Chief of Staff Edwin Meese, reported in The New York Times, February 23, 1981.

53. Fidel Castro, op. cit.

54. Ibid.

55. Ibid.

56. The Washington Post, April 8, 1981.

5

U.S. Policy

Objectives and Options

EDWARD GONZALEZ

This chapter begins by assessing the Cuban challenge to U.S. security and foreign policy interests, the range of objectives that U.S. policy toward Cuba should strive for in the 1980s, and the accomplishments as well as failures of recent U.S. policy toward Castro. The study then examines two conventional policy alternatives, the punitive and conciliatory approaches, with regard to their respective strengths and weaknesses in advancing U.S. objectives toward Cuba. Finally, the concluding part of the study explores the way in which the United States might devise and apply a long-term strategy for gaining increased leverage against Cuba and, directly or indirectly, the Soviet Union, with the aim of promoting a range of minimum-maximum objectives toward Cuba in the 1980s.

CUBA: U.S. INTERESTS AND OBJECTIVES

Beginning with President Eisenhower, every U.S. administration has been confronted with the "Cuba problem." After six months in office, the new Reagan administration is similarly faced with devising a policy toward Castro's Cuba

AUTHOR'S NOTE: This chapter is based on the author's larger study of Cuba under a project on Caribbean Basin security issues underway at The Rand Corporation.

that will advance U.S. interests and objectives. As a starting point, therefore, we must first ascertain what U.S. interests are affected by Cuba's presence and activities.

CUBA'S CHALLENGE TO U.S. INTERESTS

Cuba's challenge to the United States in the 1980s consists of three interrelated elements involving U.S. security, global, and regional interests. First, U.S. security interests are directly endangered in the Caribbean and elsewhere by Cuba's close military and political ties with the Soviet Union. While Cuba's alliance with the USSR could be viewed as largely defensive in character during the 1960s, Cuban-Soviet military ties have assumed an increasingly offensive *and* coordinated dimension since the mid-1970s. Thus, Cuba's Angolan operation was facilitated by Soviet logistical support beginning in late 1975. Two years later, the Soviets supplied not only logistical support but also the strategic command for Cuba's expeditionary forces in Ethiopia, and Soviet pilots flew Cuban Migs on the island to enable Cuban air force pilots fly combat missions in Ethiopia.[1]

Moreover, the Soviet Union has vastly increased its overseas military capabilities since the 1960s with its blue-water navy, whose ships now pay port calls and conduct oceanic surveys in the Caribbean. In this regard, Soviet submarines have a repair and rest facility in Cienfuegos; a Soviet, 3,000-man brigade evidently remains in Cuba; and Soviet reconnaissance planes and electronic surveillance facilities now use the island for monitoring the U.S. and Caribbean area. The Soviet reach into the Caribbean is also significantly augmented by Cuba's own military capabilities.

Having already engaged in overseas combat operations supported by and coordinated with the USSR, Cuba's Revolutionary Armed Forces (FAR)—consisting of 142,000 active duty and 60,000 ready reservists—continue to be advised by some 1,500 or more Soviet advisors on the island. Since the mid-1970s, the Army has been modernized and reequipped with Soviet T-62 tanks, BMP infantry combat vehicles, BM-21 multiple rocket launchers, and ZSU-23-4 self-propelled anti-aircraft guns. Additionally, the FAR has developed a modest airlift capability with the delivery of Soviet AN-26 short-range military transport planes capable of carrying forty fully equipped paratroopers on round-trip missions of 600 nautical miles each way, thereby placing many Caribbean islands and parts of Central America within reach of Cuban airborne troops. The Navy is also developing the potential for a regional presence in the Caribbean, having recently acquired two *Foxtrot* class Soviet submarines and a Soviet frigate, while its *Osa* and *Komar* class missile attack boats have a 400 and 200 neutical mile radius, respectively. Most critically, the Air Force possesses an inventory of some 200 advanced jet aircraft, consisting of MiG-21 fighters and a lesser number of MiG-23 attack fighters. With its combat radius of 520 neutical miles, not only can the MiG-23 command much of the Caribbean and all of Florida, but it can also strike at targets as far away as Mobile, Alabama, Savannah, Georgia, and the Yucatan Peninsula.[2]

An impending military conflict with the Soviet Union would thus require that the United States divert air, sea, and naval units from other military theaters in order to cope with the growing Cuban and Soviet military presence in the Caribbean. Combined with successful Cuban-supported insurgencies in Central America or elsewhere in the Caribbean Basin in the years ahead, such a presence could eventually result in the United States becoming outflanked along its southern perimeter. In that event, the United States could no longer view the Caribbean Basin as an "economy of force" region. Instead, it would have to greatly expand the U.S. military presence in the Basin, thereby restricting its capacity to project U.S. power globally.

Second, U.S. global interests continue to be undermined by Cuba's role as a military-political paladin in Africa, where the Cuban military presence in particular has greatly advanced Soviet interests and objectives in the continent. To be sure, Cuba has had its own interests to promote in Africa by greatly expanding its military and political presence there.[3] Still, the initial dispatch of 36,000 Cuban combat troops to Angola in 1975-76, followed by the dispatch of another 12,000 to Ethiopia in 1978,[4] were both indispensable to the advancement of Soviet objectives in Africa, in that the Cuban operations consolidated the power of the two pro-Soviet Marxist regimes in these countries while securing the Soviet, East European, as well as the Cuban presence in southern Africa and the Horn. In this respect, an estimated 15,000-19,000 Cuban military personnel remained stationed in Angola, and another 11,000-13,000 in Ethiopia at the end of 1980. Cuban military personnel in these two African states and elsewhere alone accounted for two-thirds of the estimated 51,555 military advisors, instructors, technical personnel, and troops that were stationed by the USSR and East European states in the Third World the previous year, excluding Soviet forces in Afghanistan.[5]

Third, Cuba's intensified "internationalist" activities in Nicaragua, El Salvador, and elsewhere threaten the stability of the Caribbean Basin, and directly or indirectly facilitate further Soviet penetration of a region of vital strategic and geopolitical importance to the United States. More so than other states, Cuba supplied the military and political support that proved essential to the victory of the Sandinista forces in the Nicaraguan civil war.[6] In the post-1979 period, Havana dispatched not only school teachers, public health, and administrative personnel to Nicaragua, but also military and security advisors that enabled the new revolutionary government to consolidate its power. By early 1981, most estimates placed the number of Cubans stationed in Nicaragua at 5,000.

Cuba also appears to have stepped up its support for the Marxist-Leninist guerrilla forces in El Salvador, beginning in late 1979. The Castro regime supplied political advice and direction to the Salvadoran guerrillas as it had done earlier with the Sandinistas. Additionally, the State Department charged that Havana organized and coordinated the transportation of upwards of 800 tons of weapons that various communist bloc countries reportedly had agreed to supply the guerrillas, and that began to arrive in El Salvador in September 1980.[7] More recently, Colombia suspended relations with Havana in March 1981, charging that Cuba had trained and armed nearly 100 guerrillas who had been captured earlier that month in Colombia.[8]

U.S. Objectives and Past Policy

At a minimum, therefore, U.S. policy should aim at, (1) neutralizing the security threat to the United States posed by the Cuban-Soviet relationship, (2) discouraging future Cuban military operations overseas, and (3) arresting Cuban efforts to destabilize and revolutionize the Caribbean Basin. At a maximum, U.S. policy might additionally seek to employ Cuba, as a highly exposed client-state of the Soviet Union, as a fulcrum for constraining Soviet international behavior. More ambitious still, a maximum set of goals might also have the objectives of fundamentally altering (1) the Cuban relationship with the Soviet Union and (2) the very composition and nature of the Cuban regime itself.

U.S. policy toward Cuba in the 1977-80 period was not effective in advancing the above minimum or maximum objectives. Instead, the major accomplishment of that policy was to reestablish subdiplomatic level ties with the Castro government in 1977, thereby ending the sixteen years of U.S. isolation from Cuba. With the stationing of the U.S. Interests Section in Havana, communication with the Castro regime was facilitated, and the U.S. government became far better informed regarding developments on the island. In themselves, these were two substantial gains for U.S. policy, ones that should be preserved in any future U.S.-Cuban policy. Additionally, a byproduct of the thaw was the return of tens of thousands of Cuban exiles to their homeland on brief visits, which in turn precipitated the surge of political unrest that suddenly confronted the regime in 1979-80, and which ended with the mass exodus of over 125,000 Cubans in the 1980 "Freedom Flotilla." Indirectly, therefore, U.S. policy contributed to developments that had significant impact within Cuba by allowing the return of the exiles.

Nevertheless, the original U.S. premise for moving toward a more normalized relationship in 1977—to provide the Castro regime with the political and economic incentive to become less beholden to the USSR, and thereby to wean it away from Moscow—was soon rendered inoperative by a succession of Cuban policies toward Ethiopia, Nicaragua, the Non-aligned Movement, and Afghanistan. Indeed, given the initial conciliatory U.S. policy at the time, these developments demonstrated the extent to which the Castro regime's foreign policy interests were not only conflictive but also intrinsically *contradictory* to those of the United States.

Contradictory interests between the two countries derive from the fact that each adheres to fundamental issues and objectives which cannot be sacrificed by either without irreparable harm to their respective international positions and roles. Hence, with the advent of the Carter administration's new Cuban policy, Havana might have secured some economic gains with the further normalization of relations with the United States after 1977. But these potential gains were by no means certain, since the restoration of commercial relations was contingent in large part upon U.S. Congressional (and public) approval, which in turn depended upon Cuba's "good behavior" on the international front. It was at this point that Cuban and U.S. interests were in direct contradiction: The Castro regime could not forego its "internationalist" role as a political-military paladin in the Third World, nor its ever closer and more supportive alliance with the Soviets, as Washington demanded, since these roles advanced the regime's *maximum* objectives of obtaining (1) greater international status and maneuverability (which the United States could not supply); (2) new Third World allies; and (3) greater leverage with Moscow as the latter's highly valued ally.[9] Although reacting negatively, Washington was thus unable to force Havana's abandonment of policies that were leading to a heightened Cuban military presence in Africa (Ethiopia), to renewed Cuban support for the Soviet Union in the Third World, the United Nations, and the Non-aligned Movement, and to the intensification of Cuba's own revolutionary activities in Central America. Unable to provide credible incentives for Cuba to detach itself from the Soviet Union, U.S. policy has become equally ineffective in discouraging the Castro regime from engaging in increasingly objectionable international behavior at the outset of the 1980s.

If recent U.S. policy was unable to advance even minimal U.S. objectives, what policy alternatives are now available toward Cuba? As will be suggested shortly, a long-term strategy of international leverage toward the Castro regime and, directly or indirectly, its Soviet patron might well succeed in promoting a range of minimum and maximum objectives. Such a leverage strategy by the United States, however, must be distinguished from two mutually opposing policy options that have been advanced as the method for dealing with Castro. Hence, we now need to look at the conventional *punitive* (or "hardline") and *conciliatory* (or "softline") approaches toward the Castro regime.

CONVENTIONAL POLICY ALTERNATIVES

The Punitive Option

The punitive policy would have the United States adopt political and military postures that would punish the Castro regime for its behavior, contain its active support for revolutionary movements, and, if necessary, eliminate the regime itself.[10] The range of political steps that could be taken involves the closing-down of the Cuban Interests Section in Washington, the termination of travel between Cuba and the United States, the reassessment of the U.S.-Cuban fishing treaty of 1977, and the resumption of a major anti-Castro propaganda campaign aimed at the Cuban people. The range of military measures includes the resumption of intelligence flights over the island, the interdiction of Cuban supplies destined for revolutionary forces in the Caribbean Basin, and the active support of Cuban exiles in the waging of a "war of national liberation" against Castro.

Although risky, the punitive option would appear to hold out prospects for realizing several minimum and maximum objectives toward Cuba. It would directly address the principal external "source" for heightened instability and insecurity in the Caribbean Basin, thereby arresting Cuban efforts to revolutionize the region, as well as checking or even eliminating entirely the Cuban-Soviet threat to U.S. security interests. By intensifying political and military pressures on Castro, the United States might also obtain a leverage hold over Moscow, and ultimately bring down the Cuban regime. At the very least, the punitive policy would raise the costs to Cuba were it to persist in its objectionable behavior.

Many of the above punitive measures would be self-defeating for U.S. interests and objectives, however. The closing of respective Interests Sections would eliminate the official U.S. presence in Havana, thereby reisolating the United States from Cuban developments. The cessation of travel between the two countries would prevent the return of U.S.-based Cuban exiles to the island, thereby shielding the Castro regime from the destabilizing effects that the exile visits have had on Cuban society. The abrogation of the fishing agreement would not hurt Cuba, except perhaps in the distant future, since U.S. fishing grounds are presently of marginal importance to the Cuban fishing industry, but it would probably further complicate the consummation of the separate boundary agreement between the two countries which still awaits Senate ratification.

U.S. "aggression" against Cuba, whether directly through U.S. naval and air actions, or indirectly through support for an anti-Castro war by Cuban exiles, could precipitate a wave of terrorist acts in this country by groups allied with Havana. Also, it could seriously undermine U.S. relations with Venezuela and especially Mexico. Both of these countries have emerged as new regional powers in the Caribbean Basin, with Venezuela currently serving as a pivotal U.S. ally in El Salvador, whereas Mexico possesses perhaps even greater potential as a stabilizing regional force. Furthermore, not only the governments of these two countries but also other Latin American and Caribbean governments as well would most likely be confronted with major domestic disturbances were the United States seen as engaged in military aggression against Cuba.

International law aside, the effective military containment of Cuban support for guerrilla insurrections might also be beyond the immediate force capabilities of the United States. The interdiction of Cuban supplies at sea would require the redeployment to the Caribbean of U.S. naval and air units that are already stretched thin in the Persian Gulf-Indian Ocean, Mediterranean, and elsewhere in the world. Both locally and internationally, such an undertaking becomes all the more hazardous since military measures can have consequences which are neither controllable nor predictable. Thus, the United States might intend to employ force selectively in order to minimize the risks of escalating the conflict with Cuba into a broader international conflict. However, there can be no certainty that Castro and the Cuban Revolutionary Armed Forces will not respond with their own punitive actions, given the present siege mentality of the Castro leadership and the modern, combat-proven capabilities of the FAR. In fact, the Flamingo incident in May 1980 provides a recent example of a rash action by the Cuban military, if not the leadership itself, under less stressful conditions. In the meantime, an expanding U.S.-Cuban conflict would create tremendous pressures on Moscow to assist Cuba at least indirectly, for example, by initiating Soviet military moves in the Middle East or against West Berlin as in 1962.

Once started, the United States could not afford to lose a war with Cuba. But a U.S. victory in Cuba would be costly internationally, especially in the Third World, in the same manner that Afghanistan severely set back Soviet diplomacy. Unlike Moscow, however, Washington would most likely be constrained by international and domestic reaction, as well as by Soviet pressure, from employing the very level of force necessary to assure a military solution to the Cuban problem. In turn, the longer the United States remains engaged in a military conflict with Cuba, the less sustainable the military action becomes, and the greater the likelihood that the United States would be forced to disengage—a development that surely would be seen by adversaries and allies alike as a triumph for Castro and a defeat for Washington.

Finally, even the mere threat of U.S. military action, or the renewal of exile attacks and landings on Cuba, is virtually certain to work to the Castro regime's advantage, not only because of its effect in galvanizing Cuban nationalism, but also because of the all-inclusive, mobilization character of the Cuban political system. Unlike traditional authoritarian regimes, Castro's political system rests on the organization and mobilization of mass support among Cuba's population of 10 million. Thus, the Committees for the Defense of the Revolution alone have a membership of 5.3 million, while the combined, overlapping membership of all four of Cuba's mass organizations—including the CDRs—numbers 10,317,000 Cubans. Although purposefully selective in their recruitment, the Communist Party of Cuba and its youth affiliate also have a membership of 434,134 and 422,000 respectively.[11] The Revolutionary Armed Forces number 142,000 active-duty personnel, plus 60,000 ready reservists, and will command upwards of 600,000 additional Cuban civilian volunteers who are to make up the new Territorial Troop Militia, while still other tens of thousands of Cubans work for the Ministry of Interior and other government agencies. Such a vast organizational network and membership has critical ramifications for the security of the Castro regime and for U.S. policy:

First, by virtue of their membership in the mass organizations and other bodies, the regime is able to command the vast majority of able-bodied males and females 14 years and up;

Second, while a significant portion of those mobilized may only be nominally committed or even opposed to the Castro regime, the mobilization structures and controls enveloping them are likely to make their mass defection or active opposition to the regime highly problematical; and

Third, at the very least the regime can count on the loyalty of hundreds of thousands of cadres who occupy low and middle-level posts in the mass organizations, the Party, the military and security organs, and the other governmental bodies, and who thus have a strong personal stake in the survival of the Castro regime.

Indeed, it is precisely the spectre of an island-wide blood-bath associated with the fall of the Castro regime, and the return of exile elements to power, that provides the regime with much of its cohesion and mass support. For example, in his speech before the National Assembly of People's Power on December 27, 1980, Castro warned of the increased possibility of U.S. aggression:

> We must raise our guard, vigilance must be increased because the attacks may not involve military action or a naval blockade; they can also consist of the introduction of animal diseases and plant blights—these people have no scruples of any kind—and they can consist of sabotaging the economy and starting the business of trying to murder leaders again and that sort of thing. . . . As we said in the Main Report [to the Party Congress], they'll have to assume responsibility for their acts. This also holds true for conterrevolutionary activity; we must use an iron fist and crush the slightest sign of counterrevolution.[12]

In turn, to defend against both external aggressors and domestic counterrevolutionaries, and to mobilize the civilian populace even further, the regime has been pushing the development of the new Territorial Troop Militia as a backup force to the FAR. In celebrating the 20th anniversary of his proclamation of the socialist nature of the Cuban Revolution, which occurred on the very eve of the Bay of Pigs invasion, Castro thus emphasized that Cuba was again being threatened:

> Hence, the similarity between this April 16 and that April 16. This is why we're again having to make a great effort to defend ourselves, to mobilize the people, men and women, all our people, to organize the Territorial Troop Militia and to accelerate the work of fortification and buttressing our defense capacity in every way.[13]

In short, the prospects of a frontal attack from the United States provided Castro with the pretext for renewed mass mobilization in defense of the Cuba *patria,* thereby helping to solidify his regime and the latter's ties to the popular masses.[14]

softline

The Conciliatory Option

The conciliatory option would have the U.S. government offer the Castro regime the restoration of trade relations, the availability of U.S. credits and technology, and the normalization of diplomatic relations on condition that Cuba (1) cease being an active military ally of the USSR in the service of Soviet expansionism; and (2) terminate support for revolutionary insurgencies in the Western Hemisphere.[15] The conciliatory approach thus aims at realizing the minimum U.S. objectives of neutralizing the Soviet-Cuban security threat, discouraging Cuba's role as a military paladin of the USSR, and arresting Cuba's promotion of revolution in the Americas. Logically, such an approach might also lead to the eventual realization of the maximum goals of fundamentally altering the Cuban-Soviet relationship and perhaps the regime itself.

The conciliatory option enjoys three advantages over the punitive alternative. First, it is a low-risk policy that would not precipitate a U.S.-Soviet military confrontation or heightened world tensions. Second, it would not require the redeployment of scarce military resources to the Caribbean, but would instead enable the United States to employ its abundant economic and technological advantages in bargaining with the Castro government. Finally, were Castro to reject U.S. overtures, the conciliatory approach would not solidify the regime and regime-mass relations as with the punitive option, but rather might undermine regime cohesion and its basis of popular support. *p 2"*

The conciliatory approach has three major difficulties, however. To begin with, it disregards the new make-up of the Castro regime, and how the recent expansion of the *fidelista-raulista* leadership increases the prospects that contradictory interests will prevent Cuba from accepting U.S. conditions under the conciliatory option. In this regard, the new *fidelista-raulista* predominance within the Castro regime today suggests that the latter will be even less receptive to a conciliatory approach than was the case four years ago under the Carter administration. At that time, the upper echelons of both the Party and the government were more representative of other leadership elements, including not only "old Communists" from the Popular Socialist Party, but also newly ascendant managerial and technocratic elites who were most concerned with expanding economic and trade ties with the industrialized West and the United States. Now, however, this earlier trend toward a broader coalition of leadership elites has been entirely reversed.

Thus, veteran *fidelista* hardliners assumed greater control of the Council of Ministers beginning in late 1979, while prominent technocratic and managerial elements were displaced, among them Foreign Trade Minister Marcelo Fernandez. The Second Party Congress in December 1980 underscored these changes as the new Political Bureau's regular and alternate membership, and the new Secretariat line-up, contained a far greater concentration of *fidelista* and *raulista* veterans than previously.[16]

As Table 5.1 indicates, the Political Bureau's regular membership was increased from thirteen to sixteen. One of the three new additions is a veteran of the guerrilla campaign, another served as liaison to Castro's guerrilla headquarters (Camacho), and all three are either *fidelista* or *raulista* in their leadership orientations. The dominance of the two Castro brothers and their respective followers was thus increased to thirteen of the 16-member Political Bureau (including Dorticos, Camacho, and Cienfuegos), while the remaining three "old Communists" from the PSP were reduced to a shrinking minority. Equally significant was the apparent rise of a *fidelista* hardliner to new leadership prominence: Reappointed as Minister of the Interior in December 1979, Ramiro Valdes was now moved from seventh (1975) to fourth place in the rank order of Political Bureau members.

The biggest change was in the creation of eleven new Alternate Members to the Political Bureau. As Table 5.2 reveals, the predominance of the July 26th Movement and

TABLE 5.1 Sixteen Regular Members of the PCC Political Bureau, December 1980 (listed in the order given by *Granma*)

Political Bureau: Name & Rank Order	Pre-1959 Political Origins [1]	Current Primary Institutional Affiliation and Positions
(c) Fidel Castro (1st. Sec.)	M-26-7:Fg	Pres., Councils of Ministers* & State; Commander-in-Chief
(c) Raul Castro (2nd. Sec.)	M-26-7:Rg	1st V. Pres., Councils in Min.* & State; Minister, MINFAR
(c) Juan Almeida (Mem.)	M-26-7:Fg	V. Pres., Councils of Min.* & State
(c) Ramiro Valdes (Mem.)	M-26-7:Fg	V. Pres., Councils of Min.* & State, Minister, MININT
(c) Guillermo Garcia (Mem.)	M-26-7:Fg	V. Pres., Councils of Min.* & State
(c) Jose Ramon Machado (Mem.)	M-26-7:Rg	PCC Secretariat
(c) Blas Roca (Mem.)	PSP	Member, Council of State
(c) Carlos Rafael Rodriguez (Mem.)	PSP	V. Pres., Councils of Min.* & State
(c) Osvaldo Dorticos (Mem.)	M-26-7:Fu	V. Pres., Councils of Min.* & State

(c) Pedro Miret (Mem.)	M-26-6:Fg	PCC Secretariat
(c) Sergio del Valle (Mem.)	M-26-7:Fg	Min. of Public Health; Member, Councils of Ministers & State
(c) Armando Hart (Mem.)	M-26-7:Fu	Min. of Culture; Member, Council of State
(c) Arnaldo Milian (Mem.)	PSP	V. Pres., Councils of Min.*; Member, Council of State; Min. of Agricul.
(n) Jorge Risquet (Mem.)	M-26-7:Rg	PCC Secretariat
(n) Julio Camacho (Mem.)	M-26-7:Fu	PCC 1st Sec., Havana
(n) Osmani Cienfuegos (Mem.)	M-26-7:Fu (ex-PSP)	Sec., Councils of Min.* & State

Key: (c) = Continuing member; (n) = New member
[1] The abbreviations in this column are:
M-26-7 = (Castro's) July 26 Movement; F = Fidelista; R = Raulista; g = guerrilla veteran; u = urban resistance; PSP = Popular Socialist Party (pre-Castro Communist Party)
*Member of the Executive Committee of the Council of Ministers. Under the governmental reorganization of January 10, 1980, the President, First Vice President, and remaining 12 Vice Presidents, who constitute the Executive Committee, assumed responsibility for designated clusters of ministries and functional areas of government.

SOURCES: Granma Weekly Review, December 23, 1979, January 13, 1980, and January 4, 1981.

TABLE 5.2 Alternate Members of the PCC Political Bureau, December 1980 (listed in the order given by *Granma*)

Alternates in the Political Bureau: Name and Rank Order	Pre-1959 Political Origins [1]	Current Primary Institutional Affiliations and Positions
Abelardo Colome (Div. General)	M-26-7:Rg	1st V. Min., MINFAR; 1st Substitute Minister of the FAR, respon. for Cuba's overseas forces
Senen Casas (Div. General)	M-26-7:Rg	1st V. Min., MINFAR; Chief of the General Staff, respon. for Cuba's home front defenses
Sixto Batista (Div. General)	M-26-7:Fg	V. Min., MINFAR; Chief, Central Political Directorate
Antonio Perez	M-26-7-Rg	PCC Secretariat
Humberto Perez	M-26-7:R	V. Pres., Councils of Min.; Min. Pres., Central Planning Board (JUCEPLAN)
Jesus Montane	M-26-7:Fg	PCC Secretariat
Miguel Cano	u.k.	PCC 1st Sec., Holguín Province
Vilma Espin (wife of Raul Castro)	M-26-7:Rg	Pres., Fed. of Cuban Women (FMC)*; Member, Council of State
Roberto Veiga	u.k.	Sec-Gen., Central Organization of Cuban Trade Unions (CTC)*; Member, Council of State
Jose Ramirez	PSP: Rg	Pres., National Assoc. of Small Farmers (ANAP)*; Member, Council of State
Armando Acosta	PSP	Coord., Committees for the Defense of the Revolution (CDRs);* Member, Council of State

Key: [1] The abbreviations in this column are: M-26-7 = (Castro's) July 26 Movement; F = Fidelista; R = Raulista; g = guerrilla veteran; PSP = Popular Socialist Party (pre-Castro Communist Party); u.k. = unknown
*Mass organization

SOURCES: Granma Weekly Review, December 23, 1979, January 13, 1980, and January 4, 1981

fidelista-raulista elements is even greater among the alternates: seven of the eleven alternates were members of Castro's July 26th Movement, seven of eleven who were under the command of Fidel or Raúl Castro, including José Ramirez of the PSP and Vilma Espin, who married Raúl in 1959. Still others, like Miguel Cano and Roberto Veiga, evidently developed close ties with the Castro brothers in the postrevolutionary period. Equally conspicuous is the institutional representation of the MINFAR, the mass organizations, and the Party in the alternate membership, with the MINFAR heading the list with Division Generals Colome, Casas, and Batista, all veterans of Cuba's Angolan or Ethiopian campaigns, and comprising the Army's top command. Only Humberto Perez, as head of the Central Planning Board, represents the more pragmatic, economic-technocratic tendency within the government.

As is readily apparent in Table 5.3, the new PCC Secretariat heightens the *fidelista-raulista* dominance even further. Of the nine members, three are *fidelista* guerrilla veterans, and five are *raulista* veterans. The "old Communists" from the Popular Socialist Party (PSP) are represented only by Lionel Soto, whereas three ex-PSP leaders were dropped, including two—Carlos Rafael Rodríguez and Blas Roca—who had been charter members of the Secretariat ever since it was first formed in October 1965.[17] As a result, the new Secretariat contains the highest concentration of *fidelista* and *raulista* leaders than at any time during its 15-year existence.

In turn, the value preferences, dominant goals, and organizational interests of the *fidelista* and *raulista* elites, as well as those of Fidel Castro himself, are virtually certain to make the present leadership far less receptive to U.S. economic and diplomatic inducements than would be true of the technocratic-managerial elites who have now become marginalized. In fact, the heightened predominance of *fidelista* and *raulista* leaders is likely to sharpen the contradictory interests between Cuba and the United States. Thus, the *fidelistas* seek maximum political and ideological goals which are contrary to U.S. global and regional interests, including increased international status, leverage, and leadership for the Castro regime, while

TABLE 5.3 Nine Members of the PCC Secretariat, December 1980 (listed in the order given by *Granma*)

Secretariat: Name and Rank Order:	Pre-1959 Political Origins [1]	Party Position and Areas of Functional Responsibility
(c) Fidel Castro	M-26-7:Fg	First Secretary
(c) Raúl Castro	M-26-7:Rg	Second Secretary
(c) Pedro Miret (Mem.)	M-26-7:Fg	Public Consumption & Serv., Basic Industries
(c) Jorge Risquet (Mem.)	M-26-7:Rg	Transp., Comm., & Construct.
(c) Antonio Perez (Mem.)	M-26-7:Rg	Educ. & Revol. Orientation
(c) Lionel Soto	PSP	Economy
(c) Jose Ramon Machado	M-26-7:Rg	PCC Org.; General Affairs; State & Judiciary; Mass Org., Adm. and Finance
(n) Jesus Montane	M-26-7:Fg	Foreign Relations & PCC Americas Dept.
(n) Julian Rizo	M-26-7:Rg	Sugar, Agriculture & Livestock
Not Reappointed:		
Carlos Rafael Rodriguez (Mem.)	PSP	
Blas Roca (Mem.)	PSP	
Arnaldo Milian (Mem.)	PSP	
Julio Camacho	M-26-7:Fu	

Key: (c) = Continuing member; (n) = New member
[1] The abbreviations in this column are: M-26-7 = (Castro's) July 26 Movement; F = Fidelista; R = Raulista; g = guerrilla veteran; u = urban resistance; PSP = Popular Socialist Party (pre-Castro Communist Party)

SOURCES: Granma Weekly Review, December 23, 1979, January 13, 1980, and January 4, 1981

both the *fidelista* and *raulista* military elites have an additional organizational interest in strengthening the Cuban-Soviet alliance, which is similarly unacceptable for the United States. Accordingly, *the conciliatory approach is doomed beforehand precisely because it requires that the dominant leadership elements within the regime abandon their most valued goals and interests as a condition for securing a less valued objective of economic development through U.S. assistance.*

The second major difficulty with the conciliatory option concerns its economic feasibility for the United States. For example, what would it "cost" the United States for Castro to detach Cuba militarily from the USSR, and to cease its revolutionary activities in the Caribbean Basin? In turn, could the United States hope to replace the USSR as Cuba's principal trading partner and subsidizer? We do know approximately how much Castro's Cuba costs the Soviet Union: The USSR provided Cuba with an estimated $5.7 billion in repayable aid between 1960 and 1979, plus an additional $11 billion in grants and trade subsidies for the same 20-year period. During the 1976-79 four-year period alone, however, Cuba cost Moscow an estimated $9.6 billion in total economic assistance, most of it outright grants and trade subsidies, which amounted to an average bill of $2.4 billion per annum, or 47 percent of the $4.567 billion that the United States provided in *total* development assistance in 1979.[18]

With regard to the second question, the Soviets supply Cuba with nearly all of its petroleum imports, and at a discounted price of approximately 50 percent of the world price, both of which the United States would be hard pressed to provide. Additionally, the USSR is Cuba's principal sugar buyer, again at a preferential price, with Cuban sugar exports to the Soviet Union due to rise 2.5 to 3 million tons in 1981-82, which the United States could not absorb, owing to the established position of domestic and other international sugar suppliers in the U.S. market. Even if Cuba were willing to realign itself, therefore, the United States could ill afford to displace the USSR as the Castro regime's principal benafactor, nor could it adequately satisfy the present requirements of the Cuban economy.

On a more modest scale, the United States might still try to provide Castro with some inducements for distancing himself from the USSR, and for curbing his revolutionary ambitions in the Western Hemisphere, by simply giving Cuba limited access to U.S. trade, technology, and credits. But limited access to U.S. largess provides only weak inducements, which in turn would give the United States little leverage in bargaining for Cuban foreign policy concessions. Indeed, as was demonstrated in 1977-78, the U.S. government has virtually no bargaining power in such situations because of the Castro regime's ability both to extract very high levels of Soviet economic support *and* to pursue its own preferred foreign policy inclinations as Moscow's most valued ally in the Third World. Hence, the United States has little to offer Cuba under such circumstances.

Finally, the conciliatory approach cannot be sustained over the long term. For it to receive sustained support from within the Executive Branch, Congress, and the public at large, a conciliatory U.S. policy would require prompt successes in terms of visible changes in Cuban international behavior. Conversely, such support rapidly dwindles when the desired changes are not forthcoming, as indeed occurred beginning in 1978 with Cuba's new military operation in Ethiopia. Given the new predominance of the *fidelista-raulista* elites, and the difficulty the United States faces in offering credible and effective economic inducements to Castro, a new conciliatory approach would thus stand little chance of triggering the required changes in Cuban foreign policy.

DEVISING A LEVERAGE
STRATEGY TOWARD CUBA

Neither the punitive nor the conciliatory option constitutes a coherent political strategy toward Castro's Cuba. Each lacks a clear definition of realizable goals; each proposes relatively simple, short-term solutions to the complex, enduring conflict with Cuba; and each is essentially a reactive policy—as has been the history of U.S.-Cuban policy since 1959—except that each responds to the perennial "Cuban problem" with a different approach. Clearly, then, there is a need for a new U.S. policy toward Cuba.

A leverage strategy would assume the initiative toward Castro; it would aim at advancing U.S. minimum and maximum goals with regard to Cuba through the employment of a spectrum of political, economic, and military policies over an extended period of time, conceivably into the late 1980s. Hence, unlike the punitive and conciliatory options, it would be sustainable within the United States, as well as politically and militarily feasible in the larger regional and international context. In this respect, a leverage strategy would be keyed to the contemporary Cuban reality, avoiding the strengths of the Castro regime while exploiting its many weaknesses and new vulnerabilities.

A leverage strategy systematically combines both pressures and inducements from the punitive and conciliatory approaches in order to create situations which will *oblige* the Castro regime to change its international behavior. But it differs from the punitive and conciliatory options: It has a long-term perspective, and most importantly, it avoids working against the strengths of the Castro regime while exploiting the latter's many weaknesses, as well as its new vulnerabilities and interests, so as to systematically advance U.S. objectives in the 1980s.

Before elaborating the strategy, we must first define international leverage and its constituent elements as they apply to Cuba and the Soviet Union. Then, we need to identify those particular conditions within the present Cuban situation that make the Castro regime (and Moscow) susceptible to the exercise of U.S. leverage. Finally, we will look at some of the leverage instruments and policies that might be available for effectively promoting U.S. objectives with respect to both Cuba and the Soviet Union.

U.S. Leverage: Cuba and the Soviet Union

On an abstract level, international leverage can be defined as State A influencing State B's behavior to A's advantage through B's recognition that it can minimize its vulnerabilities and maximize its interests only by satisfying A.[19] As the leverage practitioner, either State A holds political, economic, or military power over State B, or it possesses an essential raw material, a geostrategic location, and/or a political or ideological relationship of great value to B that *obliges* the latter to provide policy concessions to A. Thus conceived, international leverage becomes available to and is practiced by "weak" as well as powerful states and can be used either in a passive manner to maintain a favorable relationship with the target state, or actively to wrest specific policy concessions from that state.[20]

Turning to the Cuban case, the United States can generate international leverage on Cuba and, directly or indirectly, on the Soviet Union as well. In the first instance, Cuba becomes the direct target of U.S. leverage, with the minimum objectives being to induce significant changes in the Castro regime's regional and international behavior, and with the maximum ones being to alter the regime's very complexion and relationship with the Soviet Union. Whatever the objectives, the attainment of leverage rests on the ability of the U.S. government to exploit actively the Castro regime's vulnerabilities *and* interests through the intensification of pressures combined with the offering of inducements.

Pressures and inducements are *both* necessary and must be coupled if maximum leverage over the regime is to be attained. Coupling is vital because U.S. pressures can exacerbate the regime's vulnerabilities but may be insufficient for gaining leverage if the vulnerabilities can be lessened by the regime's own counter measures on the domestic and foreign policy front. On the other hand, if the pressures are combined with major inducements from the United States, the regime itself— or key elite elements within the regime—may conclude that the leadership's primary interests can best be satisfied over the long term only through accommodation with the United States. Thus, *whereas pressures exacerbate regime vulnerabilities, inducements promote regime or specific elite interests in order to obtain maximum U.S. leverage over Cuba.*

What are the regime's growing vulnerabilities that can be exploited by the United States to intensify regime-mass tensions and interelite conflict? Among the more obvious ones are the following:

- two decades of poor economic performance, with the outlook for the rest of the 1980s remaining bleak according to the regime itself;
- a tendency toward renewed centralization and authoritarianism since 1979, reversing the earlier liberalization trends associated with the "institutionalization of the revolution" in the early to mid-1970s;
- an overextended foreign policy that has syphoned off Cuba's scarce material resources, entailed war casualties in Angola and Ethiopia, and compromised Cuba's international standing in the Third World because of subordination to Moscow and because of Afghanistan;
- perpetuation of a political oligarchy in which the newly enlarged 1980 Party Central Committee still remains unrepresentative of much of the island's population in terms of race (blacks and mulattoes make up only 12 percent), generations (Castro's 1953 generation still accounts for 56 percent), and provincial origins (Castro's province, Oriente, alone continues to account for 37 percent); and
- continued dominance by a guerrilla elite at the highest levels of the Party, state, and government, with the nonguerrilla elites having become more marginalized in these top policymaking organs than at any time since the 1960s.

In turn, the United States is in a position to exacerbate these vulnerabilities through political, psychological, and military pressures.

Although a discussion of these measures is outside the scope of this chapter, some suggestions are in order. For example, the United States could beam radio and television programs to the island which would provide Cuban audiences there with alternative sources of information on developments within Cuba and in the world at large, and which would systematically expose the deficiencies of the Cuban economy and polity as well.[21] The United States could undertake joint political and military measures with friendly governments in the region, not only to constrain Cuban support for revolutionary groups but

216

CUBA

also to discredit the regime internationally and to raise the political costs of its activist foreign policy within both Cuba and the regime itself. The U.S. government could also probe for regime weaknesses and divisions by cultivating dissident or potentially dissident civilian and military circles within the government. The aim of these and other measures would be to intensify the pressures on Havana in order to wrest major changes in Cuban foreign policy and behavior.

Such pressures would not necessarily provide the United States with leverage, however, if the Castro leadership sees that it can effectively neutralize its vulnerabilities and thereby assure its paramount interests in regime survival through domestic measures which tighten internal security, mobilize mass support, and develop the Territorial Troop Militia, and through external measures that commit the Soviet Union to higher levels of economic and military support. Thus, together with pressures that intensify the regime's concern over survival, and that raise the costs of its objectionable behavior, the United States also needs to offer major inducements to the regime to alter its behavior.

Inducements would be keyed to the *primary* interests that the regime—or elite elements within the regime—have in assuring regime security and survival, in restoring international autonomy, and in promoting long-term economic development. The United States would be in the position to assure security and survival by virtue of its ability to ease up on U.S. pressures. Also, unlike the Soviets, only the United States could offer Havana sufficient maneuvering room to enable it to regain Cuba's autonomy internationally. Finally, even though it could not replace the Soviets as Cuba's economic benefactor, the United States nevertheless might be in a position to provide Cuba with sufficient increments of additional trade, technology, and possibly capital investment advantages so as to advance the island's developmental prospects. In any event, such inducements would aim at convincing Cuban leaders that their primary interests, especially that of regime survival, would be better served in the long run by foregoing Castro's maximum foreign policy objectives, and thus by compromising with

Washington. Among the key inducements needed to enhance U.S. leverage, therefore, would be the readiness of the U.S. government to accept a socialist-oriented regime in Cuba, with or without the Castro brothers, in return for fundamental changes in Cuba's regional and international behavior.

Cuba can also become a fulcrum for obtaining leverage on the Soviet Union, either directly or indirectly. For example, if the USSR becomes the direct target of U.S. leverage, then Cuba would serve as the means by which to constrain Soviet expansionism elsewhere in the world by virtue of its vulnerability as the most exposed salient of the Soviet bloc. Or Cuba could remain the target state, in which case U.S. leverage would be indirectly exercised on Moscow as a result of U.S. policies toward the Castro regime. In either instance, Cuba provides the United States with a fulcrum for leveraging Moscow because of a range of Soviet interests in Cuba as a client-state of the USSR, and because of the new vulnerabilities of the Castro regime resulting from domestic problems, rising East-West tensions, and U.S. pressures on Cuba itself.

The Soviets have a strong vested interest in the preservation of Cuba as a client-state because they have made an immense political, economic, and military investment in Cuba over the years; because the Castro regime has become a valued international ally that has been especially effective in the Third World; and because communism as a historical process is allegedly irreversible. Additionally, the Soviet commitment to Cuba since 1960 serves as testimony of the Soviet Union's emergence as a genuine world power, capable of extending its political, economic, and military power globally, with Cuba also serving to advance the Soviet strategic outreach into the Western Hemisphere itself. Precisely because of this large Soviet stake in Cuba, Moscow's increased concern over the viability of its distant client-state should thus make it susceptible to Cuba-derived leverage being employed by the United States, particularly if the latter actively sought to exploit the Castro regime's vulnerabilities and interests through the kinds of pressures and inducements described earlier.

Seen in this context, Cuba would become hostage to U.S.-Soviet relations. However, Washington would have to take great care in not overplaying its "Cuba card," thereby provoking Soviet retaliation against U.S. allies contiguous to the USSR.[22] Thus, Washington might need to avoid direct military threats against Cuba in trying to leverage Moscow and to confine its Cuba-derived leverage to resolving Cuban related problems. Accordingly, such leverage might best be used by the United States to secure Soviet cooperation in minimizing the Cuban-Soviet security threat in the Caribbean, and in otherwise moderating Cuba's regional and international postures, which are policy areas over which Moscow has some control.

As described above, leverage ought not to be equated with diplomatic "bargaining" and "persuasion," nor with the concept of "power" as traditionally conceived. Bargaining and persuasion will occur in the operationalization of leverage, while power relationships or the invocation of sanctions may become an integral part of a leverage situation, particularly in the exploitation of a state's weaknesses and vulnerabilities. But none of these constitute a political strategy that systematically aims at the creation of a condition whereby the target state (Cuba) becomes obliged to advance its primary interests by altering its behavior to satisfy the objectives of the leverage state (the United States). A leverage strategy would strive to create such a condition through the combined application of pressures *and* inducements that are keyed to the target state's vulnerabilities and interests. What awaits further research, therefore, is a careful assessment of the types of vulnerabilities and interests that potentially make the Castro regime susceptible to U.S. leverage, and of the types of leverage instruments and policies that the U.S. government could employ toward Cuba in the long run.

NOTES

1. In the Ethiopian operation, Cuba's expeditionary forces that spearheaded the successful offensive against Somalia in February-March 1978 were led by Div. Gen. Arnaldo Ochoa, but were under the overall command of Lt. Gen. Vasiliy Ivanovich

Petrov of the USSR. On Cuban-Soviet policies in Africa, see Edward Gonzalez, "Cuba, the Soviet Union, and Africa," in David E. Albright, ed., *Communism in Africa* (Indiana University Press, 1980), pp. 145-167. See also William M. LeoGrande, *Cuban Policy in Africa, 1959-1980* (Policy Papers on International Affairs, Institute of International Studies, University of California, Berkeley, 1981).

2. Data on the capabilities of the FAR have been taken from an unclassified study prepared by the Office of Cuban Affairs, Department of State, "Cuban armed forces and the Soviet military presence," (Washington, DC, 1981). It should be noted that this study places the number of armed forces personnel, including ready-reservists, at 225,500, as opposed to my figure of 202,000.

3. See Gonzalez, loc. cit., and LeoGrande, loc. cit.

4. The Angolan and Ethiopian troop figures were mentioned by Fidel Castro in his "secret speech" of December 27, 1979, before the National Assembly of People's Power.

5. National Foreign Assessment Center, CIA, *Communist Aid Activities in Non-Communist Less Developed Countries, 1979 and 1954-79, A Research Paper (ER 80-10318U, October 1980), p.* 15.

6. The first of several Cuban arms shipments began in September 1977, with the May 1979 shipments proving indispensable to the FSLN spring offensive. Havana also dispatched Julian Lopez, allegedly a DGI officer and currently Cuban Ambassador to Nicaragua, to Costa Rica in March 1978 to coordinate Cuban operations.

7. See the text of the "State Department report on Communist support of the Salvadoran rebels," New York Times, February 24, 1981, p. A8. In recent months, however, the State Department's "White Paper" has been criticized by the Wall Street Journal, the New York Times, and others for exaggerating the amount of communist bloc arms funneled by Cuba into El Salvador.

8. Los Angeles Times, March 24, 1981, p. 2.

9. For a further elaboration of the "logic' of Cuba's international position at the time, see Edward Gonzalez, "Institutionalization, political elites, and foreign policies," in Cole Blasier and Carmelo Mesa-Lago, eds., *Cuba in the World* (University of Pitsburgh Press, 1979), pp. 3-36.

10. This essentially is the position taken by the Committee of Santa Fe, made up of L. Francis Bouchey, Roger Fontaine, David Jordan, General Gordon Sumner, and Lewis Tambs, in their report, *A New Inter-American Policy for the Eighties* (Council for Inter-American Security, May 1980). Despite its title, a recent report provides a relatively balanced assessment of the difficulties confronting the implementation of the punitive approach. See "Reagan's goal: cutting Castro down to size," *U.S. News and World Report,* April 6, 1981, pp. 20-22.

11. The membership figures on the mass organizations and party are taken from Fidel Castro's "Main report to the Second Party Congress," Granma Weekly Review, December 28, 1980, pp. 10-12.

12. Ibid., January 11, 1981, p. 2.

13. Ibid., April 26, 1981, p. 3.

14. Apart from evoking the threat of an external enemy, the regime is also able to generate considerable mass support for ideological, political, and social reasons. See Jorge I. Domínguez, "Cuba in the 1980's," *Problems of Communism,* March-April 1981, esp. pp. 57-58.

15. See Abraham F. Lowenthal, "Reagan's best weapon against Cuba may be the threat of peace," Los Angeles Times, April 5, 1981, Part V, p. 3. In contrast to

Lowenthal's position, the conciliatory approach has been advocated in the past without any conditions being attached. This is not a realistic option for U.S. policy, however.

On the other hand, elements of the conciliatory approach reportedly form part of the new Cuban policy being formulated by the Reagan administration. Thus, were Castro to acquiesce to a U.S ultimatum regarding the cessation of Cuba's destabilizing activities in Central America and elsewhere, "he can count on compensation in the form of normalization of relations with the United States, trade, technology and other economic benefits" (U.S. News and World Report, April 6, 1981), p. 20.

16. The distinction between *fidelista* and *raulista* officers initially derives from their primary associations with the Castro brothers during the anti-Batista struggle. Generally, the *fidelistas* joined Fidel in the Moncada attack of 1953, and/or later remained with him on the First Front during the course of the guerrilla struggle, whereas the *raulistas* later joined the younger Castro brother in establishing the Second Front in 1958. In the post-1959 period, several of the most prominent *fidelista* guerrilla veterans eventually became civilianized as they assumed permanent leadership positions in the party and government, and thereafter constituted the core of the inner circle around Fidel. A number of other *fidelistas* remained with the FAR, however, and became professional soldiers. Although some *raulista* officers were reassigned to civilian posts in the late 1960s and 1970s, the majority remained in the FAR as close associates of Raúl. Within the top ranks of the professional military, therefore, there are nearly as many *fidelista* senior officers as there are *raulistas*. However, the younger, middle-grade officer corps could well be considered *raulista* in orientation, given Raúl's direct control of the FAR.

17. Another PSP leader, Raul Valdes Vivo, had been a Secretariat member until December 1979, when he was released to join the editorial board of the *World Marxist Review* in Prague.

18. The data on Soviet economic assistance are from National Foreign Assessment Center, CIA, *The Cuban Economy: A Statistical Review—A Reference Aid,* ER 81-10052/PA 81-10074, March 1981, p. 39. The U.S. aid figure is from The World Bank, *World Development Report,* 1980, p. 140.

19. With but a few notable exceptions, "leverage" remains an elusive and much neglected concept in the literature on international politics. For an early, pioneering effort to develop leverage as a distinct analytical concept, see Richard W. Cottam, *Competitive Interference and Twentieth Century Diplomacy* (1967). For other relevant studies, see Thomas Schelling, *The Strategy of Conflict* (1960); Robert O. Keohane, "The big influence of small allies," *Foreign Policy,* Spring 1971; and Robert Keohane and Joseph S. Nye, *Power and Interdependence—World Politics in Transition* (1977).

20. While it is commonly believed that the superpowers exercise leverage over small states, the reverse is also true. Thus, Finland has used passive and, on occasion, active forms of leverage to forge a relationship with the Soviet Union that maximizes Finnish internal autonomy and safeguards national integrity. Cuba, too, has been a highly successful leverage practitioner in its 21-year relationship with Moscow, using both active and passive leverage to ensure the Soviet commitment. On the U.S. side, Israel has stood out as a skilled player of leverage politics in its dealings with Washington, employing active as well as passive leverage to maintain and strengthen U.S. support for Israel. The Shah was also adept at leveraging the United States, even prior to the energy crisis that began in 1973, and even during the height of the Iranian

Revolution when his regime began to unravel. All these states possessed meager conventional "power" capabilities, and were either vulnerable to or dependent upon the superpower. Yet each was able to leverage the respective superpower by exploiting the value(s) the latter attached to them: Finland (strategic, political), Cuba (strategic, ideological, political), Israel (strategic, political), and Iran (strategic, raw material, political). For additional information, see David F. Ronfeldt, "Super-clients and superpowers—Cuba: Soviet Union/Iran: United States," *Conflict,* 1, 4, 1979, pp. 273-302; Steven Spiegel, *The War for Washington: The Other Arab Israeli Conflict (forthcoming);* and George Maude, *The Finnish Dilemma (1975).* The author is also currently at work on a comparative study of international leverage that focuses on Cuba, Iran, Finland, and Mexico.

21. Although commercial Spanish-language radio and TV programs from Miami are received in Cuba, especially in Havana and surrounding regions, there are no information programs expressly directed to audiences in Cuba that are currently being transmitted on standard frequencies.

22. Bordering on the Soviet Union, and dependent upon the United States, the Shah's Iran previously was the U.S. client-state that was most analagous to Cuba, and against whom the Soviets could have retaliated in response to U.S. moves against Castro. Although lacking the same kind of symmetry, Turkey and especially Pakistan today present the most likely Soviet targets for checkmating U.S. moves against Cuba, owing to their respective internal problems and external vulnerabilities, while West Berlin also remains a logical target.

Index

About the Authors

JORGE I. DOMINGUEZ is a Professor of Government, Chairman of the Committee on Latin American and Iberian Studies, and a member of the Executive Committee of the Center for International Affairs, all at Harvard University. He is President of the Latin American Studies Association. His books include *Cuba: Order and Revolution, Insurrection or Loyalty: The Breakdown of the Spanish American Empire* (both from Harvard Press), *Economic Issues and Political Conflict: U.S.-Latin American Relations* (from Butterworth), and *Mexico's Political Economy: Challenges at Home and Abroad* (from Sage).

EDWARD GONZALEZ is Professor of Political Science at the University of California—Los Angeles and a Resident Consultant at The Rand Corporation. He is the author of *Cuba Under Castro: The Limits of Charisma* (1974), as well as numerous articles and monographs on Cuban domestic and foreign affairs. He is currently completing two major studies on Cuba and U.S.-Cuban policy at The Rand Corporation.

WILLIAM M. LEOGRANDE is a Professor and Director of Political Science in the School of Government and Public Administration at The American University in Washington, DC. He received his Ph.D. from the Maxwell School, Syracuse University, in 1976. He has written widely in the field of Cuban studies and U.S. foreign policy toward Latin America.

CARMELO MESA-LAGO is Distinguished Service Professor of Economics and Latin American Affairs and Director of the Center for Latin American Studies at the University of Pittsburgh. He was President of the Latin American Studies Association in 1980 and has served as a consultant to many international, regional, and national institutions. He is the author or editor of more than fifty scholarly articles and a dozen books, among them *Revolutionary Change in Cuba* (1971), *Cuba in the 1970s: Pragmatism and Institutionalization* (1974, 1978), *Cuba in the World* (1979), *The Economy of Socialist Cuba: A Two-Decade Appraisal* (1981), and *Cuba in Africa* (1982). He also founded the journal *Cuban Studies/Estudios Cubanos* in 1970 and continues as its editor.

JOHN SPICER NICHOLS is an Assistant Professor and Director of Graduate Studies at the School of Journalism, The Pennsylvania State University. He is the author of *Cuban Mass Media: Organization, Control and Function* (Journalism Monographs, 1982) and of chapters on the Cuban media in *World Press Encyclopedia, Keeping the Flame: Media and Government in Latin America,* and *Case Studies of the Mass Media in the Third World.* A Ph.D. in journalism and mass communication from the University of Minnesota, he interviewed President Fidel Castro, media policymakers, and a variety of journalists while conducting field research in Cuba in 1977 and 1979.

**The
Center
for
International
Affairs**

**Harvard
University**

1737 Cambridge Street, Cambridge MA 02138
Cable Address : HUCFIA   (617) 495-4420

HARVARD STUDIES IN INTERNATIONAL AFFAIRS